Petra Eckhard, Klaus Rieser,
Silvia Schultermandl (Eds.)

Contact Spaces of American Culture

American Studies in Austria

edited by

Astrid M. Fellner
(Saarland University)

Klaus Rieser
(University of Graz)

Hanna Wallinger
(University of Salzburg)

Volume 12

LIT

Contact Spaces of American Culture

Globalizing Local Phenomena

edited by

Petra Eckhard, Klaus Rieser,
and Silvia Schultermandl

LIT

Cover image: © ddpimages/AP/Stephan Savoia

Printed with the support of the University of Graz

Bibliographic information published by the Deutsche Nationalbibliothek
The Deutsche Nationalbibliothek lists this publication in the Deutsche Nationalbibliografie; detailed bibliographic data are available in the Internet at http://dnb.d-nb.de.

ISBN 978-3-643-50434-0

Wien 2012
Krotenthallergasse 10/8
A-1080 Wien
Tel. +43 (0) 1-409 56 61
Fax +43 (0) 1-409 56 97
e-Mail: wien@lit-verlag.at
http://www.lit-verlag.at

LIT VERLAG Dr. W. Hopf
Berlin 2012
Verlagskontakt:
Fresnostr. 2
D-48159 Münster
Tel. +49 (0) 2 51-620 320
Fax +49 (0) 2 51-23 19 72
e-Mail: lit@lit-verlag.de
http://www.lit-verlag.de

Auslieferung:
Deutschland: LIT Verlag Fresnostr. 2, D-48159 Münster
Tel. +49 (0) 2 51-620 32 22, Fax +49 (0) 2 51-922 60 99, e-Mail: vertrieb@lit-verlag.de
Österreich: Medienlogistik Pichler-ÖBZ, e-Mail: mlo@medien-logistik.at
Schweiz: B + M Buch- und Medienvertrieb, e-Mail: order@buch-medien.ch

CONTENTS

Localizing Global Phenomena of American Culture: Contact, Space, Representation

Petra Eckhard, Klaus Rieser und Silvia Schultermandl

In the midst of all the hobnobbing at his boss's pool party, the Pakistani American protagonist Changez in Mohsin Hamid's novel *The Reluctant Fundamentalist* (2007) becomes aware of his ambivalent position within post-9/11 American culture. Changez, a once successful agent within the globalization strategies of the New York City based company Underwood Samson, feels strangely alienated from his colleagues who symbolize a society which has set roots in America to a degree that he cannot, especially now that 9/11 positions him in an assumed ideological opposition to his meritocratic colleagues. This pool party, despite its connotations of luxury and leisure, symbolizes to Changez a kind of mobility which is contained within and limited by a fixated space. It exemplifies to Changez and to the reader the subtle demarcations between the inside and the outside in American culture. In other words, it functions as a representation of American society at large.

Like Nick in F. Scott Fitzgerald's *The Great Gatsby*, Hamid's protagonist finds himself entangled in a complex social web which comes into focus in this concrete space. The exclusionary practices performed within the social mingling around the swimming pool are indicative of myriad contacts which bring about American culture. While before 9/11 Changez's Princeton educational background and stellar career at a major American corporation signal his inclusion into the American social fabric, his unrequited love for Erica (read: AmERICA) and his growing resentment toward the capitalist exploitation of smaller businesses in the global South by Underwood Samson (read: the U.S.) position Changez in-between two concepts of American identity: individualism and conformism. Changez's feeling of alienation is more complex than that of other protagonists in American literature, such as the Chinese American protagonist Ralph in Gish Jen's short story "In the American Society." Ralph confronts an obvious hostility when the party host throws his jacket and car keys into the swimming pool in a act of xenophobia and social ostracizing, an act which shatter's Ralph's American dream of social upward mobility and prompts his resignation at the end of the short story that his American-born daughters are hopefully "better swimmers" than he is. For Changez, the swimming pool is a space of ambivalence in which his American identity constantly shifts like the small ripples of the water's surface in the pool itself.

The swimming pool in Fitzgerald, Jen and Hamid is one of many spaces within and outside the United States which facilitate interpersonal contact that reflects the perimeters of American culture. In this collection, such spaces include tent cities, basketball courts, pirate ships, settlement houses and social network sites. In all of these spaces, global phenomena manifest themselves on a local basis and encapsulate aspects of American culture.

That global and local are not merely oppositional or contradictory notions of cultural spaces is one of the underlying premises of the essays within this collection. It examines the myriad and complex configurations of culture along that spatial axis. To this end, the individual chapters consider the relevance of space, place and non-place as acutely historical and cultural situated; they examine border phenomena and transnational thinking and a meaning of "America"; they pay attention to cultural constructions but also embodied social actors; they highlight fluidity and difference without forgetting about the large structuring forces and politics along the lines of race, class, gender, ethnicity. Throughout the individual chapters, there are tendencies to read America as an inside, as a lived reality and as an outside, as an idea continuously to be realized. Such a plethora of partly contradictory models is indispensable but tends not only to question national borders but also the possibilities of a publication project such as ours. Thus, while the contributions were invited to think within this multiplicity, we chose some keywords to structure the field: Contacts with and in American culture; an attention to space, the interrelated but opposed aspects of representation.

While the contributions to this volume treat contact spaces and localization of global phenomena in a very concrete way, most of them also—and in some cases exclusively—treat the rendering of such spaces in representations. This is not surprising since the formation and interpretation of American contact spaces is usually rendered through a medium to a wider public. In other words, the connection between the local and the global regardless of the direction of translation is generally mediated. Thus, the articles in this volume not only offer close readings of particular texts but are also implicitly and explicitly interpretations of representation and mediation. In this light, one line of inquiry studies metaphors in various texts, the other one reads media texts *as* contact spaces and investigates the role of mediation as a transition point.

Contact in American Culture

The key variable in these interactions is contact. Contact is, in fact, a vector through which to analyze American culture, how it emerged, how it shifts and where it may be going in a global context. These are the main aspects we seek to connote with the term "contact space," a term which acknowledges the spatial dimension of contact in and with American culture. Contact spaces are spaces with/in American culture where an idea of Americanness emerges through a concrete form of contact on the one hand and through its mediated representation on the other. Contact spaces are spaces of and for interpretation which exemplify the myriad ideas of Americanness produced in global and local contexts and rendered visible through aesthetic representation; they not only make possible dynamic cultural contact but both embrace and enforce cultural variability and exchange.

Our use of the term "contact space" builds on Marie Louise Pratt's understanding of the dialectical cultural encounters that shaped colonial America. In *Imperial Eyes: Travel Writing and Transculturation* (1992), Pratt coins the term "contact zone" to refer to "the space of colonial encounters, the space in which people geographically and historically separated come into contact with each other and establish ongoing relationships, usually involving conditions of coercion, radical inequality, and intractable conflict" (6). Pratt's idea of the contact zone acknowledges the "interactive, improvisational dimensions" underlying the cultural encounters with/in American culture in ways that earlier approaches to the emergence of American culture did not. Almost a century before Pratt, Frederick Jackson Turner establishes with his famous frontier thesis a line of demarcation at which the old, European world meets the new, American world. Turner concludes that "[t]he frontier is the line of most rapid and effective Americanization" and that "the advance of the frontier has meant a steady movement away from the influence of Europe, a steady growth of independence on American lines" (56). Turner sees the development of American culture in strictly one-dimensional terms, as his idea of the line as a metaphor for the geographical exploration and cultural commodification of the American West suggests. Moreover, the movements he envisions within these parameters are one-dimensional, the cultural encounters unilateral. Pratt extends the limited scope of Turner's frontier thesis to include the interactions between and among various cultures; her concept of the contact zone is two-dimensional, her transcultural model of Americanization interactive.

It is no coincidence that Pratt's reformulation of Americanization occurred so close to the 500 year anniversary of Christopher Columbus's arrival in "America" perhaps no less than it is a coincidence that the completed annexation of the American West occasioned Turner's publication of his *The Frontier in American History* (1893). With Columbus and the beginning colonial encounters of America, contact has taken a geographical and geopolitical dimension and, if one thinks of Columbus's faithful reporting on his discoveries to the King and Queen of Spain, has been shaped by a cultural imagination which translates the local into a global context. In Native American studies, Columbus's landing in "America" constitutes the first contact between indigenous America and the European colonizers. While this idea of a first contact suggests the beginning of colonization, it also privileges the cultural exchanges the Europeans initiated. In contrast, Annette Kolodny's article "Letting Go Our Grand Obsessions: Notes Toward a New Literary History of the American Frontiers," which, appearing in the same year as Pratt's *Imperial Eyes*, shares the understanding that early practices of defining American culture failed to recognize the dialectical relationship inherent in these early encounters:

> Although we have only recently marked the one-hundredth anniversary of the supposed closing of the frontier, I am recommending that we reopen it, thematizing frontier as multiplicity of ongoing first encounters over time and land, rather than as a linear chronology of successive discoveries and discrete settlements. (13)

This revision brings about new perspectives on American culture and reevaluates previous assumptions about the emergence of American culture. Thus is also Paula M. L. Moya and Ramón Saldívar's contention in "Fictions of the Trans-American Imaginary," an article which appeared a decade after Pratt's study.

> The transnational imaginary is thus to be understood as a chronotope, a contact zone, that is both historical and geographical and that is populated by transnational persons whose lives form an experiential region within which singularly delineated notions of political, social, and cultural identity do not suffice. As we understand it, the trans-American imaginary is an alternative and epistemologically valuable way of describing our place in the world and the literature we teach. (2)

What becomes clear from this brief historical overview of the idea of contact in American culture is a tendency to explore not the lines of demarcation between cultural entities but their linkages and interconnected areas.

In a contemporary context, such linkages can be drawn between a variety of manifestations of American culture in strictly local terms. The individual essays in this collection query and challenge the ways in which contact produces and deconstructs notions of American-ness at the same time. Whether certain spaces such as that of the settlement house, the tent city or the shop window are more immanent expressions of American culture than social network sites, the basketball court, or the gentrified New York neighborhood is not a question which motivates our study. Instead, this collection offers analyses which draw from spatial theory and representational aesthetics for our investigation of the kinds of notions of American culture these and other spaces produce in a global context and the textual representations which shape and communicate these contact spaces.

Our project largely follows the "transnational turn" which Shelley Fisher Fishkin propositioned as an imperative for contemporary American Studies. Fishkin's definition of the transnational turn as a critical practice which sees "the inside and outside, domestic and foreign, national and international, as interpenetrating" (21) highlights the complex dynamics that underlie cultural contact with/in American culture. The specific spaces in which these cultural contacts occur rely on a repositioning of the United States within a critical framework that suggests its interconnectedness with other geographical areas. In all of the various fields of New American Studies—Border Studies, Hemispheric American Studies, Inter-American Studies, Atlantic Studies, Pacific Rim Studies—there is reference to a spatial dimension in which these forms of contact occur. All of these fields acknowledge that the United States is an integral part of a larger geographical and geopolitical conglomerate and that by embracing this conglomerate as a category for critical analysis, the US loses some of its exceptionalist status. At the same time, these fields of study refuse to stop their inquiries at national borders and detail the interconnectedness of cultural practices and traditions in their, more organically, transnational context; they reposition our critical lenses of observation. As a result, we now see American Studies differently, and we look at different conceptual spaces when doing American Studies based on the many different forms of contact that generate American culture in different global spaces.

Space: A (Very) Brief History

What exactly are we talking about when we talk about *space*? From earliest antiquity onwards, a great variety of spatial concepts emerged that have led to much confusion, not only in terms of unstable terminology (how to distinguish *topos* from *chora* or *space* from *place*?) but also in terms of a multi-layered web of spatial discourses that makes impossible a single and clear-cut definition. This confusion about the nature of space is largely due to two reasons: First, theories of space developed out of a plethora of disciplines—philosophy, theology, mathematics, geography, architecture, sociology, political science, aesthetics, psychology—and second, these spatial concepts have been subject to constant historical and systematic change ever since its first theoretical formations by Plato and Aristotle.

These early discussions about space were marked by a philosophical dilemma that centered on the question whether space *is* or *is not* part of our material reality (Aristotle). Also the seventeenth century saw a fundamental matter of dispute concerning the nature of space: Was it to be understood in *absolute* (Gassendi, Newton) or *relative* (Locke, Leibniz) terms? In other words, was space to be conceived as independent of the bodies it contained, or in relation to the bodies that filled it? With Kant's *Critique of Pure Reason* (1781) this philosophical struggle received a new and interesting twist: Reading space through the lens of aesthetics, Kant held the view that space is nothing but the result of sensual experiences or impressions, "a necessary *a priori* representation," (50) as he formulates it. Kant's negation of a physical-geometrical conception of space is often exemplified with Brunelleschi's invention of the linear perspective, whereby the human eye is fooled into seeing a three-dimensional space on a plane surface. Space, Kant contends, only exists in relation to the subject's cognitive capacities and thus becomes a category of thinking.

At the beginning of the twentieth century, and, most significantly with Einstein's theory of gravitation (1905), the conception of absolute space, i.e. the argument that space was fully independent of its content, finally lost its persuasive power. Instead, spatial theories became more and more anthropological in nature, exploring the interrelationship between the human subject and his/her position in space. Space, thus, became relevant as a social category. Durkheim's sociological approach, for example, convincingly argued that space is the result of social facts and conditions, implying that space is always dependent of cultural parameters, as alterations of geographical space (in the form of borders or monuments) always originate from political, economical, and cultural relations. Along similar lines, Simmel's early twentieth century theory of space held that spatial boundaries are "not a spatial fact with sociological consequences, but a sociological fact that is formed spatially" (143). However, unlike Durkheim, Simmel was more concerned with the interactions of different social groups and organizations, so that space functioned as the formal precondition for social reciprocities.

Modern and postmodern spatial theory largely understands space as the product of social practices (Park, de Certeau, Lefebvre), thus further developing the sociological theories introduced by Durkheim and Simmel. Among the most influential scholars of the twentieth century is Henry Lefebvre, who, in his well-known work *The Production of Space*, argues that every society produces its own space. "Space is permeated with social relations," Lefebvre writes, "it is not only supported by social relations but it is also producing and produced by social relations" (286). More specifically, Lefebvre conceives of (urban) space as a lived experience and criticizes dominant conceptions that are purely abstract (graphic representations of space). In similar terms, Michel de Certeau posits space as the result of social practices, thus also privileging sociological content over form. In *The Practice of Everyday Life*, for example, he contends that the act of walking alone transforms and develops the urban fabric.

The *spatial turn* of the 1990s marked a heightened interest in exploring the spatiality of human life. This philosophical return to space, which also spelled the end of the privileging of time and linear historiography, involved a new consciousness of spatiality that took into account all the manifold conceptions that "being in space" involved. This, in turn, initiated a heightened interest in disentangling the chaotic web of terminology. Hence, the spatial turn also saw a debate about the distinction between the terms *space* and *place*. While there are still wild variations in definitions, it is Marc Augé's influential study *Non-Places* (1995) that provides the most coherent and comprehensible distinction. For Augé, a *place* comes into being through human relationships and thus is filled with recognizable identities and histories. In contrast, *non-places* lack these identities and histories that have been inscribed in space. They are 'supermodern' sites of transit (like airports, freeways, shopping malls or refugee camps) that are marked by a certain fleetingness and do not allow stable human relationships to grow. *Space*, for Augé, is something purely abstract, often used to "designate unnamed or hard-to-name places . . . the non-symbolized surfaces of the planet" (82). In fact, what differentiates place from space is a matter of scale and perspective: Place is anything that signifies "the clarity and distinctness of the near and small" (Casey 295) while space points to "the emptiness of the far and enormous" (ibid.). From this it follows that *place* (being endowed with a personality) connotes the category of the *local*, while *space* (being endowed with anonymity) connotes the category of the *global*.

It was the ongoing processes of globalization (i.e. the homogenization of social and economical contexts) during and after the spatial turn which altered the spatial concepts and theories of the twentieth century. Largely, these concepts and theories grew out of the new politics of subjectivity that resulted, on the one hand, from "time-space compression" (Harvey) induced by new communication technologies and, on the other hand, from processes of migration and transculturation. Jameson's "postmodern hyperspace" (44), for example, denotes a radically new form of space which "transcend[s] the capacities of the individual human body to locate itself, to organize its immediate surroundings perceptually, and cognitively to map its position in a mappable external world" (ibid.). This hyperspace that Jameson describes here is a space made of virtual networks of communication and capitalism in which the subject can no longer orient him- or herself. Also Augé's aforementioned *non-places* count among the dehumanizing consequences of late capitalism.

In this connection, Foucault's influential text "Of Other Spaces," originating from a lecture given in 1967, is relevant in the sense that it already foreshadowed this connectivity between real and imagined spaces. Foucault termed these spaces of difference "heterotopias" (or respectively, "counter-sites") and located them between real and utopian spaces. Foucault illustrates the concept of heterotopia by comparing it to a mirror which, through the process of reflection, makes it possible for the subject to locate him/herself in a place where s/he is not. For example, Foucault lists cemeteries or museums as examples, as they are material spaces that merge the past and the present and thus are real but at the same time simulate a reality. Heterotopias, being part of every culture, often lie beyond conventional social structures and power relations. As such, they can also be defined as alternative sites that often clash with the dominant social order.

Following a postcolonial approach, Homi Bhabha argues that space must be conceived of along the lines of cultural hybridity and cultural translation. His notion of *thirdspace* denotes spaces of betweenness (i.e., spaces which neither belong to the colonized nor to the colonizers), thus creating an ambiguity that eludes the politics of cultural and racial polarity. "This thirdspace," Bhabha writes, "displaces the histories that constitute it and sets up new structures of authority, new political initiatives, which are inadequately understood through received wisdom" (211). Bhabha's influential concept was further developed, for example, with Avtar Brah's coinage of the term *diaspora space* denoting the "intersectionality of diaspora, border and dis/location as a point of confluence of economic, political, cultural and psychic processes" (615). This implies that any postcolonial discussion of space, being mainly concerned with processes of (forced) dispersal or displacement from a homeland, must necessarily involve mental conceptions that are, for example, evoked by memory, trauma, or dreams. Hence the legitimization of Edward Soja's famous claim that any contemporary understanding of space must involve the material (*firstspace*) as well as the imagined (*secondspace*) dimension, thus culminating in a *thirdspace* that, even though different to Bhabha's *thirdspace* in terms of the theoretical frame and argument, also connotes hybridity and openness. Thus, pure imaginations of "space" can be as valuable as abstract cartography, especially when dealing with the formation of cultural identities.

Postmodern identities are constructed via alterity and difference, which, in turn, also forges the spatial patterns that these identities are concerned with. Spaces in the "here and now" can only be fully understood in consideration of the "there and then" and are always marked by spatial transitions, made concrete through thresholds, barriers, or borders

(Geilsdorf 31). It is these spaces of liminality, spaces in which contact with the "Other" occurs, that this volume is concerned with.

The Representation of Contact Spaces

While the contributions to this volume treat contact spaces and the localization of global phenomena in very concrete ways, most of them also—and in some cases exclusively—analyze the rendering of such spaces in representations (books, films, artistic interventions, internet sites, photographs, performances). This is not surprising since the formation and functioning of American contact spaces has to be transmitted through a medium to reach a wider public. In other words, regardless of the direction of translation, the connection between the local and the global is generally mediated. As many contributors point out, if we want to understand globalization, also the analytical approach has to resort to some form of representation, be it metaphorical or allegorical.

If read through this lens, the contributions can be grouped into three categories, corresponding to their approaches to representation. The contributions to this volume offer *close readings* of specific literary works or films to reveal their treatment of contact spaces. Most articles in this volume not only pay attention to individual texts, but also analyze their potential to offer interpretations of representation and mediation. Two topics in particular shape the critical emphases of the contributing essays: an interest in either *metaphors* or in reading representations as intermediaries and *mediations*.

The contributions of Georg Drennig, Laura R. Fisher, Alexandra Ganser, Lisa Lowe, Ana Maria Manzanas Calvo, Sina A. Nitzsche and Susanne Wegener are studies which depict the various contact spaces. Georg Drennig, for example, reflects on the intersection of rioting, protest, racializing and public space through a reading of the movie "Do the Right Thing" (1989) and a photograph taken at the Seattle WTO riots of 1999 that depicts a protester entering a Starbucks through a smashed window. Laura R. Fisher conducts her historiographical study of the settlement house movement in part through Vida Dutton Scudder's 1903 semi-autobiographical novel, *A Listener in Babel*. Alexandra Ganser uses Michel Maxwell Philip's novel *Emmanuel Appadocca* (1854) to substantiate her claim that the pirate ship is a prime example of heterotopic space. Within her wider argument concerning the representability of globalization and the possible pitfalls of metaphorical concepts, Lisa Lowe analyzes Stephen Frears' "Dirty Pretty Things" (2003) and Alejandro Gonzáles Iñárritu's "Babel" (2006). Ana Maria Manzanas Calvo, too, has turned to Alejandro González Iñárritu's "Babel," next to Tom MacCarthy's movie "The Visitor" (2007) and Neill Blomkamp's "District 9" (2009) in her analysis of contemporary representations of encounters with the "Other." Finally, Sina A. Nitzsche is interested in the dissemination potential of the hip-hop movie "Wild Style" (1983), and Susanne Wegner examines the power of literary devices such as magical realist techniques in Karen Tei Yamashita's novel *Tropic of Orange* (1997) for their potential to open up binaries such as North-South. The close readings zoom in on concrete contact spaces in and outside the United States.

Beyond the close readings mentioned above, many contributions seek to clarify how we can grasp that elusive thing we call globalization and, in particular, how it is manifested in local contexts. Likewise, they ask how local contacts and their ramifications are distributed to a wider public. A key role in this translation process is attributed by many to the use of metaphors. In this volume, Lisa Lowe, Laura R. Fisher, Alexandra Ganser and Susanne Wegner all trace how literary or filmic texts employ metaphors.

Lisa Lowe here lays the theoretical foundation in her reflection on the representability of globalization. From a critique of metaphors of globalization in the social sciences (AIDS, "Chinese takeover," "Greenpeace"), Lowe analyzes two films and their different use of metaphors. Her essay reflects on the possibilities and limits of representation: how to represent the contradictory and enormous process that is called globalization. Lowe argues that the social sciences revert to metaphors in the face of the challenge that globalization posits, because they are faced with the discursive limits of rational language and rationalized concepts such as "the nation." Through her textual analysis she then shows how cultural texts (i.e., films) do employ metaphors in a different way, not as shorthands for complex processes, but as embedded allegories, which challenge the audience to analyze and to co-construct the meaning both of the local contacts and of the grander structures of globalization. Thus, Lowe offers a metareflection on the representability of globalization through the lens of metaphor and allegory. Alexandra Ganser looks at one particular example of localization. She takes the pirate ship not only as a metaphor for slavery, but also as a fictional site where different discourses meet, a site also of resistance and dialogue, a heterotopia. As such, the pirate ship also reveals the limits of literary representation since the pirate ship in *Emmanuel Appadocca* is a site of potential and instability. Susanne Wegner, similar to Lisa Lowe's argument, discloses the strength of literature (in her case Karen Tei Yamashita's novel *Tropic of Orange*) to highlight what non-fictional globalization discourse and its metaphors tend to efface. Specifically, Wegner claims that in this fictionalization, "the gap between the cultural and the economic" can find an adequate form of representation. For example, the wrestler SUPERNAFTA in this novel represents NAFTA, but obviously also exceeds the literal meaning, thus both functioning as metaphor *and* making the reader aware of the process of representation. In sum, these contributions bring the tools of textual study to bear not only on analysis of fictional texts, but also turn them towards (not against) a social science discourse. They thereby elevate fictional texts from the status of cultural artifact to implicit theorizations. Thus on a different level than the concrete spatial, these essays not only analyze but themselves contribute to contact (e.g., between fields of enquiry) and border diffusion (e.g., between literature and science).

Other essays in this collection focus on media in their original sense: as intermediaries and mediators. In fact, the local and the global are generally connected through some form of representation and are thus intrinsically mediated. As our contributors point out, this mediation is very different from mimetic representations, because in general, the "representations" shape the "real" spaces. The relationship between places and their mediation may sometimes be quite direct, at other times they form an intricate web of mutual shaping. The contributions of Ana Maria Manzanas Calvo, Eric C. Erbacher, Laura R. Fisher, Louis J. Kern, Sina A. Nitzsche, Georg Drennig, and Kathy-Ann Tan all are involved in such analyses of the tangled web of signification.

Ana Maria Manzanas Calvo's argument that contemporary representations of the "Other" render contact spaces as camps sets the tone for this group of essays which investigate how representations shape real spaces. Manzanas Calvo, for one, extends the spatial metaphor issued by the Bush administration in the aftermath of 9/11, namely, the emergence of an "axis of evil" which separates the patriotic American self from the terrorist Other, and applies this notion to Tom MacCarthy's "The Visitor," Alejandro González Iñárritu's "Babel," and Neill Blomkamp's "District 9." The heterotopic spaces in these films, so Manzanas Calvo's contention, are transnational and highly stylized in their cinematographic realization.

Some of them focus on the influence of mediations on the real spaces they claim to merely represent. For example, Eric C. Erbacher stresses that media promotion is a central aspect of the "third wave" gentrification of Williamsburg. Mediation is thus not a representation which accompanies the hard facts of gentrification, but shapes its field in a Foucauldian discursive style. In quite a different approach, Laura R. Fisher's study of settlement houses also looks at how representation, in her case literature, both partakes and intervenes in many different ways in "reality." She points out that literature was important within the settlement movement as a tool for cultural sophistication and acculturation but also furnishes one of the prime modes of access to the historical reality. In her study of an autobiographical text, Laura R. Fisher does not fail to uncover the privileged author's intentions from her descriptions of the settlement houses. Finally, the literary representation is compared and contrasted to a museum representation as a different form of mediation. Louis J. Kern, in his study of NBA basketball, is interested in the questions of violence and spectator pleasure in relation to three levels of contact spaces. First, there is the contact space on the court, characterized in U.S. basketball by a high degree of violence. Secondly, surrounding this space, the NBA is itself a contact space, characterized, among other things, by the necessity to integrate players from around the world and to adapt itself to international situations and developments. Thirdly, U.S. basketball's heavy mediation also shapes basketball's popularity worldwide and thus, again the practice on its courts. Turning to the contribution by Sina A. Nitzsche means changing from the regulated and almost overdetermined space of the basketball-court to the supposedly blank slate of the street. In Nitzsche's essay, the Hip-Hop movie "Wild Style" is a "medial" contact zone that shaped and transformed Hip-Hop culture worldwide. Here, the New York City street is the real contact zone, represented in the fiction film, which foregrounds the conflict between street and art scene. The movie's success, then, has spawned a number of diverse hip-hop movements and styles, but has also accelerated the global commodification of Hip-Hop. When, finally, people who were inspired by the film come to see the shooting locations, titled as "Birthplace of HipHop," contact returns full circle. The "real" street then is both real and mediated. This is also the contention of Georg Drennig's chapter which compares Spike Lee's "Do the Right Thing" (1989) to the WTO riots in Seattle and the now-iconic photo of a smashed Starbuck's window. While the ghetto riot in Lee's film is largely localized, as Drennig points out, the Seattle protest makes anti-globalization endeavors visible within the gentrified downtown, a place which is usually not associated with rioting. In both, the real and the mediated spaces of the movie and the riot, the glass windows function as boundaries between the commercial and the non-commercial spaces; their destruction, in turn, symbolizes the collusion of private and public spaces at large. A similar case can be made for tent cities, according to Kathy-Ann Tan. In her study of tent cities as heterotopias she highlights representation and mediation even further, pointing out dominant as well as resistant media interventions. She claims that there are at least three different kinds of mediations. Firstly, there are mass media representations such as TV news. As Tan points out, they can bring visibility to the plight of the homeless, but they also tend to romanticize the homeless or naturalize their situation in a dystopian scenario. Secondly, artist's projects are seen as particular interventions that transcend mere representation, attempting to shape the discourse and thus the real form of tent cities. Finally, media outreach on the part of the inhabitants themselves takes a variety of forms, from individual blogs via websites such as "The Golden Door" to instructional DVDs. We can thus see the media convergence as an overlay of the tent cities themselves, equally mobile, equally contradictory, and equally attempting to hold their ground.

Finally, two contributions reconceptualize this already complex relationship between mediation and "real" contact spaces in their investigations of virtual contact spaces. In their cooperative contribution, Eugen Banauch, Astrid M. Fellner, and Susanne Hamscha look at social network sites as virtual forms of localization. They claim that the virtual connection taking place in social network sites amounts to a localization *within* the medium, a simulated locality. In other words, rather than representation of mediation, according to these authors, the current situation is one of a simulacrum of space. In a different take, Leo Lippert discards the spatial metaphors themselves in a turn to performance as analytical mode. Based on a reading of an obscure Austrian singer who appears in local Austrian settings wearing traditional Native American costumes, Leo Lippert's theorizing points beyond the issue of representation (and that of American Studies, and that of transnationality), arguing we should understand all aspects of contact with/in US culture as performance.

Doing American Studies in Open Space

Looking back at the contributions to his volume, it has been surprising to discover the constancy of this trend to look at representation and mediation: While not originally stressed in the call for papers, the present volume, beyond its contribution to the understanding of space, place, locality and globalization, has also turned out to be a contribution to questions of cultural representation, consistently pointing out that if we want to understand the space that is called "America" or even small sub-segments thereof (baseball courts, a tent city, a settlement house) we have to be aware of their mediation—and of our own analytical remediation as metaphors, allegories, and performances.

For the most part, the contributors to this collection were participants in a very open forum, a conference organized according to "Open Space" principles. This method in itself encapsulates many of the above mentioned theoretical stances: an attention to *contact* over form, to flexible place/space construction (groups resign to different spaces and decide themselves how much time they want to spend on their topic). Perhaps this openness of the format was in part responsible for the author's interest in intersections, heterotopias, etc., not only on the level of the American spaces covered, but also of the forms of thinking, speaking, and writing about them.

Some of the spontaneity that the Open Space format of the conference provided is also reflected in this collection. We intentionally did not divide the contributing chapters into various categories or sections; what we suggest in our introduction is merely one of many ways of establishing a thematic link among the individual contributions. We hope that our readers will find many more rich and invigorating dialogues between the chapters. For this purpose, we wrote chapter abstracts that provide a more general overview of the themes running through the chapters. With these abstracts at the beginning of each chapter, we invite the reader to read against the grain of our suggested thematic arrangement. In this sense, our volume, too, is a contact space through which individual chapters interact with each other in multiple ways.

Works Cited

Augé, Marc. *Non-Places: Introduction to an Anthropology of Supermodernity*. London/New York: Verso, 1992.

Bhabha, Homi. "The Third Space. Interview with Homi Bhabha." *Indentity, Community, Difference.* Ed. Jonathan Rutherford. London: Lawrence and Wishart, 1990. 207-221. Print.

Brah, Avtar. "Diaspora, Border and Transnational Identities." *Feminist Post-Colonial Theory: A Reader*. Eds. Lewis Reina and Sara Mills. Edinburgh: Edinburgh UP, 2003. 613-634. Print.

Casey, Edward S. *The Fate of Place: A Philosophical History*. Berkeley: U of California P, 1997.

Damir-Geilsdorf Sabine, and Béatrice Hendrich. "Heuristische Potenziale einer Verknüpfung der Konzepte Raum, Mental Maps und Erinnerung" *Mental Maps – Raum - Erinnerung*. Eds. Sabine Damir-Geilsdorf, Angelika Hartmann and Béatrice Hendrich. Münster: LIT, 2005. 25-48.

Fishkin, Shelley Fisher. "Crossroads of Cultures: The Transnational Turn in American Studies – Presidential Address to the American Studies Association, November 12, 2004." *American Quarterly* 57.1 (2005): 17-57.

Fitzgerald, F. Scott. *The Great Gatsby*. 1925. London: Arnold, 1976.

Hamid, *The Reluctant Fundamentalist*. London: Hamilton, 2007.

Jameson, Fredric. *Postmodernism or the Cultural Logic of Late Capitalism*. London: Verso, 1991.

Jen, Gish. "In the American Society." *Whose Irish?* New York: Vintage, 1999. 114-32.

Kant, Immanuel. *Critique of Pure Reason.* [1781] London: Dent, 1991.

Kolodny, Annette. "Letting Go of Our Grand Obsessions: Notes Toward a New Literary History of the American Frontiers." *American Literature* 64.1 (March 1992): 1-18.

Moya, Paula M. L., and Ramón Saldívar. "Fictions of the Trans-American Imaginary." *Modern Fictions Studies* 49 (2003): 1-18.

Pratt, Marie Louise. *Imperial Eyes: Travel Writing and Transculturation.* London: Routledge: 1992.

Simmel, Georg. "The Sociology of Space." *Simmel on Culture*. Eds. David Frisby and Mike Featherstone. London/Thousand Oaks: SAGE, 2000. 137-169.

Turner, Frederick Jackson. *The Frontier in American History.* [1893] New York: Henry Holt, 1945.

Metaphors of Globalization

Lisa Lowe

Lisa Lowe analyzes metaphors of globalization both in the social sciences and in cultural representations. She notes that globalization has forced social sciences to abandon the idea of the nation as a bound rational unity and has fostered the use of metaphor. Such metaphors include "AIDS," "migration" (in particular the transnational Chinese), a "Chinese takeover," global NGOs such as "Greenpeace" and the "U.S. war on terror." While earlier metaphors such as Coca-Colonization or McWorld tended to symbolize aspects of homogenization and cultural uniformity, globalization has actually also brought a host of disparities. Thus the new metaphors emphasize a multiplicity of worlds and global inequalities. Lowe also counterpoints this referential use of metaphors as it is practiced in the social sciences with that in culture and the humanities, where they tend to be used in an allegorical mode, which implicates readers in the interpretation. Lowe exemplifies this in an analysis of Stephen Frears' "Dirty Pretty Things" (2003) and Alejandro Gonzáles Iñárritu's "Babel" (2006). In the first example, a heart found in a toilet bowl does not stand for a "whole," be it trafficking in human organs or undocumented immigrants, but rather allegorically opens possibilities of interpretation around the "stolen heart." Similarly, In "Babel" a rifle takes on such allegorical functions and, beyond that, entwined but different stories of human encounters with the law traces social and spatial differences in global movements that do not produce a totalized meaning but have to be interpreted.

> A second class of words in which comparisons are made. The pond after rain, a lily. Watershed and water level. Coinciding glint of scales and scrapers. Conjectural poles. -Myung-mi Kim, "Exordium"

In London 2003, I viewed Anish Kapoor's sculpture "Marsyas" at the Tate Modern Museum. Kapoor's astonishing piece occupied the entire length of the enormous 150-meter long and 35-meter high Turbine Hall that had once been the Bankside Power Station. Because of its impressive size, made of three steel rings joined together by a single span of dark red PVC membrane, and occupying the entire length of the enormous hall, it was impossible to view "Marsyas" in its totality from any single position; it was necessary to take up a number of perspectives, it evoked, all at once, *both* the vast hulls and masts of the seventeenth-century ships that had brought African slaves and then Asian indentured workers to the colonized Americas, *and* the twenty-first-century telecommunications technologies whose reaches permit the worker in the metropolis to call her mother back "home." The ensemble of fabric and steel textures evoked both a pre-modern sense of nature and the late modern devices of industry. Furthermore, the dramatic contrasts of the physical presence of the massive red sculpture and the negative space of the cavernous hall in which it was built thematized the violent material contrasts of the last three centuries: the promises that progress, development, and expansion would bring increasing freedom and prosperity, contradicted by the terrors of genocide, poverty, and war.

Figure 1

Figure 2

Figures 1 and 2: Marsyas, 2002 Anish Kapoor, PVC and steel, Inst: Tate Modern, 2002-2003 Photo: John Riddy, Courtesy: Tate, London

I open my discussion with this work because it not only captures the scale, movement, uncertainty, and contradictions that are indices of what we have termed for some decades now "globalization," but it thematizes the problem of representation itself with respect to our late modern present. That is, we would hardly expect artists to represent the contemporary global condition through realist notions of verisimilitude. Rather, the sculpture by Kapoor, a Bombay-born son of a Hindu father and Iraqi mother and émigré to Britain, uncannily evoked the "structure of feeling" of a globalization simultaneously riven and interconnected (Lowe, "Immigrant Literatures"; Raymond Williams), Raymond Williams having elaborated the concept of a "structure of feeling" as "a record of the felt sense of the quality of life at a particular time and place…social experiences *in solution*, not yet *precipitated*." (Williams, 133-34) The sculpture as viewed from both above and below mediated in a striking manner not merely the multiperspectival, but the geohistorical condition of globalization (Taylor). By geohistorical, we mean that globalization is not merely a contemporary stage, but rather the longer extended set of diverse processes that have linked multiple spaces through logics at once political, economic, and cultural. Neither evenly integrating, nor rendering homogeneous all parts of the world, these processes have varied in time and location, and taken place quite differently in unlike parts of the world. Each space, perspective, and temporality brought together through global processes has a presence in making and transforming our contemporary world. Globalization encompasses captive enslaved Africans, Asian "coolies," early northeastern American garment workers, women assembling VCRs in Baja California *maquiladoras,* indigenous shrimping practices in Colombia, and the latest biomedical technologies for genetic engineering. It includes the Nigerian village, the Los Angeles suburbs, and the global cities of New York, London, Tokyo, or São Paolo. In this sense, globalization cannot be represented iconically or totalized through a single developmental narrative; it is unevenly grasped, and its representations are necessarily partial, built on the absence of an apprehensible whole. There is no single history of who or what is global, but rather it requires a more complicated set of representations that not only mediates its "structure of feeling" but also inaugurates a critical genealogy of the representational traditions that have constituted, however inadequately, the manners of knowing its diverse conditions.

If Kapoor's sculpture explicitly thematizes that representing globalization is an aesthetic problem, I am suggesting that representing globalization constitutes implicitly an epistemological problem of what can be known, as well. Observing that the empirical social sciences within the U.S. university have resorted to metaphors to describe globalization, I distinguish this referential use of metaphor from the aesthetic practices of metaphor in culture, and observe that cultural works often include a diversity of critical hermeneutics for reading globalization's conditions of both possibility and impossibility. In the last twenty-five years, the scholarly disciplines of sociology, political science, economics, history, and geography, among others, have sought to define "globalization," describing a condition of unprecedented global exchange, interpenetration, conflict, and connection, characterized by movements of goods, peoples, and money. Yet mere global connection is hardly a recent phenomenon; in the ancient world, there were empires, conquests, slavery, trade, diasporas;

European colonial expansion began in the sixteenth century, reaching its heights in the nineteenth century. Hence with their representations of globalization, late twentieth-century social scientists desired to name a specific shift: the way in which, since World War II and decolonization, there has been a transformation of nation-states into an international network of linked political economies, and within the last three decades, an acceleration in the scale, mode, volume and degree of exchanges and interdependency. Scholars have sought to translate the unknowability of postmodern globalization into the terms of what modernity has known. Sociologists note that the worldwide reach of capitalism has exacerbated the cleavages and contradictions between traditional forms of human society and instrumental rational bureaucracies that Weber had already observed of the late nineteenth century (Wallerstein, *Modern World-System*; Sklair; Sassen). Economists measure increased gross domestic product, a consequence of processes like mixed production and flexible accumulation that, since the 1970s, have permitted very mobile capital to lay hold of specific forms of sometimes quite immobile labor, markets and materials in locations like export processing zones in Asia or Latin America, or immigrant enclaves in industrialized Europe or North America (Greider, Gray). In other instances, economists put forward data on consumption, employment, real wages, or imports and exports, however much of this data cannot represent or measure the social costs of globalization, the destruction or depletion of community, environment or resources over time (Rodrik). Political scientists study governments, parties, and interactions of levels of state, as well as international law, diplomacy, and international organizations, and develop scientific models for understanding international political systems. In each of these, political scientists are guided by liberal political theory and its classic story of freedom acquired through the joining of like-minded individuals into a political society or state in order to protect their individual liberties (MacPherson); hence, liberal forms of government and state become an *ideal type* for measuring societies as they enter the international fold (Keohane and Nye). Historians excavate the past through the study of archives, and form coherent narratives from linked sequences and patterns in events. Whereas nineteenth-century historians represented the progress of the modern era by documenting the development of the nation from its earlier unenlightened past, global processes of the second half of the twentieth century have demanded of historians new forms of study that reach beyond the nation-state, which seek to represent relationships between cultures, regions, and economies that formed the conditions out of which the modern world emerged (Chakrabarty). Since the late 1980s, anthropologists, who once employed the ideal type of Western industrialized society to study "traditional" non-Western cultures, have discussed the discrepancy of knowledge between modern and nonmodern cultures (Clifford; Clifford and Marcus; Asad). Cultural anthropology now references modernization as a history of asymmetrical power, and has developed new ethnographic methods for studying the cultures that have emerged from the history of encounter.

If the vast, shifting processes and conditions of globalization are in excess of the efforts to represent them, then perhaps all descriptions or explanations of globalization are either fragmentary, partial, or rhetorically displaced; that is, they are metaphors for globalization itself. Aristotle defined metaphor as "giving the thing a name that belongs to something else; the transference being either from genus to species, or from species to genus, or from species to species, or on grounds of analogy"(Preminger 490). The modern rhetorician Kenneth Burke discussed metaphor, and its variants, metonymy, synechdoche, catachresis, and so forth, as devices for seeing something in terms of something else: It brings out the thisness of a that, or the thatness of a this. It involves the "carrying over" of a term from one realm to another, a displacement that necessarily involves varying degrees of incongruity or lack of equivalence; the metaphor depends upon an implicit acknowledgment that two realms compared are never identical (Burke 504). The "frisson" of the metaphor is that sensation in which similarity and difference coincide, or the sensation of the coincidence of both similarity and its "excess." Traditionally, metaphor has been represented as a trope of transference in which an unknown, or an imperfectly known, is described in terms of a known. Metaphors can also convey spatial orientations, like near-far or center-periphery. The linguist George Lakoff employs the term "ontological metaphors" to convey those instances when the experiences of those far away are rendered as if they were immediate, as if we experience their experiences ourselves (Lakoff and Johnson). Current electronic media and visual culture are, of course, replete with these metaphorical experiences. I use metaphor, then, not only as a versatile figure that attempts to translate globalization's unknown into the mundane terms of the known, but also as a figure that states the irreducibility of what it attempts to represent. The "metaphoricity" of globalization is the rhetorical proliferation of figures that attest to the desire to render what is not yet fathomed as objectively known. If the U.S. social sciences have been dramatically challenged to revise their paradigms in light of the processes and conditions of late twentieth- to early-twenty-first century globalization, in what sense is metaphoricity the sign of this revision? To renew the argument made quite persuasively by Hayden White some years ago about the poetics of nineteenth-century historical narratives: We commit a serious error if we understand metaphor to be the exclusive province of literary, cultural, or aesthetic language, a presumption that was at the heart of the nineteenth-century separation of science and art, and the consequent division of humanistic and scientific knowledge (White). Histories have forms, styles for "telling" the past, and conventions through which they successively reproduce what White called "the explanatory effect." Revising the narrative frameworks for understanding American slavery, Walter Johnson has termed this sometimes violent process the "historical politics of time-making" (152). Modern history often portrays a single, secular human experience developed over time, putatively shared by all. Historians may aspire to realism, and to represent events "as they actually happened," but they perform poetic, stylistic and rhetorical acts to do so, and the manner in which they resort to such literary conventions changes over time, in relation to the forces and imperatives of their moment. So it is not simply that late twentieth-century social science descriptions of globalization must be understood as rhetorical and figurative, but also that the social sciences resort to metaphor precisely for the purpose of addressing "globalization," that is, exactly at the point at which the conditions they seek to explain exceed the modernist empirical social science paradigm.

Modern sociology emerged in the late nineteenth century as the scientific study of human social behavior and the structure of societies. Durkheim's pioneering use of empirical evidence and statistical material in the study of society, and Weber's methodology of historical comparative study based upon the analytic construct of an *ideal type,* were fundamental to twentieth-century sociology and influenced other social sciences, like political science and economics (Durkheim, Giddens, Lemert). Weber's well-known thesis was that social behavior had come to be dominated more and more by goal-oriented rationality and instrumentality, and less and less by traditional values or emotions, a tendency he named the "iron cage" of industrial society. For the larger part of the twentieth century, social scientific paradigms relied upon this unit of industrial society bounded within one nation, and presumed what Akhil Gupta and James

Ferguson have called the "isomorphism" of place, culture, language and state. In this sense, the Weberian paradigm of comparison advanced an implicit narrative emplotting a development of societies from pre-modern to modern, investing a positive value in the trajectory of modernization. The "modern" became not merely the *ideal type* to be measured against, but the universal apex of development to be attained and achieved. In the first half of the twentieth century, social sciences not only privileged Western modernity, but produced evidence that non-Western societies needed industrial development and social modernization. With the founding of area studies in U.S. universities during World War II and in its vast expansion and institutionalization in the postwar period of Soviet-U.S. confrontation, social science methodologies were adopted for the study of "areas" of keen interest to the United States, such as East Asia, Southeast Asia, South Asia, the Middle East and Latin America (Breckenridge and van der Veer; Cumings; Miyoshi and Harootunian; Rafael)

Modernization studies epitomized the Western-centered developmentalism that cast societies in these non-Western "areas" as culturally different "latecomers." In the work of Marion Levy or Talcott Parsons, for example, the Asiatic or "oriental" was cast as successful "latecomer" to Western modernity, as opposed to the African or Muslim "deviance." Sociologists of religion like Robert Bellah (*Beyond Belief*; *Religion and Progress*) differentiated between the "this-worldly asceticism" of Protestant Christianity in the industrial West, and the less modern, "world-rejecting" belief systems of non-Christian societies, going so far as to argue that the social and economic development in China and Japan was due to a "Protestant ethic analogy in Asia." Despite the many critiques of orientalist knowledge productions by Edward Said, Rey Chow, Talal Asad, and others, the contemporary "clash of civilizations" thesis revitalizes precisely this historical demonizing of Islam as an irrational "culture of violence" antagonized by the pressures of modernization. Contemporary comparative sociologists of religion (Juergensmeyer) frequently recur to this model of cultural difference, casting Islam as a resurgent religious fundamentalism in critical protest to the current materialism of globalization. Modernization approaches in area studies in effect created a global hierarchy of societies in which "non-modern" and "less modern" spaces were distinguished as *racially* different. "The *racial* [was] articulated as the category distinguishing modern technological and cultural conditions from those which are spatially adjacent to but temporally distant from modernity," Denise da Silva has observed.

This modernization model was firmly established in the U.S. sociological study of race and ethnicity, as well. As Henry Yu and Roderick Ferguson have asserted, Chicago School sociologists in the early and mid-twentieth century studied "orientals" as *ethnic* groups who could become an assimilable "model minority," in relation to Negro *racial* difference constructed as irremediably, or "pathologically," deviant. Insofar as increased international immigration in the late twentieth century has rendered the U.S. national discussion of race and ethnicity more global and diversified, we might also say that a pluralistic discourse of "difference" continues to work through a governmentality that assimilates immigrant newcomers who resemble the normative *ideal type* and "racializes" those whose "cultural differences" seem too "different"—whether the alleged cultural difference inheres in a lack of literacy or education, or a suspected threat to national security.

In the 1990s, the Gulbenkian Foundation commissioned a study (Mudimbe et al.) in which sociologists argued that changed geopolitical conditions in the post-World War II period both issued from and contributed to the radical altering of the social sciences, naming three developments after 1945 that profoundly affected the structure of the social sciences put into place in the preceding hundred years. The first was the change in world political structure, including the emergent economic strength of the United States after World War II, within a world politically defined by the so-called Cold War between the United States and USSR, and the decolonization movements and historical reassertion of non-European peoples in the world. The second development was the largest expansion of the world's productive capacity and population it had ever known, between 1945 and 1970, involving a scalar expansion in nearly all spheres of human activity. The third was the quantitative and geographic spread of the university system, leading to a multiplication, however unevenly realized, across the developed and developing worlds, of the numbers of professional social scientists. Each of these three new global social realities, the commission argued, posed a problem for the social sciences, how they had been institutionalized, and how they explained "society."

As the social sciences attempt to keep pace with the shift, and to account for the history of relationships between cultures, regions, and economies that formed the conditions for the contemporary period, new ethnographies perform reciprocal or comparative studies of the people, places, and discoveries that had been "forgotten" in former accounts. If modern sociology before postwar globalization described society as rational, bureaucratic, separated into public and private spheres of activity, and bound within a single social world in one nation, then the global interdependencies and connections between and among regions and activities previously conceived as separate, have challenged the sociological paradigm. For a sociology that tacitly assumed that human beings live in one national, rationally integrated social world at a time, cross-border relations, subcultures, transnational multilingual communities, and religious syncretism, were all seen as idiosyncratic or problematic (Calhoun). Yet with contemporary globalization, the social sciences are increasingly pressured to make these the very phenomena through which the social must be understood. Not only is the notion of the individual moving in a linear fashion through a single stable social order eclipsed within the world of globalization, in which travel, transnational production, and international media make the world global and multiple, but many people may have always lived in multiple spaces and among differences of nation, language, religion, gender, race and class (Lowe, "Utopia"). Faced with the challenges of describing these historical and contemporary phenomena, the social sciences have turned to metaphors.

Metaphoricity, then, names a tropological, but ultimately, epistemological, dilemma of representing postmodern globalization; the rhetorical surplus expresses the still very "modern" desire to master what will not be mastered, to rationalize as comprehensible the incomprehensible. Among the range of social scientific discourses in which globalization is most commonly explained, we find metaphors of various kinds of accelerated motion: from the migration of workers, refugees, or cosmopolitans to the circulation of goods, products, and commodities; to the rapid electronic transfers of capital and commerce; from the contagion of diseases, from SARS to AIDS, to the telecommunication flows of images, information, and ideas; from the spread of world religions, from evangelical Christianity to fundamentalist Islam; from the flexibility of capital and post-Fordist mixed techniques that permits increases in both production and accumulation to the flux of shifts in national, regional and international sovereignty, alliance, interdependence and coalition. To convey, for example, the unprecedented migrations of laborers required for the global economy, social scientists employ metaphors that reference fluids in the human body, traffic on streets, routes of highways, speed of jet travel, the rootlessness of the nomad, and so forth. Yet, more frequently, the figurative strategies characterizing globalization are metonymic and synechdochic, that is, they employ variants of metaphor in which the ensemble is reduced to one idiom, or the part used to symbolize the whole.

Sociologists, for example, have invoked AIDS as a metaphor for globalization. Roland Robertson identified six phases of globalization—from early global exploration through European dominance up to the Cold War—and invoked the figure of the AIDS epidemic to represent the sixth phase. For Robertson, the advent of AIDS represented not merely the rise of actual diseases and pandemics, but it symbolized a "new" phase of risk and peril at a global level that included the revival of ethnic divisions and wars, the influences of global media, and the rise of militant fundamentalisms; AIDS was Robertson's metaphor for the insecurity of a world in which the older certainties associated with European modernity had been displaced. AIDS figured a range of "globalization panics," from global environmental dangers to fear about financial volatility. When AIDS was first identified in the U.S. in 1981, about four hundred thousand people were identified with the disease; during the next ten years, more than 10 million people became infected with the HIV virus; research now documents that more than 33 million people worldwide are living with HIV and AIDS (Smith and Naím). In a sense, AIDS began as a metaphor that represented the confounding of medical science by a disease that penetrated bodies and defied national boundaries; yet as medical treatment became available in the United States and wealthier European nations, the understanding of AIDS as a catastrophic third-world epidemic has swiftly become a metaphor for the range of dangers associated with globalization (Patton, Irwin). It singles out one aspect of a greater, undetermined set of processes, in which disease is meant to stand in for the entirety of the larger complex of risks and effects of global contacts; like SARS or avian flu, it is a metaphor for a foreign contagion of deleterious, unforeseen effects of globalization, whose reach is as yet beyond the apprehension or control of rationalizing science.

The movement of migrants, in particular, transnational Chinese, has been another common *metaphor* of globalization. The essays collected in Aihwa Ong and Donald Nonini's, *Ungrounded Empires: The Cultural Politics of Modern Chinese Transnationalism*, for example, study the "some 25 million Chinese outside of China, the bulk of whom are concentrated around the fast-growing Pacific Rim…well-placed to play a key role in realizing the potential and promise of globalization" (4). Drawing from a wealth of ethnographic research conducted in sites throughout the Asia Pacific, the editors and essayists contended that it is impossible to understand globalization without examining transnational movement and settlement as part of the strategies of accumulation by Chinese under capitalism. They began their analysis with a discussion of the limitations of the Cold War era Parsonian social scientific explanation of Chinese culture that emphasized "norms" and values" of "Chinese culture," from entrepreneurial spirit to loyalty to native place, to studies of family firm behavior. They connected this "culture and personality" bias to later business school discourses from the 1980s that sought to explain the "East Asian economic success" through likewise culturalist explanations of neo-Confucianism discipline. *Ungrounded Empires* discussed a range of Chinese transnationals in Taiwan, Hong Kong, Singapore and Malaysia; the Chinese "astronauts" and "parachutists" (who vault to other countries while their families "stay in place"), who study in the United Kingdom or the United States obtaining educational "capital," or who work as mobile industrialists, financiers or manufacturers throughout Asia. Ong and Nonini argue that "Chinese transnationalism" emerged in the 1970s, alongside the regimes of flexible accumulation and mixed production, and its new modes of social organization, as Chinese adapted to new configurations of the production and distribution of goods and services, moving and connecting intraculturally across the diaspora. In light of the reorganization of labor processes and practices, including subcontracting and outsourcing, Ong and Nonini argue that "the distinctive transnational strategies of diaspora Chinese have converged even more closely with the circuits of accumulation within flexible capitalism across the Asia Pacific" (19-20). In the discussions of globalization in the last three decades, transnational Chinese immigration figured not only as a metaphor for the economic modernization of China, Taiwan, Singapore and Hong Kong, where Chinese are the largest cultural or ethnic group, but "Chinese transnationalism" became the privileged metaphor for a range of trends associated with the larger area of East, South and Southeast Asia, of the "Pacific Rim" or the "Asia Pacific" as a general political economic region (Connery, Dirlik, Gourevitch). This metaphor not only left Asia undifferentiated, but it also obscured the role of U.S. and multinational capital invested in the development of specific industries, on the one hand, and the ramifications of this rapid development in different countries—from Malaysia to the Philippines to South Korea—in terms of their local labor, environment, and technology bases, on the other.

In 2004 and 2005, economists began to issue ominous warnings about China's economic growth and the U.S. trade imbalance with China, and since the "success" of the 2008 Beijing Olympics, the current figure of a "Chinese takeover" has now eclipsed that transnational Chinese migrant as the sign of globalization. Thomas Friedman's *The World is Flat,* for example, employed the metaphor of a "flat" world to capture the sense that the playing field of competition between China and the United States has evened. But whereas the flat world metaphor may convey the U.S. anxiety about China's productivity, it obscures of course the "unflat" inequality that continues to exist between the industrialized G-8 and Latin America and Africa. Friedman uses the metaphor to caution U.S. policy makers and economists that they have not realized the dramatic erosion of the U.S. science and technology base relative to the social and political support for education and training in China and India. Although many countries—ranging from those in Western Europe and Canada, to China and India—provide for social welfare (education, health care provisions), Friedman argues that the U.S. withdrawal from this commitment disadvantages U.S. industries. He makes the neoliberal recommendation that market-friendly attention to social welfare will advance U.S. ability to compete in a "flat world." When, in 2004, *Business Week* reported a massive shift in economic power created by "the China Price" and heralded that the U.S. trade deficit with China would soon likely pass $150 billion, the "Chinese takeover" became the newest metaphor for globalization. Since then, a storm of books have taken up this theme, from Alexandra Harney's *The China Price* to James Kynge's *China Shakes the World* to Barry Naughton's *Chinese Economy*.

We might reflect that in the 1990s, just a decade earlier, the pervasive circulation of U.S. commodities, like Coca-cola or McDonald's, was the metaphor of choice for globalization: from George Ritzer's claim that contemporary society is afflicted by "McDonaldization," the spread of American consumerism that reduces all tastes and experiences to a single pattern, to Benjamin Barber's argument that characterized globalization in terms of an exacerbated struggle between religious revivalism and the accelerated profit-driven market, for which "McWorld" was the moniker. McDonald's was the metaphor for not only cultural homogenization, the mass production that converts everything into equivalent units for consumption, and the global reach of commercial saturation by media conglomerates, like Sony, Nike, and Microsoft, that have eroded the distinction and autonomy of "traditional" cultures, both Western and non-Western. Metaphors that previously implied global uniformity and homogeneity dramatically underestimated the ways in which global processes widen historical disparities and proliferate new forms of difference. Today's metaphors of globalization more often emphasize the deepening of cleavages between rich and poor, and the multiplicity of worlds linked by unpredictable processes: whether natural disasters like earthquakes, tsunamis, and hurricanes, or environmental disasters like global warming, whether the hazards of linked financial markets in which a regional stock market crash affects the global economy or acts of "terrorism" and the terrifying condition that the overextended military ambitions of one nation, the United States, could bring the entire world into war.

Social scientists who do conceptualize globalization as deepening the cleavages between rich and poor perceive a worldwide struggle between those who seek more equitable, sustainable development for the global poor, and the private economic interests of transnational corporations. They study global social movements and transnational advocacy networks that have addressed issues like medical aid for the world's poor, human rights violations, or women's rights (Keck and Sikkink). A group like Greenpeace, once a small group of activists protesting the nuclear bomb tests in Alaska in the 1960s, is now a massive transnational organization that can call on millions of supporters to carry out highly publicized actions, and has played a significant role in creating a global ecological sensibility, and a cultural awareness of environmental destruction threatening human extinction (Wapner). Global environmentalism has become a global social movement in the face of degradation from acid rain, air pollution, tropical deforestation, and the thinning of the ozone layer, but it is also a metaphor—the figure of global warming, in particular—that captures both the peril of apocalyptic destruction and the promise of collective means for imagining survival (Pellow, Oreskes). If the world at the end of the nineteenth century was one in which some spaces of nature remained still untouched, our present historical moment is one in which resources have reached depletion, have been utterly used and spent. Wastefulness has proliferated new toxins, new diseases, and new hazards to fear, and there appears to be nothing left to extract, waste, or spoil. Insofar as the depletion and pollution of our physical world has resulted in climate change, global warming itself has also become a *metaphor* alluding to the varieties of limits and possibilities of this moment of globalization: overextended military ambitions that have given rise to desperate, bloody opposition; excessive luxury for the few create the desperate poverty and destitution of the many. Global warming is at once a *metaphor* for catastrophic degradation of the environment, and for the understanding that greed and self-interest are entirely inadequate for the creation of a global ethic that might adequately address or adjudicate the means for collective human survival.

Finally, since September 2001, in the U.S., the "war on terror" has been the most frequently invoked metaphor for globalization, calculated to figure and condense wide-ranging anxieties about national security and survival within an incomprehensibly complex world order, conjuring a lethal enemy whose threatening presence has justified the revival of U.S. militarism and nationalism reminiscent of its policies and practices of the Cold War period. The metaphor of the "war on terror "references two schools of political science that address international relations: the "neo-realist" school that believes states are the major actors in world affairs, that international anarchy is the principle force shaping states, that states in anarchy are predisposed toward conflict and perpetual struggles for security and power; and the "neoliberal" school that understands international relations in terms of "complex interdependence" among nations, and multiple channels and institutions of cooperation and collaboration (Baldwin, Keohane, Keohane and Nye). Neoliberals envision a global society that functions alongside individual states by means of regional treaties or hemispheric economic trade agreements, to institutions such as the United Nations, to increasing numbers of international non-governmental organizations addressing issues from environmental protection to human rights to nuclear deterrence; this latter "institutionalist" approach had come to represent the mainstream analysis in the political science of international relations, in the two decades after the Cold War (Kahler and Walter). Yet after September 2001, the U.S. under the George W. Bush administration pursued a foreign policy that rejected international diplomacy and justified military force as a rational instrument of power, harking back to understandings of "national security" from the political realist approach of the Cold War period. Neoconservatives argued that, unlike Europe, the U.S. should not have reduced their military power after the Cold War, and that the aggressive unilateral stance in Iraq, was necessary for the U.S. recuperation of its global stature (Kagan and Kagan).

The Bush administration stated its prerogative to use preemptive force by pointing to the "terrorist" threat of September 11 to justify its declaration of a "state of exception" (Agamben, *State of Exception*) in which international institutions like the United Nations, regional economic alliances, and multilateral diplomacy were inadequate to achieve global cooperation. This state of exception rationalized the use of force and suspension of civil rights to maintain domestic order, and was used to justify the invasions of Afghanistan and Iraq. The global unilateralism of the U.S. invasion of Iraq broke with the "international regime"—the principles, norms, and governing arrangements of interstate interdependence—which had been in effect for at least three decades. Moreover, the representation of the war in Iraq as a "necessary" war drew on the concept of just war defined by circumstances in which a state has been attacked or invaded, when there has been a violation of international laws. Yet what is called "terrorism" is often the uprising of subjugated people fighting against state-sanctioned violence; they are named "terrorists" not only to delegitimize their actions and to justify "war" against them, but also to gain popular support for the exercise of state and military violence as means for dominating regions, populations, and resources. Thus, the processes and conditions of globalization in the last two decades have challenged the certainty and efficacy of a nineteenth-century notion of the modern nation-state that informed the *ideal type* in sociology, political science, economics, history, and geography. Insofar as the modern concepts of state, society, sovereignty, production, history, territory and culture persist, they are gradually and increasingly eclipsed by the simultaneous emergence of altogether new conditions. The social scientific turn to metaphors to describe our present global conditions precisely registers this paradox. Of all the modernist legacies, it is perhaps the concept of a future guaranteed by social progress that still persists within our present context; it continues to abstractly organize many of the social and political activities of our contemporary world. We uphold the promise of modern progress within conditions that raise the gravest questions about its eternal or universal validity. The presumption of a future guaranteed by progress is troubled everywhere by the realization that for the last half century, we have lived in a world that survived the use of nuclear weapons, and that we cannot know if and how a world with such destructive capability can continue to survive. Maintaining its survival will not come about through a refortification of nationalism and the nation-state or through concepts of diplomacy or militarism from a former era now incommensurate with our own. Unanswerable questions, like that of imagining a future within the global conditions of the last decades, have pressed the empirical social sciences to their epistemological limits.

The ethical and epistemological difficulties of globalization are thus registered by the rhetorical excess that becomes apparent when empiricism reaches a threshold and the social sciences turn to metaphors to figure globalization. The purpose of observing this turn is not to discredit metaphorical language as "less true," but to make some distinctions between the uses of metaphor in the different contexts of the social sciences and culture, and to suggest that these distinct projects entail quite different definitions of "culture" and understandings of culture's place on the horizon of meaning. Although we traditionally associate metaphor with aesthetic culture, the social scientific recourse to metaphor actually often indicates an underestimation of culture. Although social scientists commonly declare that culture is an important barometer of globalization, their analyses have tended to subordinate culture as a passive effect of political economic processes, whether relegating culture to the waning sphere of tradition within modernization, or in conceiving of culture as commodified entertainments, in claims that globalization has either homogenized or hybridized culture. In either case, culture is conceived as secondary and ephemeral to, rather than constitutive of, the social, and it is largely understood to be a static repertoire of symbols that merely reflects the social structure. To the contrary, we can appreciate that the cultural mediations of globalization are much more than inert effects or symptoms of an *a priori* social structure or political economy, and may provide us with profound diagnoses and prescriptions of our condition. Arjun Appadurai has elegantly persuaded us that the migrations and interdependencies of globalization have created new cultural maps, giving rise to new social identities, overlapping affinities and worldviews, while Ulf Hannerz has argued that global cultural processes are far more complex than earlier ideas about cultural flows from center to margin, and that they exceed the simplifications of global homogenization or corruption of the periphery. In mediating the "structure of feeling" of this global epoch, works of literature, journalism, film and visual culture, music, monuments, or electronic digital culture not only represent the most dominant social trends, but they also express residual traditions and emergent ideas, as well. Moreover, culture includes not only forms of expressive culture, but the variety of practices that range from the conduct of households to the inhabiting of public space, to attitudes and presumptions about belonging to township or community, homeland or world. Material and situated, cultural practices of representation enunciate and organize subjectivity, affect, memory and imagination within the social; through cultural practices, the social is understood and interpreted, and ultimately, it is through the representational media of culture that social change is newly conceptualized and desired. Culture provides languages and spaces for critically interpreting what can be known about the history of global processes and their reorganization of that world.

I close with a consideration of two recent films that have portrayed globalization, which I hope might permit me to be more specific about metaphors in cultural texts and social scientific explanation: Stephen Frears' "Dirty Pretty Things" (2003) and Alejandro Gonzáles Iñárritu's "Babel" (2006). Some metaphors mask the nonequivalence between the figure and what it represents, contributing to misrecognition and the naturalization of the social relations under globalization; others implicate us in the incommensurability, and generate alternative analyses and critiques of the social order presented as naturalized. "Dirty Pretty Things" and "Babel," I would suggest, in different ways go beyond the referential use of metaphor within an empirically given totality, to present allegories of globalization that implicate the viewers in a hermeneutic for reading those processes. Like Kapoor's sculpture with which I began, they each thematize the problem of representation itself with respect to the comprehension of the geohistorical conditions of globalization.

"Dirty Pretty Things" portrays the perilous existences of illegal immigrants, refugees, and asylees who survive in the margins of urban London. They are the most vulnerable and transient immigrants, who work in the interstitial midnight spaces of the city, cleaning hotel rooms, driving and delivering black market goods, prostituting, tending to cadavers in hospital morgues—invisible until identified by immigration authorities or illegal profiteers for regulation or extortion. The protagonist Okwe, forced to flee his former Nigerian life as a doctor, is now an illegal driving a taxi cab by day and working as a hotel desk clerk by night, chewing on *khat* to stay awake. He bunks on the couch of Senay, a Turkish Muslim woman who has asylum but works illegally as a chambermaid at the same upscale hotel. With no time for romance between work shifts or evasions of immigration authorities, their relationship is one of quietly reciprocated loyalties and protections, much like the friendship Okwe shares with Guo Yi, a Chinese hospital mortician with whom he shares an occasional game of chess. Upon leaving the hotel one night, Juliette, a prostitute reports an overflowing toilet bowl in one of the rooms. Arriving to clean it up, Okwe discovers a human heart has clogged the plumbing of the toilet. Several days later, he finds an elderly Somali man with an open, unstitched side from where his kidney has been roughly removed. Okwe quickly realizes that his boss at the hotel, Señor Juan, operates a black market trade in human organs, taking kidneys from illegal immigrant donors in exchange for passport or citizenship papers. When Señor Juan glimpses Okwe ministering to the old man, he discovers Okwe's past as a doctor and seeks to blackmail him to perform the kidney surgeries. Once he senses Okwe's attachment to Senay, Señor Juan seeks to coerce Okwe by alternately threatening and tempting the chambermaid. Okwe is presented with a choice, and despite the desperation of those who inhabit the illegal margins of a metropolis whose only law is the survival of the fittest, "Dirty" presents the narrative conditions for Okwe to bring about poetic justice.

The plight of the illegal immigrants preyed upon by a black market trade in human organs is a metaphor for the shifting, perilous world of globalization, in which the priorities of the transnational economy take precedence over those of the liberal nation, and vulnerable foreign workers are drawn from Africa, Asia, the Middle East, and Eastern Europe, to work and live in London. In this allegory, sovereignty resides neither in the nation-state nor in the individual person; a prior notion of a single national culture gives way to the plural languages, religions, and mores of innumerable immigrant groups; and the bourgeois conventions of work in the daytime public sphere and domestic intimacy in the evening private sphere have never existed for the immigrants cleaning, driving, and maintaining the streets and buildings during the night hours of the city. For these illegals, unprotected by the British state, processes of adjudication or ethical action are spontaneous and provisional, and necessarily take place outside of British law. The black market organ trade is an allegory for the fragility of human life in this context, in which the drive for profit and gain disrespects borders and boundaries of all kinds, from those of the political nation and cultural community to that of human embodiment. Okwe's dilemma, the choice that he must make once Señor Juan threatens him and others, is an allegory for the possibility of justice for stateless peoples within the transnational operations of globalization.

"Dirty Pretty Things" refers allegorically to a wealth of earlier narratives—moral, philosophical, religious, political, criminal and scientific—but it also creates another "scene" beyond the film that opens the possibility of interpretation after the failures and devaluations of those traditional narrative meanings. By placing the viewer in the position of reading Okwe's ethical dilemma, the film gives the viewer the responsibility for imagining the possibility of ethical action and political community within the lawless, parasitic, denationalized conditions of globalization. In choosing to remove Señor Juan's kidney to sell to the expectant buyer, rather than permitting Señor Juan to take Senay's, Okwe delivers Senay, Juliette and himself to safety. With this action, Okwe refuses to submit to fear and refuses to accept the order of the world as it is presented to terrorize the immigrant. He takes an action that struggles for a new order, another world, instead.

We may further appreciate that the use of metaphor in a text like "Dirty" is rather different than its use in the social science of globalization, if we consider the instance of Okwe finding the human heart in the hotel room toilet. The human organ trade upon which Okwe stumbles does not involve hearts, after all, but kidneys. Because the illegals can exist, however poorly, with a single remaining kidney, Señor Juan extorts the kidneys by exploiting the imperiled immigrant's need for papers. That Okwe finds the heart before he discovers the kidney scheme makes little sense in terms of the film's plot or narrative; in this sense, the human heart appears in "Dirty" as a deictic metaphor that points to its own metaphoricity, that directs the viewer to interpret the narrative of the organ trade allegorically, rather than as practically referential within an empirical framework. In "Dirty," the metaphor of the human heart fished out of a toilet bowl by a frightened immigrant hotel clerk announces itself *as metaphor*, and codes the story of the organ trade it inaugurates as *allegorical*. The heart cannot stand for the "whole"—neither for the absent, anonymous body from which it originated, nor for the organ trade of which it is the remains. The heart's "impossibility," its inability to refer because it is always already displaced, signals that globalization is a meaning that cannot be reached metaphorically. By pointing to the incommensurability of globalization with any other order of meaning, the heart opens out into allegory and the possibilities of interpretation.

In making a general distinction between the social scientific and aesthetic uses of metaphor, I mean to differentiate between an instrumental use of metaphor as a practical, referential symbol, and its deployment as a principle of allegory. The film presents the moment Okwe fishes out the organ with a coat hanger in a dirty, grisly naturalism, which contrasts the prettier romantic allusions that are inevitably called forth by the more conventional metaphor of the "heart;" the implied juxtaposition states the exclusion of the illegal from the sentiments of bourgeois intimacy for which the "stolen heart" would be the most cliché association. Where the organ trade allegorizes, all at once, the immigrant wrenched from her former circumstances, the pitiless violence to which the poor and migrant communities are subject, the indignities of waste, the transience of work, dwelling, and rest, the heart is the figure of possibility: its appearance ruptures the nightshift at the hotel, it leads to the provision of Okwe and his friends with the means to survive a deteriorating public sphere, abandoned by the state, without gods—a social world that lacks "a heart."

Iñárritu's "Babel" employs intersecting stories that link the U.S.-Mexican border, Morocco, and Japan, portraying globalization as the simultaneous production of social and spatial differences. As its title suggests, the film alludes to the biblical story of mankind's hubris in building the Tower of Babel, after which man was divided into languages, confounded, and scattered across the world. The allusion to the biblical Babel suggests that the contemporary project of global universality through modernization is a new Tower, and that rather than the universal extension of freedom, justice, or prosperity, globalization reproduces instead difference and division, sundering anew communities and nations, separated by language, wealth, technology, and militarized borders. While "Babel" was advertised as a movie with a simple message of common humanity that transcends national borders, we might observe, to the contrary, that the film precisely allegorizes the perils of universal human community, demonstrating its brutal economy of representation, the labors of articulation and translation, and the violences of misreading—across and within national languages, between states and its citizens, parents and children, husbands and wives. It presents an allegory of the processes through which entitled communities have been recognized as the proper subjects deserving of human rights, while others are constructed as those from whom humanity must be protected, the multitude legible not as humanity but only as its violators. As allegory, the film introduces the viewer to this critical framework through which we can interpret the processes of "globalization" as the promise of universality that masks the division of human communities, what Randall Williams (2010) terms "the international division of humanity." It instructs us in reading these processes.

"Babel" introduces several apparently distant stories that it slowly reveals to be related. It opens with the sale of a Winchester rifle to a Moroccan goatherd so that his young sons may kill the jackals attacking the herd. As the boys Yussef and Ahmed practice shooting, they dare one another to try to hit a vehicle in the distance. One shot hits an American woman traveling in the bus filled with French and British tourists passing through a small village called Tazarine, and she and her husband cannot return to their children in San Diego, whom they have left in the care of the undocumented Mexican housekeeper who has raised the children since they were infants. We are introduced to a deaf-mute high school girl in Tokyo, and learn eventually that on a hunting trip in Morocco, her father had given the Winchester rifle as a gift to his guide. As the Moroccan village shelters the American woman until her embassy can send a helicopter to transport her to a hospital, the housekeeper brings the children to Tijuana so she can attend her son's wedding, where she is detained by the border patrol on the morning of their return. There are no facile continuities or discontinuities in the portrait of globalization that these linked but disconnected stories convey; industry, media and technologies have profoundly altered publics and their intimacies, but they have also left particular conditions unchanged; the repetition of state violence toward, and forcible underdevelopment of, the subaltern poor of the global South reiterate the divides of nineteenth-century colonialisms. "Babel" suggests that if globalization promises universality through the social, political, or economic interconnection of worlds, it has not only failed, but also that the sites of encounter and exchange precisely pronounce the deepened exclusions of subaltern groups from representation.

Through the device of the Winchester—the U.S.-made "gun that won the West"—the film elaborates how reading and misreading threat and violence are historically critical operations in the legibility of an international division of human populations. The passage of the rifle would appear to be a metaphor for violence and its global crossings, yet this reference is from the start destabilized in the social order allegorized in the film. The rifle is *not* a metaphor for violence, I would contend, but rather the sign of the opacity of violence, a figure stating that violence is not given to transparency, a figure whose role in the film is to introduce the question of the attribution of violence. By means of the rifle, we see that the distinction between who is violent and who must be protected from violence is central to the global economy of legitimate humanity and dehumanized humanity. From the nineteenth-century colonial state to the late twentieth to early-twenty-first-century imperial nation-state, the state has exercised sovereignty through its monopoly on violence. This has meant not only that the state possessed the political and military power to determine the nature of the state of exception in which violence was necessary, but it has also consisted of a monopoly of biopolitical power "to make live" (*faire vivre*): the power to name the humanity entitled to protection in order to make live, and simultaneously, the power to "let die" (*laisser mourir*) those it deemed "violent," named as those who threaten the state's sovereign power (Agamben, *Homo Sacer*; Foucault). What the state deems a "threat" may range from open dissent or revolution to the articulation of grief, the refusal of invisibility, silence, poverty or hunger. In the political/juridical sphere of enfranchisement of the citizen in the nation, the "maternity" of the North American woman Susan who has been shot is recognized precisely as "endangered life," yet Amelia, the undocumented Mexican housekeeper who has raised her own adult son and now provides domestic care for Susan's children, is only legible as dangerously "illegal." The anxious French and British tourists are respected by the economic logic of development that recognizes the industrialized G-8 nations, yet the subaltern desert goat herders are either invisible or absurdly misread as "terrorists." The supranational global telecommunications order promises to transcend national and local linguistic particularity through extending sounds and images that travel across distances. The divisions are not exclusively enacted at national boundaries, but comprise the misreading of the agrarian world by the industrialized, rural life by the urban, the youth by the elders, and the speechless by those who speak.

The film "Babel" ends with several "speech acts" in which those who have been constructed as "outlaws," encounter and entreat the law. There are three linked scenes in which different subjects each attempt to speak to a representative of the law, in whose terms they are not represented: Chieko has bared herself to the Japanese detective investigating the rifle; Yussef smashes the rifle before the Moroccan police, and raises his arms in surrender; Amelia runs across the desert toward the Border Patrol, crying for help. These instances of embodied speech, beyond language, I would contend, are not seeking recognition from the law. Rather, their articulations are constituted as in excess of the terms of the law, whose agents view them as "in violation," as inhuman. These scenes, in which various agents of the law refuse these marginal subjects' attempts to speak, direct us as viewers towards the critique of the state, and its monopoly on violence. "Babel" implicates viewers in this attribution and instructs us that to represent globalization is to return continually to the impasse of deciding who is violent and who must be protected from violence.

Thus, I have observed that the detour to metaphor within the social sciences occurs at the point at which these studies confront the mandate of explaining globalization. In making a general distinction between the social scientific and cultural uses of metaphor, I differentiate between an instrumental use of metaphor as a practical, referential symbol, on the one hand, and its deployment as a principle of allegory, on the other. In the former, the use of metaphor is static, in the latter dynamic; one assumes a stable social totality, and the other invents an alternative out of the ruins of historical loss of such totality. In ways that poststructuralist theory never could, the material conditions of globalization have brought the social sciences to epistemic crisis, revealing the limits, the occlusions, and the constructedness of disciplinary claims. We need not conceive this crisis as "failure," but rather as an opportunity for interdisciplinary collaboration. I am not, in any sense, arguing that it is inappropriate for empirical social sciences to resort to metaphor. Quite the opposite, my provocation is rather for the social sciences to take metaphors much more seriously. Instead of casting the superior "truths" of social science against the "fiction" of aesthetic works, perhaps there is much for the social sciences to draw from in the richer, developed critical future that one finds in culture and the humanities.

Works Cited

Agamben, Giorgio. *Homo Sacer: Sovereign Power and Bare Life*. Stanford: Stanford UP, 1998.

---. State of Exception. Chicago: U of Chicago P, 2005.

Appadurai, Arjun. *Modernity at Large*. Minneapolis: U of Minnesota P, 1996.

Aristotle. *Poetics* 1457b.

Asad, Talal. *Genealogies of Religion: Discipline and Reasons of Power in Christianity and Islam*. Baltimore: Johns Hopkins UP, 1993.

Baldwin, David A. Neorealism and Neoliberalism: the Contemporary Debate. New York: Columbia UP, 1993.

Barber, Benjamin. *Jihad vs. McWorld*. New York: Times Books, 1995.

Bellah, Robert. Beyond Belief: Essays on Religion in a Post-Traditional World. New York: Harper, 1970.

---. ed. *Religion and Progress in Modern Asia*. Glencoe: Free Press, 1965.

Breckenridge, Carol A. and Peter van der Veer, eds. *Orientalism and the Postcolonial Predicament: Perspectives on South Asia*. Philadelphia: U of Pennsylvania P, 1993.

Burke, Kenneth. *A Grammar of Motives*. Berkeley: California, 1969.

Business Week. "The China Price." December 6, 2004.

Calhoun, Craig. *Critical Social Theory: Culture, History and the Challenge of Difference*. Oxford: Blackwell, 1995.

Chakrabarty, Dipesh. *Provincializing Europe: Postcolonial Thought and Historical Difference*. Princeton: Princeton UP, 2000.

Chen, Kuan-Hsing and David Morley, eds. *Stuart Hall: Critical Dialogues In Cultural Studies*. New York: Routledge, 1996.

Chow, Rey. *Woman and Chinese Modernity: The Politics of Reading Between West and East*. Minneapolis: U of Minnesota P, 1991.

Clifford, James. *The Predicament of Culture*. Cambridge: Harvard UP, 1988.

---. and George Marcus, eds. *Writing Culture: the Poetics and Politics of Ethnography.* Berkeley: U of California P, 1986.

Connery, Christopher. "Pacific Rim Discourse: The U.S. Global Imaginary in the Late Cold War Years." *Boundary 2* 21.1 (1994): 31-56.

Cumings, Bruce. *Parallax Visions*. Durham: Duke UP, 1999.

da Silva, Denise. "Towards a Critique of the Socio-logos of Justice: The Analytics of Raciality and the Production of Universality." *Social Identities* 7.3 (2001): 421-454.

Dirlik, Arif. "The Asia-Pacific Idea: Reality and Representation in the Invention of a Regional Structure." *Journal of World History* 3.1 (1992): 55-79.

Durkheim, Émile. *The Rules of Sociological Method.* 1938. Trans. Sarah Solovay. Glencoe: Free Press, 1950.

Ferguson, Roderick. *Aberrations in Black: Toward a Queer of Color Critique*. Minneapolis: U of Minnesota P, 2004.

Foucault, Michel. *'Society Must Be Defended': Lectures at the Collège de France, 1975-1976*. Trans. David Macey. New York: Picador, 2003.

Frears, Stephen (director). *Dirty Pretty Things* (2003).

Friedman, Thomas. *The World is Flat: A Brief History of the World.* New York: Farrar, Strauss, 2005.

Giddens, Anthony. *Capitalism and Modern Social Theory: An Analysis of the Writings of Durkheim, Marx and Weber.* Cambridge: Cambridge UP, 1971.

Gray, John. False Dawn: *The Delusions of Global Capitalism.* New York: New Press, 1998.

Greider, William. *One World Ready or Not: The Manic Logic of Global Capitalism*. New York: Simon and Schuster, 1997.

Gupta, Akhil and James Ferguson. "Beyond 'Culture': Space, Identity, and the Politics of Difference." *Cultural Anthropology* 7.1 (February 1992): 6-22.

Gourevitch, Peter A. "The Pacific Rim: Current Debates." *The Pacific Region: Challenges to Policy and Theory*. Ed. Peter A. Gourevitch. Newbury Park: Sage, 1989.

Grossberg, Lawrence, et al., eds. *Cultural Studies: A Reader*. New York: Routledge, 1992.

Hall, Stuart. "Cultural Studies: Two Paradigms." *Media, Culture, Society* 2 (1980): 52-72.

Harney, Alexandra. *The China Price: The True Cost of Chinese Competitive Advantage*. New York: Penguin Books, 2008.

Hannerz, Ulf. "Scenarios for Peripheral Cultures." *Culture, Globalization, and the World-System*. Ed. Anthony D. King. Oxford: Blackwell, 1990.

Harvey, David. *The Condition of Postmodernity*. Oxford: Blackwell, 1990.

Iñárritu, Alejandro Gonzáles (director). *Babel* (2006).

Irwin, Alexander, et al. *Global AIDS: Myths and Facts, Tools for Fighting the AIDS Pandemic*. Brookline: South End, 2003.

Johnson, Walter. *Soul by Soul: Life Inside the Antebellum Slave Market*. Cambridge: Harvard UP, 1999.

Juergensmeyer, Mark. *Terror In the Mind of God*. Berkeley: U of California P, 2000.

Kagan, Donald and Frederick Kagan. *While America Sleeps: Self-Delusion, Military Weakness, and the Threat to Peace Today*. New York: St. Martin's, 2000.

Kahler, Miles and Barbara Walter, eds. *Territoriality and Conflict in an Era of Globalization*. Cambridge: Cambridge UP, 2006.

Kapoor, Anish. *Marsyas*. London: Tate Publishing, 2002.

Keck, Margaret and Kathryn Sikkink. *Activists Beyond Borders: Advocacy Networks in International Politics*. Ithaca: Cornell UP, 1998.

Keohane, Robert O. and Joseph Nye. *Power and Interdependence*. Glenview, Il.: Scott, Foresman, 1989.

Keohane, Robert O. ed. *Neorealism and Its Critics*. New York: Columbia, 1986.

Lakoff, George and Mark Johnson. *Metaphors We Live By*. Chicago: U of Chicago P, 1980.

Lemert, Charles. *Sociology After the Crisis*. Boulder: Paradigm, 1995/2004.

Levy, Marion. *Modernization and the Structure of Societies*. Princeton: Princeton UP, 1966.

Lowe, Lisa. "Immigrant Literatures: A Modern Structure of Feeling." *Literature on the Move: Comparing Diasporic Ethnicities in Europe*

and the Americas. Ed. Dominique Marçais et all. Heidelberg: Carl Winter, 2002.
---. "Utopia and Modernity: Some Observations from the Border." *Rethinking Marxism* 13/2 (Spring 2001): 10-18.
MacPherson, C.B. *The Political Theory of Possessive Individualism: Hobbes to Locke*. Oxford: Clarendon, 1962.
Miyoshi, Masao and Harry Harootunian, eds. *Learning Places: the Afterlives of Area Studies*. Durham: Duke, 2002.
Mudimbe, V. Y. et al., eds. *Open the Social Sciences: Report of the Gulbenkian Commission on the Restructuring of the Social Sciences.* Stanford: Stanford UP, 1996.
Naughton, Barry. *The Chinese Economy: Transitions and Growth.* Cambridge: MIT Press, 2007.
Ong, Aihwa and Donald Nonini, eds. *Ungrounded Empires: The Cultural Politics of Modern Chinese Transnationalism.* New York: Routledge, 1997.
Oreskes, Naomi. "The Scientific Consensus on Climate Change." *Climate Change*. Eds. Joseph F. DiMento, Pamela Doughman. Cambridge: MIT Press, 2007.
Parsons, Talcott. *The Evolution of Societies*. Englewood Cliffs: Prentice-Hall, 1977.
Patton, Cindy. *Globalizing AIDS*. Minneapolis: U of Minnesota P, 2003.
Pellow, David Naguib. *Resisting Global Toxics: Transnational Movements for Environmental Justice*. Cambridge: MIT Press, 2007.
Preminger, Alex, ed. *Princeton Encyclopedia of Poetry and Poetics.* Princeton: Princeton UP, 1974.
Rafael, Vicente. "Cultures of Area Studies in the United States." *Social Text* (Winter 1994): 91-111.
Ritzer, George. *The McDonaldization of Society*. Thousand Oaks: Pine Forge, 1993.
Robertson, Roland. *Globalization: Social Theory and Global Culture.* London: Sage, 1992.
Rodrik, Dani. *One Economics, Many Recipes: Globalization, Institutions, and Economic Growth.* Princeton: Princeton UP, 2007.
Said, Edward. *Orientalism*. New York: Random House, 1977.
Sassen, Saskia. *Globalization and Its Discontents: Essays on the New Mobility of People and Money.* New York: New Press, 1998.
Sklair, Leslie. *The Sociology of the Global System.* Herfordshire: Harvester Wheatsheaf, 1991.
Smith, Gordon and Moisés Naím. *Altered States: Globalization, Sovereignty and Governance*. Ottowa: International Development Research Centre, 2000.

Taylor, Peter. *Modernities: A Geohistorical Interpretation*. Minneapolis: U of Minnesota P, 1999.

Wallerstein, Immanuel. *The Modern World-System*. New York: Academic, 1976.

---. *Capitalist World-Economy*. Cambridge: Cambridge UP, 1979.

Wapner, Paul. *Environmental Activism and Civil Politics*. Albany: SUNY P, 1996.

Weber, Max. *Economy and Society*, 3 volumes. 1922. New York: Bedminster, 1968.

White, Hayden. *Metahistory: The Historical Imagination in Nineteenth-Century Europe*. Baltimore: Johns Hopkins UP, 1973.

Williams, Randall. *The Divided World: Human Rights and Its Violence*. Minneapolis: University of Minnesota, 2010.

Williams, Raymond. *Marxism and Literature*. Oxford: Oxford, 1977.

Yu, Henry. *Thinking Orientals: Migration, Contact and Exoticism in Modern America*. Oxford: Oxford, 2001.

The Pirate Ship as a Black Atlantic Heterotopia: Michel Maxwell Philip's Emmanuel Appadocca

Alexandra Ganser

Alexandra Ganser explores how Michel Maxwell Philip's Emmanuel Appadocca *fictionalizes the pirate ship as a transnational and multiethnic contact zone. Ganser argues that Emmanuel Appadocca, which is widely considered to be the first Caribbean novel, exemplarily presents the pirate ship as a heterotopic space in which various discourses of legitimacy and illegitimacy meet and in which piracy and slavery are discursively intertwined in order to question dominant conceptions of law, might, and right. Ganser concludes that Philip's design of the pirate ship as an embodiment of an ideal and harmonious state of trans-ethnic solidarity thus powerfully gives voice to subaltern subject positions and allows for a discursive questioning of the dominant order.*

In the early modern Atlantic world, from the sixteenth century onwards, one of the major sites of cultural contact and encounter were the ships that were circulating between Europe, Africa, and the Americas. A large share of Atlantic seafaring took place in the service of the circum-Atlantic slave trade, thereby serving European empire-building in the Americas. Ships were important not just politically or economically, however. Because of their central position in the colonial economy in general, and for slavery in particular, ships also became a popular literary topos, especially for writers critiquing slavery. Ships have been cast as important sites of struggle and as symbols of escape in the context of a fledgling Black Atlantic consciousness, from Olaudah Equiano's *Interesting Narrative* (1789) to nineteenth-century Atlantic abolitionist literature such as Fredric Douglass's *My Bondage and My Freedom* (1855) or Martin Delany's *Blake* (1859-62). In these texts, the ship serves as a paradoxical symbol of both terror and freedom and as a site on which the foundational violence of the triangular trade is critiqued with regard to the enslavement and the forced relocation of Africans as well as to the unequal labor relations in the seafaring trades.[1]

One subset of nineteenth-century maritime fiction of the Black Atlantic are narratives that fictionalize the pirate ship as a transnational and multiethnic contact zone. Often inspired by early modern accounts of piracy, texts such as Michel Maxwell Philip's 1854 *Emmanuel Appadocca; or, Blighted Life: A Tale of the Boucaneers* (1854) [2], sometimes claimed to be "the first Anglo-Caribbean novel" (Cudjoe, "Preface" xiii-xiv), or Melville's "Benito Cereno" (1856) characterize the pirate ship as a mobile site of fluidity and uncertainty,[3] of crisis and deception. These authors articulate the pirate ship as a site that allows for social critique, dialogue, and the destabilization of binary constructions of difference, one of the prime qualities Mary Louise Pratt attributes to cultural contact zones. Philip, a Trinidadian jurist of mixed descent, whom C.L.R. James described as "the most brilliant native of his time and within memory," "[p]erhaps the greatest of all creoles" (255; 269), published the autobiographically inspired *Emmanuel Appadocca* as a protest against slavery in the U.S., lamenting the cruelty of "the slave holders of America" against "their slave-children" (6), by which the author particularly refers to the "illegitimate" offspring of white masters and black enslaved mothers.[4] The book presents "Philip and his character [as] ... vindicators who, like Frederick Douglass and C.L.R. James, would outread and outdignify the white oppressor" (Smith 171). Philip wrote and published the book while he was reading for the bar and working as a correspondent for a Trinidadian newspaper in London; the text, influenced by Sir Walter Scott's and James Fenimore Cooper's sea romances, is a transatlantic narrative that transcends national borders through its critique of race relations, connecting Great Britain, the United States, the Caribbean, and Africa on both

1 Thus also the introduction of the term "Red Atlantic" by Marcus Rediker (see Rediker,"Atlantic," as well as Linebaugh/Rediker).

2 I would like to thank Gesa Mackenthun for the inspiring thoughts and insights she has shared with me both in person and through her seminal study *Fictions of the Black Atlantic in American Foundational Literature*, in which she discusses *Emmanuel Appadocca* in the context of Gilroy's Black Atlantic paradigm.

3 On the link between discourses of piracy and mobility, see Ganser (forthcoming).

4 For biographical accounts of Philip's life, see the various publications by Selwyn Cudjoe as well as one of C.L.R. James's earliest writings, a biographical essay on Philip published in *The Beacon* in 1931. In this essay, James points to "some future occasion" (255) on which he would discuss Philip's novel, but the occasion apparently never arrived (Nielsen 4).

the fictional and the metafictional level. Part swashbuckling adventure, part philosophy, *Emmanuel Appadocca* mixes social critique and emancipatory claims on behalf of Philip's fellow creoles. In this essay, I place Philip's understudied novel within the context of Paul Gilroy's concept of the Black Atlantic and, in a further step, critically discuss it as an instance of heterotopia, a space in which dominant conceptions of law and justice are questioned and refigured.

As I will argue in the following, the novel exemplarily presents the pirate ship as a space in which various discourses of legitimacy and illegitimacy meet. Piracy and slavery are discursively intertwined in order to question dominant conceptions of law, might, and right. This discursive entanglement of slavery and piracy had begun with earlier fictional accounts of piracy such as Daniel Defoe's *Captain Singleton* (1720) on the one hand, and with political writings such as the first two drafts of the United States Declaration of Independence on the other, relegating the responsibility for the slave trade exclusively to the British monarch and criminalizing the King by calling it his "piratical warfare."[5] What makes Philip's novel such an important narrative intervention is the fact that it was the first to voice a subaltern subject position by placing at its center a creole protagonist of mixed descent, who references the racial trope of the "tragic mulatto," while at the same time introducing a heroic "colored" pirate and intellectual whose perspective is emphatically presented to the reader. In this way, the text negotiates the transatlantic phenomena of piracy and slavery through the perspective of a Black Atlantic consciousness by imagining the pirate ship as an imaginary site of resistance and dialogue.[6]

---

5 In both the first and the reported draft of the Declaration, the British monarch is accused of waging "cruel War against human Nature itself, violating its most sacred Rights of Life and Liberty in the Persons of a distant People who never offended him, captivating and carrying them into Slavery in another Hemisphere, or to incur miserable Death, in their Transportation thither. This piratical Warfare, the opprobrium of infidel Powers, is the Warfare of the Christian King of Great Britain" (www.ushistory.org/declaration/document/compare.htm). During the Civil War, the Union also used this rhetorical strategy against the Confederate States in a variety of representations of Jefferson Davis as a pirate, stealing Africans into slavery.

6 Jeffrey W. Bolster has briefly examined the historical relation between African Americans and piracy in the first chapter of Black Jacks: African American Seamen in the Age of Sail (1997). For a critique of Bolster through an economic reading of black mariners' narratives such as Equiano's, see Kazanjian 35-84.

The Ship as Heterotope

In his oft-quoted lecture on the spatial concept of the heterotope, Michel Foucault mentions the ship not only as a *potential* instance of heterotopia—a concrete, materialized utopian space governed by alternate systems of organization and thus disturbing systems of representation—but as a heterotopian site "par excellence" (27). Foucault had introduced the concept in 1966 in the preface to *Les Mots et Les Choses* (Engl. *The Order of Things*; xviii) and further expanded on the concept in "Des Espaces Autres" (Engl. "Of Other Spaces"), a lecture delivered to an audience of architects in 1967 and published in 1986.[7] In this lecture, he examines heterotopian sites as relational sites which "have the curious property of being in relation with all the other sites, but in such a way as to suspect, neutralize, or invert the set of relations that they happen to designate, mirror, or reflect" (24).

Foucault avers a close relationship between utopia and heterotopia, viewing them as two different types of such paradoxical sites that invert yet also mirror their designated relations in social space. While utopias have "no real place" (he distinguishes between "site" and place, which is defined as an "emplaced site," or a site that is materially manifested), heterotopia refers to emplaced counter-sites: "A kind of effectively enacted utopia in which ... all the other real sites that can be found within the culture, are simultaneously represented, contested, and inverted. Places of this kind are outside of all places, even though it may be possible to indicate their location in reality" (ibid.).[8] Foucault thus does not conceive of utopia and heterotopia in a structural opposition, but argues that between

7 Though the lecture was never revised, Foucault agreed to its publication shortly before he died (see Harvey 159).

8 In The Order of Things, Foucault's distinction between the two is drawn out in the field of representation. In contrast to utopias, "[h]eterotopias are disturbing, probably because they secretly undermine language, because they make it impossible to name this and that, because they shatter or tangle common names, because they destroy 'syntax' in advance, and not only the syntax with which we construct sentences but also that less apparent syntax which causes words and things (next to and also opposite one another) to 'hold together.' This is why utopias permit fables and discourse: they run with the very grain of language and are part of the fundamental dimension of the fibula; heterotopias ... desiccate speech, stop words in their tracks, contest the very possibility of grammar at its source; they dissolve our myths and sterilize the lyricism of our sentences" (xviii).

utopias and "these quite other sites ..., there might be a sort of mixed, joint experience" (ibid.).[9]

The utopian impulse is strong in Foucault's conception; yet, as David Harvey reminds us,

> Foucault appealed to heterotopia to escape from the 'no place' that is a 'placeful' Utopia ... This directly challenged rational urban planning practices of the 1960s, along with the utopianism that infused much of the movement of 1968. By studying the history of spaces and understanding their heterogeneity, it became possible to identify absolute spaces in which difference, alterity, and 'the other' might flourish or ... actually be constructed. (159-60)

"Of Other Spaces" begins by historicizing heterotopia, stating that as a first principle, every cultural context constitutes its specific heterotopias, which take varied forms. It is at this point that Foucault singles out the "crisis heterotopias" of "so-called primitive societies" (25), sites reserved for individuals in an assumed state of crisis; these have been increasingly replaced in modern societies by "heterotopias of deviation" (ibid.), into which individuals whose behavior is marked by a transgression of social norms are placed (such as the prison). This social and legal dimension also defines the pirate ship, which was both a transgressive by-product of early modern colonial politics and racial relations and an emblematic site of struggle about legitimacy and legality. The pirate ship, mirroring colonial relations while simultaneously inverting them in critical moments, can thus be read as a heterotopia of the crisis of colonial legality and of deviation: a site outlawed by a dominant order that labels it "piratical," thus placing the enslaved or otherwise "colonized" subject, whose economic and military actions are unsanctioned, into a realm of illegitimacy and disenfranchisement. Unlike the prison, however, the pirate ship functions as a mobile inversion of dominant social relations and hence is also a site of social experimentation and potential empowerment. This quality is arguably why the pirate ship was attractive for abolitionist writers.

Foucault's second principle of heterotopology also relates to the historicity of heterotopia, emphasizing the potential of functional change of cultural counter-sites when the actual site remains the same (ibid.). The third principle holds that heterotopias are "capable of juxtaposing in a single real place several spaces, several sites that are in themselves in-

9 For Foucault, this mixture is best exemplified by the mirror, both a utopian and heterotopian site where the imaginary meets the material.

compatible" (ibid.); here, the theatre and the garden are Foucault's selected examples, but the ship could be seen in the same manner as hosting a variety of spaces marked by race, gender, and class / rank. The fourth principle looks at the heterochronous dimension of heterotopia, its "absolute break with ... traditional time" (ibid.), as both the accumulation of time in the cemetery, the library, and the museum and the absolute temporality of the festival and fairground demonstrate. The pirate ship, as a tentative and temporary site of social experimentation, is also marked by such a discontinuous temporality.

The fifth principle is also important for a heterotopological reading of the pirate ship, as it holds that "heterotopias always presuppose a system of opening and closing that both isolates them and makes them penetrable" (26). The entry is either forced or ritualized, according to Foucault; the pirate ship combines the two entry forms, as most pirates had a history of naval impressment behind them and articulated, with the ritual of swearing to the pirate code, the changing of sides and the entry into the counter-culture of piracy. The sixth and final Foucaultian principle concerns the function of the heterotope that unfolds between two extremes: it either creates a "space of illusion that exposes every real space … as still more illusory" (27) or, in what he calls the "heterotope of compensation" (ibid.), compensates for the messiness of ordinary social space in a site that is more perfectly and meticulously arranged and ordered; as examples, Foucault mentions the heterotopia of Puritan New England or the Jesuit South American colonies (ibid.).

It is significant that Foucault ends his lecture with the maritime heterotopia of the ship:[10]

> … [T]he ship is a floating piece of space, a place without a place, that exists by itself, that is closed in on itself and at the same time is given over to the infinity of the sea … [F]rom port to port, from tack to tack, from brothel to brothel, it goes as far as the colonies in search of the most precious treasures they conceal in their garden. … [T]he ship has not only been for our civilization, from the sixteenth century until the present, the great instrument of economic development ... but has been simultaneously the greatest reserve of the imagination. The ship is the heterotopia par excellence. In civilizations with-

10 I have altered the translation slightly, using "ship" instead of "boat," as the French *bateau* of the original text can mean both; it is obvious that Foucault, by evoking colonial ship-faring, does not refer to boats here.

> out ships, dreams dry up, espionage takes the place of adventure, and the police take the place of pirates. (27)

In an uncharacteristic, almost lyric romanticism, Foucault associates piracy with dreams (that have not "dried up") and adventure here. He generalizes the ship, disregarding those vessels that in fact dominated colonial seafaring (i.e. slavers and the ships of the various Navies and mercantilist charter companies), and assumes the viewpoint of the maritime colonizer, praising his civilization as somehow freer (pirates instead of the police), superior in its cultural imagination and as more economically advanced. For the enslaved subject on the Middle Passage, the search for "precious treasures" ended in death, trauma, and dislocation; Foucault entirely obliterates the problematics of "our civilization"'s maritime imagination. Carried away by exoticist desire, it seems, Foucault's formulation becomes poetic rather than analytical and neglects, due to an assumed structuralist oppositionality, that the ship has never "existed by itself" but has always depended on its economic, political, discursive, and material-technological environment and on unequal power relations.

Critics such as Edward Casey or David Harvey are certainly right when they diagnose Foucault's essay with sketchiness and opacity.[11] David Harvey has also criticized Foucault for the formulation discussed above, arguing, with poignant sarcasm, that the entire concept of heterotopia is flawed: "The commercialized cruise ship is indeed a heterotopic site if ever there was one; and what is the critical, liberatory, and emancipatory point of that? Foucault's words could easily form the text of a commercial for Caribbean luxury cruises" (160-61). For Harvey, Foucault's heterotopia is incoherent, as the theoretical principles set forth do not justify his ultimate association of the heterotope as liberatory and emancipatory. In Harvey's reading, Foucault conceives heterotopic spaces as absolute and static, as "somehow outside the dominant social order," as if "their positioning within that order can be severed, attenuated or, as in the prison, inverted on the inside" (160). This is his biggest point of critique: "Whatever happens within them is then presumed to be subversive and of radical political significance" (ibid.), a conjecture he finds uncon-

11 In *The Fate of Place* Casey argues that "Of Other Spaces" is not a detailed analysis of the complexities of place but a rather sketchy proposal of heterotopology that is assumed to open a new field in which spatial modalities disclose and express specific distributions of power in society.

vincing and simplistic. His verdict, in the end, attests banality and escapism to Foucault's lecture.

As an alternative, Harvey proposes Henri Lefebvre's view of heterotopia, which he articulated in *The Urban Revolution* (1968) a year after Foucault's lecture. Like Foucault, Lefebvre understands heterotopias—he prefers the term "heterotopy"—as spaces of difference and potential transformation yet keeps the concept "in tension with (rather than as an alternative to) isotopy (the accomplished and rationalized spatial order of capitalism and the state), as well as with utopia as expressive desire" (Harvey 161). Although the difference between Foucault and Lefebvre is mainly one of gradation and has much to do with the fact that Foucault never expanded on his concept beyond its mentioning in *The Order of Things* and the lecture cited above, Harvey is right in upholding the dialectic dynamism with which Lefebvre infuses his heterotopy, a dynamism foreclosed by Foucault's invocation of absolute spaces: "The differences captured within the heterotopic spaces are not about segregation and separation, but about potentially transformative relations with all other spaces ... The political problem is to find ways to realize their ephemeral potentialities in the face of powerful forces that work to reclaim them for the dominant praxis" (Harvey 162). Lefebvre formulates this as follows:

> The isotopy-heterotopy difference can only be understood dynamically. ... Relations change. Differences and contrasts can result in conflict, or are attenuated, erode, or corrode ... Anomic groups construct heterotopic spaces, which are eventually reclaimed for the dominant practice. (129)

Lefebvre's interpretation and correction frees the Foucaultian heterotope from problematic romanticist implications and the air of absoluteness. From such a perspective, even the pirate ship is not beyond the grasp of "dominant practice." For literary stagings of this heterotope in the Black Atlantic context, this reconception is crucial, as they articulate the dynamism and instability of experimental social spaces whose inversion of the dominant order is always already marked by that order. Without colonialism, without slavery, without political and economic disenfranchisement, no piracy; and yet, piracy became the liminal legal status that was used as a trope to criticize and counter colonialism and slavery.

In sum, Harvey's verdict is perhaps too general. Foucault does highlight, for instance, the double function of the ship as both a "great instrument of economic development" and "the greatest reserve of the imagination" (27), thus pointing to the fact that Western dreams were colonial and economic dreams rather than innocent imaginations of maritime adventure—even though he does not critically discuss the problematics of this double function, which is foundational for the dialectics Harvey finds wanting: without these colonial dreams, the advancement of ship-building and navigation would have severely slowed down; ships became both experimental and conservative sites at once. In an updated Lefebvrian version, the Foucaultian heterotope is apt to point to the intricate relationship between heterotopic spaces, history, and power as well as to sites that are both reflective and constitutive of cultural production. With Foucault and Lefebvre, we can further focus our analytical lens by distinguishing between different heterotopias of the ship and locate them in specific historical circumstances within the history of colonialism and slavery. The pirate ship can then be seen formally as a site resulting from a crisis of legality within the mercantilist colonial Atlantic, usually caused by mutiny or theft, a vessel that is only a temporary, short-lived, and transitional home for the deviant and the subaltern and often simultaneously served diverse colonial projects.

Narrative articulations of the pirate vessel such as Maxwell Philip's eventually adopt a view from aboard ship reminiscent of the heterotope of compensation, as they try to envision a maritime order different from that of the institutionalized Marines: more equal, humane, and just, accommodating plurality rather than embracing uniformity, but also more efficient and strict. The pirate ship thus becomes an attractive literary site due to its specific heterotopic nature: a place home to maritime subjects in the waters of various colonization projects, subjects illegalized in an ostracization from humanity,[12] and a moveable place that existed and functioned by rules and orders different from the dominant ones.

The Ship and the Black Atlantic

Abolitionists across the Atlantic world were imagining a different social order revolving around the issues of resistance, liberty, (human)

12 Already in classical antiquity, Cicero defined the pirate as "*communis hostis omnium*," the enemy of all. For an examination of the development of the term piracy in the field of international law since ancient times, see Daniel Heller-Roazen's recent study *The Enemy of All: Piracy and the Law of Nations*.

property, and (il)legality; it is not surprising that the nineteenth century would take up the motif of piracy in order to question the legitimacy of slavery in literary and other writings. In general, ships have been emblematic, ambivalent literary symbols for abolitionist and Black Atlantic literature due to the crucial transatlantic experience of the Middle Passage and their function as a contact zone between different cultures, between masters and slaves; the literary use of the pirate ship teases out these characteristics by creating a heterotopic, dialectical, and dynamic site of rebellion against the colonial order on the one hand and by emphasizing this site's tenuousness, fragility, and ultimate implication in that order on the other.

In the Black Atlantic context, the ocean, like the ship, similarly functions as an ambivalent, heterotopic site, "a trope marking the unruly space between the past memory of Africa and the present reality of slavery in terms of active resistance" (Pedersen 48). Both the ship and the sea represent zones of cultural contact of a "motley crew" of subjects (Mackenthun; Klein; Birkle and Waller); both are spaces characterized by fluidity and mobility, but they are also paradoxical spaces marked by both oppression and liberation. In *The Black Atlantic: Modernity and Double Consciousness* (1993), Paul Gilroy reads the ship and the sea in a double-edged manner as both a vehicle of exploitation and resistance. "[T]he image of ships in motion across the spaces between Europe, America, Africa, and the Caribbean" (4) is evoked by Gilroy to highlight transnational movement within the sphere of the black diaspora. Ships, for Gilroy, not only recall the Middle Passage, but also subsequent travels of Afrodiasporic individuals and activists such as Martin Delany or Fredrick Douglass. Furthermore, the moving ship, as a symbol, represents "the moving to and fro between nations, crossing borders" and denote "micro-systems of linguistic and political hybridity" (Gilroy 12) due to their constant state of being in-between (nations, continents, cultures, etc.) at sea. Along with these forms of personal movement associated with the symbol of the ship, Gilroy foregrounds "the circulation of ideas . . . as well as the movement of key cultural and political artefacts" as highly important means of Afrodiasporic cultural and political exchange within the black Atlantic world (4). James Procter summarizes that "[c]irculation, movement, passage and journeying are Gilroy's preferred metaphors here, allowing him to move beyond what he takes to be the narrow, sclerotic confines of the nation" (152). Gilroy calls attention to the ideas of movement and mobility, which are key components of transnational cultural exchange, as opposed to stasis and the supposedly secure harbor of the nation-state.

In his book, Gilroy analyzes a number of literary works written by Afrodiasporic authors such as W.E.B. DuBois or Richard Wright. Yet, as Gesa Mackenthun has shown, the Black Atlantic paradigm can also provide new perspectives on maritime fiction by writers like James Fenimore Cooper or Herman Melville. Already in the late eighteenth and early nineteenth centuries, a number of Barbary captivity narratives had fuelled the development of a national U.S.-American literature by narrating the experience of being captured and enslaved by Muslim pirates on the North African coast during the War with Tripoli, the young nation's first armed conflict after independence from Great Britain; many Barbary captivity narratives in fact used accounts of piratical enslavement in order to criticize the inhumanity and brutality of chattel slavery in the U.S (such as Royall Tyler's *Algerine Captive*, 1797; Mackenthun 38-47). In addition, Daniel Defoe's popular eighteenth-century pirate novels depicted pirates who liberated slave-ships, implying that the real criminals were slave-traders rather than pirates while simultaneously they emphasized that pirates themselves often profited from the triangular trade. Philip's novel *Emmanuel Appadocca* is thus certainly not the first to bespeak a Black Atlantic consciousness in tackling slavery and its consequences through the trope of piracy, nor would it be the last. But, while Philip is not the first to critique slavery through the figure of the pirate, his novel may well be the earliest contribution by an African American to this literary tradition; its radical innovation was its sympathetic portrayal of a colored "pirate"; in addition, "it was the first Anglo-Caribbean novel to [examine the subject of miscegenation] from the point of view of a colonized person" (Cudjoe, *Boundaries* 123).

Emmanuel Appadocca; or, Blighted Life: A Tale of the Boucaneers

In *Emmanuel Appadocca*, piracy is constructed as a result of disenfranchisement on the one hand and as a source of empowerment and strength in the struggle against inequality and injustice—particularly against slavery and its consequences—on the other. In the novel, the piratical vessel enacts a different sort of "imagined community" (Benedict Anderson's term) than that of a nation-state, which excluded various groups of people due to its racist and classist colonial structures. *Appadocca* is Philip's only novel and articulates the injustice suffered by American children of mixed descent, whose white fathers abandon them, as well as by their mothers, using the topic of filial revenge, the trope of piracy, and the discourse of natural law.[13] The novel can thus be read, as Gesa Mackenthun argues, as a "meditation of how an enslaved person ought to behave under the crushing weight of slavery" (ibid.).

Emmanuel Appadocca is autobiographically inspired. While Philip's parentage is not entirely clear, it is known that he was an illegitimate child, offspring of a white owner and a colored woman on his father's estate on Trinidad. In recognition of his intellectual capacities, he was sent to a Jesuit school in Scotland, where he received a classical education, learned many foreign languages, and entered a solicitor's office upon his return home (James 254-55). In 1851, he went to England to read for the bar; around this time, he wrote to his father asking for help, a plea refused or at least neglected (ibid. 255). Although Philip—a man famous for both intellectual wit and artistic temperament (ibid. 263)—later became an esteemed member of Trinidad society, a powerful orator, and an important legislator and commissioner, *Appadocca* proves, as C.L.R. James argued, "the powerful effect with which the misfortune of his birth weighed upon his mind" (ibid. 255).

The text is a result of the Black Atlantic and its racial relations which fundamentally shaped Philip's biography: he crossed the Atlantic a number of times and actually wrote the novel in London as a response to the slavery crisis in the U.S. that followed the Fugitive Slave laws of 1850.[14] The novel, "located within the literary, cultural, and socioeconomic context of the Atlantic world system" (Cain xv), is a "triangulated text" (ibid. xvi) that discusses slavery and piracy from a transnational, ex-centric perspective. Though it was apparently a popular book in its own times—

13 According to Cudjoe, Philip had encountered the motif of revenge in Euripides's play *Hecuba*, which is cited in the novel's epigram (see *Boundaries* 124; also Cain xxxviii). Cynthia James places Philip's novel in the context of the "maroon paradigm," referring to the runaway slaves of African origin in the Americas (50-53). This critical paradigm, according to Caribbean cultural theorists such as Edward Kamau Brathwaite, revolves around tropes of abandonment, flight, and resistance, as well as around questions of ancestry and filiation. James emphasizes Appadocca's restlessness, homelessness, and multicultural emphases.

14 For a detailed account of the book's historical context as it relates to slavery, see Cain xxiv-xxxiv.

Philip made enough money with it so as to finance months of traveling through Europe—the text had been largely forgotten until the 1997 publication of the University of Massachusetts Press edition (prepared by Selwyn Cudjoe). Partly historical romance, partly slave narrative,[15] partly swash-buckling adventure narrative, it is told in the third person and weaves together "the ideology of organized piracy" (Cudjoe, "Preface" xiii) as parallel to the "pirating" of African slaves by whites and turns this ideology on its head when the colored creole hero becomes a pirate himself.

The plot concerns the desertion of the protagonist's mulatto mother (she is most likely of black and Spanish descent)16 by his father, the wealthy British sugar planter James Willmington, and the son's attempt to restore his then deceased mother's honor. The story begins when Appadocca's pirate ship, significantly named The Black Schooner, captures Willmington's British merchant ship on which the creole pirate discovers his father. Following his plan of revenge, Appadocca punishes Willmington for leaving his mother and his illegitimate offspring by casting him out upon the sea, tied to a barrel. But he unexpectedly survives and has Appadocca imprisoned on a British Navy's man-of-war, anchored close to the Danish colony of St. Thomas. Aboard ship, he encounters Charles, the son of the ship's admiral and an old friend and former fellow student at Paris. Appadocca tells Charles the story of how he had to leave Paris after his mother's death: without money to sustain himself, he had to return to the Caribbean instead of finishing his education, where he then formed his pirate crew with the Caribbean "buccaneers" in order to take revenge on his father. Appadocca escapes from the Navy ship by swimming to the Venezuelan coast, where he rejoins the pirates and yet again takes his

15 The generic affiliation with slave narratives is especially evident in the book's endorsement, written by Philip's supervisor and "Her Majesty's representative" (*EA* 10) to counter contemporary racist claims against black authorship, which presents not only Philip's authorial skills, but also his integrity as a Trinidadian citizen. In this context, William Cain writes that the novel "is not only about a character of imposing strength of will, but also is . . . intended as an act of will against the claims that persons of African descent are incapable of authorship . . . " (xlii).

16 As Gesa Mackenthun argues, the fact that his mother is of part-Spanish descent means that Appadocca assumes two subaltern (or at least marginal) positions at once. The trace of his Spanish heritage is visible in the protagonist's name, probably inherited from his mother, which combines Jesus's first name and that of the legendary Spanish Vice-Admiral Don Sebastian Ruiz de Apodaca, who had surrendered Trinidad to the British in 1797 (Cudjoe's note in the 1997 edition of the novel, 3).

father prisoner on his ship. In a terrible hurricane, Willmington sinks with her, going "down into the Caribbean sea like slaves on the middle passage trade he has profited from" (James 51), while the creole pirate-protagonist commits suicide by jumping off board, convinced that his mission is fulfilled. The trope of the tragic mulatto is rehearsed here as a "tragic tale of loss that Atlantic slavery endlessly repeated" (Cain 5), although Appadocca's death is narrated as a self-determined reunion with the ocean rather than as a suicide out of despair; hence, his end functions as a foil to Willmington's involuntary drowning: Appadocca bids farewell to his crewmembers Jack Jimmy and Lorenzo and "[w]ith a spring ... jumped from the rock and threw himself headlong into the thundering waves below" (EA 244).

One of the central discourses in *Emmanuel Appadocca* is that of legitimacy, of rights and lawfulness, of both slavery and piracy, focusing on the natural right to resistance, which is here translated into violent, even self-destructive vengeance. The most crucial scenes for *Emmanuel Appadocca*'s inversive Black Atlantic commentary on slavery and piracy are the protagonist's conversations with his friend Charles. Notably, they take place on the Navy ship on which he is imprisoned. Coming from the pirate schooner, a site of countercultural agency for Appadocca and his crew, he transfers its heterotopian and dialogic qualities onto this imperial vessel, trying to infuse it with a spirit of resistance that fundamentally questions the legal definition of piracy (which defines him as a criminal). About midway into the book, Appadocca gives a powerful speech in which he argues that colonialism itself is a piratical system:

> If I am guilty of piracy, you, too—the whole of mankind is guilty of the very same sort of crime. . . . [T]he whole of the civilized world turns, exists, and grows enormous on the licensed system of robbing and thieving, which you seem to criminate so much . . . The people which a convenient position . . . first consolidated, developed, and enriched, . . . sends forth its numerous and powerful ships to scour the seas, to penetrate into hitherto unknown regions, where discovering new and rich countries, they, in the name of civilization, first open an intercourse with the peaceful and contented inhabitants, next contrive to provoke a quarrel, which always terminates in a war that leaves them the conquerors and possessors of the land. ... [T]he straggling and weakest portions of a certain race, whose power of bodily and mental endurance, renders them the likely objects to answer this end, are chosen. The coasts of the country on which nature has placed them, are immediately lined

> with ships of acquisitive voyagers, who kidnap and tear them away ... (EA 112-14)

In his astute analysis, slavery appears as a direct consequence of the colonial venture encompassing the entire "civilized" world, and "powerful ships"—he refers to the slavers here—are this world's empire-builders. Appadocca's vehicle of revenge, in contrast, is a highly mobile site of deviation and crisis, an embodiment of an inverted colonial order in which, in this case, the colored subject is the captain rather than the cargo, and formerly impressed sailors find relief in a community of almost-equals.

Yet *Emmanuel Appadocca*'s pirate ship is by no means devoid of racial or class hierarchies. Her captain is a Byronic hero, a stoic scholar-philosopher and highly articulate "Quadroon," as contemporary racial terminology would have had it (Mackenthun 143), whose light complexion is emphasized time and again to set him apart from the few blacks that are identified as such in the book, most notably the coon-figure of Jack Jimmy, who is frequently compared to a monkey (*EA* 38, 82) and whose physiognomy is repeatedly designed as the grounds for his typologically fixed role of a figure of comic relief (as he is abused by the crew for their amusement, for instance; ibid. 29-30).

The alleged violence of the Caribbean pirates—more specifically, the French boucaneers of the novel—is of special significance in the context of the text's discursive appropriation of piracy as a means of heterotopic resistance.[17] As William Cain has pointed out, *Uncle Tom's Cabin* of 1852, a book Philip doubtlessly knew when he crafted *Appadocca*, had made the diabolic Simon Legree an apprentice among these pirates (xxxv), and *Appadocca* takes up and refashions this motif of piracy as a response to the Fugitive Slave Act. Moving from the Caribbean background toward the ocean in its setting, Philip's novel inverts the significance of this Atlantic motif through the association of piracy with a rough, quasi-democratic, revengeful Robin-Hood principle (Cudjoe, *Boundaries* 125; Lewis 81), "waging war against the exploiting classes" (Mackenthun 140) by redistributing the wealth of the colonies. Piracy, for

17 Another significant appropriation concerns the protagonist's use of the "cultural property of the white, Western world, making it equally his as a resource for the composition of literature that both will and will not be part of the classic tradition" (xxxix), as Cain comments on the text's frequent use of quotes from the classical canon of Western literature.

Philip, signifies a just rebellion, a private, legitimate war against colonial exploiters and economic inequality—he repeatedly invokes their solidarity as misfortunate outcasts, indeed as the "wretched of the earth," as Frantz Fanon would later call it.[18] To the colored pirate, the pirating of goods is considered just as legitimate, or perhaps more legitimate even, than the pirating of human beings:

> Because organized piracy presumed its own values, bespoke a particular kind of autonomy on the part of the pirates, validated a sense of courage in the pirates' undertakings, and cultivated a righteous indifference toward official society, Philip found it a fitting vehicle to carry forward the slave's sentiments about his condition. Because organized piracy inverted the notions of justice sanctioned with the civil state—that is, the purported respect for private property (which includes slaves)—it offered Philip an apt metaphor to advance an alternative system of values that differed from that of the slave-owning class. In other words, while the slave-owning class robbed Africans of their lives . . . , the pirates robbed the slave-owning class of its illusions about their system and themselves and sought to destroy them at any cost. (Cudjoe, "Afterword" 257)

This aptness of organized piracy as a metaphorical vehicle to advance humanitarian values forbidding the enslavement of human beings leads Philip to the anachronistic representation of the buccaneers as Appadocca's allies and the "machinery" of the text, as the preface states (6). In fact, the buccaneers were Protestant hunters-settlers in the seventeenth century Caribbean on Tortuga and Hispaniola, who became anti-Spanish pirates when the Spanish colonists tried to drive them from their islands. Usually, these all-male societies not only formed alliances with the natives but also exploited indigenous groups. Their stories were widely publicized with the 1684 translation of Alexander Olivier Exquemelin's *De Americaensche Zee-Roovers* (1678) into English as *The Buccaneers of America*, a text Philip might have known as it underwent various reprints and was widely available in the Americas and in Europe. Buccaneers became a generic term for pirates, and Philip might not have made any distinction here; but his choice of the word *boucaniers* in the subtitle, deriving from the Arawak word "bukan" that referred to the wooden crates used for smoking meat (a technique the pirates learned from the surviving natives), draws a parallel conflict between a colonial empire

18 See also Mackenthun 146.

and its subalterns: first with regard to the predominantly poor settlers driven to piracy and to native peoples on the verge of genocide in the seventeenth century, and second, regarding disenfranchised African Americans in the nineteenth.

It is therefore remarkable that Philip blends various historical contexts in his representation of the *boucaniers*: the novel tells us that they are quasi-aristocratic exiles disgusted with the 1789 French Revolution (rather than banished Huguenots and escaped servants in the 1600s), while their society is paradoxically described in analogy with Exquemelin's 1678 account: "The French revolution had torn up whole families together, from the soil on which they had been rooted for generations, and had driven them to distant countries for protection and subsistence. They had carried with them, to their new homes, a strong hatred for their then democratic country, in particular, and for the whole world in general" (*EA* 109), the pirate captain recounts, thus contradicting his description of life aboard the pirate ship, which is made up by subjects of various nationalities (most notably French, Spanish, and English) who we meet as Gregoire, José, or Jack, to name but a few, and whose manners are all but aristocratic. That Appadocca describes "those boucans" as his "fellow students of the French University . . . belonging to the old aristocracy" (ibid. 110) is a significant anachronism. Still, for Philip, "boucanier" is better apt than "pirate" in the title because revenge is the driving force of the plot as it specifically refers to a historical phenomenon in the Caribbean the narrative thus evokes, since the foundational motives for the original buccaneer associations were defense and revenge against the Spaniards. In contrast, fictional pirates, by the 1850s, would have triggered less serious associations in Philip's readers as they had mostly turned into rather flat figures of cheap novels and the popular stage, associations Philip's certainly wanted to avoid with respect to the gravity of his subject matter.

The leitmotif of revenge as the multi-racial pirate's prime motivation also refers to a different aspect of the Atlantic contact zone, namely the meeting and mixing of different cultural traditions and hence also of different understandings of legality and right. In this context, Appadocca's interpretation of the *lex talionis*, the right to revenge, is that "this theological law is an integral part of ancient Africa's philosophical and theological system . . . even though Europeans came to associate it with Hebraic Law. He suggests that this African theological borrowing was applied incorrectly within the Judeo-Christian system" (Cudjoe, *Boundaries* 126).

Ancient cosmic laws provide him with philosophical legitimation for his actions because he is unable to find justice under colonial law; his only confidence is that of God's justice attainable solely through the human execution of cosmic and "natural," positivistic laws (Mackenthun 145). Voicing his marginal perspective with the help of natural rights philosophy, Appadocca deems this approach as a necessary ethical bulwark against the immoral capitalist materialism characteristic of the Atlantic triangle: "[C]ommerce makes steam engines and money—it assists not the philosophical progress of the mind," he says (*EA* 116).[19] Thus, *Emmanuel Appadocca* partakes in what Derek Walcott has called the Caribbean predilection for a "literature of recrimination and despair, a literature of revenge written by the descendants of slaves or a literature of remorse written by the descendants of masters" (2; qtd. in Smith 166). The question of descent, of the "descendant of the master" (Smith 166), is of particular importance for the questioning of dominant discourses of legitimacy in *Appadocca*; while Philip refines his protagonist with an aquiline nose, light complexion, and intellectual abilities and thus seems to deny the African component in favor of the Indian and Spanish element (present in Appadocca's looks and name), an "Africanist presence" (Toni Morrison's term) pervades the narrative in a number of respects and hence emphasizes the importance of the Atlantic as a contact zone. Faith Smith argues that this presence in *Appadocca* caused "particular kinds of anxieties" (175) in nineteenth-century Trinidadian literature, disturbing nationalist discourses. Yet the novel is less concerned with the striving for a national (black) literature of revenge—after all, Trinidad, at this time, "was a place where racial oppression was less entrenched than in other colonies" (ibid. 176)—but rather voices a transnational, diasporic appeal to justice by a creole child of mixed heritage on behalf of all "illegitimate" children and their mothers, imprisoned by the racist and class structures of the Atlantic world.

In the context of this essay, what is most significant is the fact that Captain Appadocca combines ancient African knowledge, especially Egyptian astronomy and cosmology, and his Western schooling not only in his legal rhetorics but also in the very act of navigation. His nautical skills, based on his astronomical and mathematical abilities, are described as superior knowledge throughout the book. "In its disguise of astronomy

19 Wilson addresses figurations of justice in the novel, hinging his argument on its liminal physical and philosophical setting.

(representing ancient civilization), then, the theme of Africa is central to a novel which almost completely bypasses the topic of race" (Mackenthun 144).[20] The qualities of the *Black Schooner* are particularly significant here. Aboard deck we find "[t]he strange vessel"'s color inverted: "The long level deck was scoured as white as snow; not a speck, not a nail-head, not the minutest particle of anything could be discovered upon it. . . [T]he tapering masts were as clean and as smooth as ivory . . . An awning, as white as the deck which it sheltered" (*EA* 20); also, everything is marked by the pirate emblem of a human skull "place on the crossing of two dead men's bones" (ibid.). Metonymically, the ship stands for both its captain and crew, then: it is / they are black and white both, it is / they are a product of Europe, Africa, and America, it is / they are illegitimate, marked always already by society's death sentence and thus need to remind themselves of the imminence of death and the temporality of life. Life aboard is described as guided by these principles: there is much feasting and merrymaking when there is time; but as soon as the ship and the crew is endangered, firm discipline and obedience reigns the ship.

Compared to the Navy ships in the book, the pirate ship is depicted as far superior in its technological equipment, efficiency, speed, and navigation; in fact, it seems to be infused with almost supernatural power reminiscent of Jules Verne's *Nautilus* (which he envisioned fifteen years after Philip designed the *Black Schooner*). The vessel is introduced as

> a low, black, balahoo schooner, whose model . . . was most beautiful. She was built as sharply as a sword, with her bows terminating in the shape of a Gar's lance, while her stern slanted off in the most graceful proportions. But the most remarkable part in her build, was her immense and almost disproportionate length, which, combined with her perfectly straight lines, low hull, and the slenderness of her make, gave her the appearance of a large serpent. . . . Her position also, and the manner in which she seemed moored . . . was strange and peculiar. She was not swinging to the wind or current, but she rode under a bow and stern anchor, which kept her head directly towards the Dragon's Mouth, while the rippling waves . . . broke playfully on her side. (*EA* 18)

20 On the trope of Ethiopian splendor and Egyptian civilization in nineteenth-century culture, see Mackenthun 144 as well as Cudjoe, *Boundaries* 126 n. 16 & 17 and 129-30.

The schooner is in harmony with the ocean's natural forces (and thus the positivist basis of natural law doctrine), and eventually even uses these natural forces as if on her Captain's behalf in order to bring Willmington to his end when it sinks in a hurricane. In symbolic union with the protagonist, the ship uses the forces of nature (wind and waves) more efficiently than her enemies do, as Appadocca draws on his knowledge of the natural sciences (astronomy, mathematics, optics and even electronics) to surpass his powerful combatants. The ship employs a system of optical deception by using mirrors and natural light to keep her enemies within sight:

> From the tall masts of the schooner, there were reared to an immense height into the air long poles of steel that were joined and joined again to each other . . . ; at the top of these were adjusted large globe-shaped metallic mirrors, that were filled with a thick white liquid, which was continuously agitated by a small electric engine, which received its power from a battery on deck. These mirrors, when the sun was at a certain height, were made, by a trigonometrical principle, to receive impressions of objects that were beyond the scope of the human eye, and by conveying those impressions to other mirrors, that were fixed in a thousand different ways, to the several parts of the vessel, gave the power to an individual on deck to see every movement of any vessel which would otherwise be invisible, while his own remained unseen. (*EA* 193)

Optical inversion makes the pirate ship superior in strength "by the force of the same genius Appadocca was enabled to excel, to be unapproachable and irresistible" (ibid.). As a heterotope of compensation, the ship is portrayed as peaceful and social relations are just, with Appadocca reigning like a benevolent patriarch over his piratical crew:

> The firmness of mind which enabled him to curb the natures of even pirates, and to establish a discipline on board the Black Schooner that made his men simultaneously act as if they were but the individual members of only one single body moved but by one spirit, might . . . have procured for him the reputation of a wise and great leader; the powers of invention, which supplied even the deficiencies of human nature, and permitted him to make almost every element his servant, could again have handed down his name to posterity as that of a profound philosopher . . . It is not Emmanuel Appadocca alone that has been thus doomed to bury a high intellect in obscurity, or been impelled by circumstances to expend its force in guilt . . . (*EA* 193-94)

Philip's description is reminiscent of the ideal state of Thomas Hobbes, the collective body of the Leviathan that is moved by a single spirit. It points to the waste of human (creole or mixed-descent) genius and intelligence through an unjust system of colonial oppression and racism that bans the "illegitimate" subject from official society directly (through laws of disenfranchisement, such as in the U.S. of the time) or indirectly (through uneven economic distribution and opportunities, as in Appadocca's case).

As a transatlantic cultural broker, Appadocca brings into dialogue Western and African philosophical traditions rather than uncritically adopting dominant Western perspectives guiding legal and scholarly discourses. Much could be said about the romantic subplots and the role of gender in *Emmanuel Appadocca*; much more analysis would be needed to spell out its protagonist's philosophy and reasoning. My main point in this essay, however, is that the pirate ship is emblematic in its heterotopian embodiment of the ideal state, a harmonious social body that is possible and secured only through the captain's hybrid knowledge and the transnational, transethnic solidarity of the "wretched outcasts" (*EA* 93) of the Atlantic contact zone. Yet, as I have also argued, this heterotopia is at the same time implicated in dominant racist and gender discourses; Jack Jimmy, the black "sorceress" Celeste, equally stereotyped, as well as the absence of women from the ship (if not from the narrative)[21] are significant in this respect. In addition, the ship's alternative, more perfect social order is short-lived and thus does not offer a permanent base on which a more equal and just Atlantic world could be based.

Conclusion

In the seventeenth century, Samuel Johnson had compared the ship to the prison and characterized sea laborers as the most miserable among workers (qtd. in Rediker, *Villains* 43). Harsh discipline and hard work, low wages that often remained unpaid, meager or rotten supplies, disease,

21 There are in fact two romantic subplots, one concerning the former captive Agnes, who eventually is united with Appadocca's Spanish mate Lorenzo (who turns out to be the respectable St. James Carmonte); the second romantic liaison concerns Feliciana, daughter of a Venezuelan *llanero*, who falls in love with Appadocca when he is rescued from the coast and tries to make him renounce his plan of revenge and piracy altogether.

violence, and the constant threat of punishment characterized the imperial ship. While the ships of the merchant marines and the Navies functioned as imperial machines in which sailors were reduced to "hands" that set it into and kept it in motion, pirate ships turned the spatial insulation and isolation of the ship, the very qualities that led Foucault to call it heterotopian, into an asset. It was in this process of physical and symbolic appropriation that the ship was turned into a vehicle for an alternative, ex-experimental order. Peter Linebaugh and Marcus Rediker argue that "within imperial hydrarchy grew a different hydrarchy, one that was both proletarian and oppositional" (153), an alternative social order from below deck that valued seafaring abilities and group solidarity higher than social class, color, or national descent. Historically speaking, pirate crews turned their ships into sites of an alternative social order based on non-hegemonic values like fraternity, justice, or equality, although they were by no means free from the racisms and sexisms that have pervaded the modern age.

When the sailing ship was the single means of transportation that connected the shores of the Atlantic, it functioned as a medium of transatlantic communication and a heterotopian contact zone between different social orders and value-systems informed by hegemonic and anti-hegemonic discourses emanating from the antithetic experiences of the Atlantic triangle. In the literature of piracy, this imperial *and* resistant site is not designed as a clear-cut entity with fixed borders, but rather as a fluid, permeable contact zone, a site of conflict and struggle. In this context, it is significant that Appadocca and his buccaneers do not envision any territorial existence by their own values and "sought no other shelter than that which was afforded us by the high and wide seas" (*EA* 160), knowing the conditionality of heterotopic space.[22] The pirate ship and the sea emerge as counter-sites that, because of their very distance to "the law of the land" are privileged both in the development of social critique and the negotiation of cultural difference:

---

22 The yearning for a more stable home surfaces near the end of the book, when, in a letter to his friend Charles shortly before Appadocca's death, the protagonist reports that he plans to "lead the men who have followed me so bravely . . . to some remote spot on the fertile and vast continent that lies on our right, and build them a city in which they may live happily, quietly, and far removed from the world, whose sympathy they cannot hope, and care not, to possess" (*EA* 236); also before his death, he arranges that "half [of his treasure] shall be devoted to "a college for abandoned children" (243).

> Appadocca's assertion of a postnational, indeed 'oceanic', identity, coupled with the fact that he and his pirates never reside on land . . . characterizes *Emmanuel Appadocca* as a multicultural, polyphonic, 'Atlantic' book . . . Philip inscribes the Atlantic Ocean as a site of 'natural' resistance against all forms of oppression, exploitation, and paternal disavowal . . . , a multicultural contact zone which witnessed the most intense experiences of horror while holding the no less intensely felt promise of human equality and freedom which was unattainable on land. (Mackenthun 145-46)

That the pirate's mobile, temporary home has to remain beyond the Caribbean shores is both evidence of an emergent counter-modernity informed by the Black Atlantic and the tragedy of Philip's text. In the nineteenth century, the heterotope of the pirate ship thus helped Black Atlantic literature like Philip's to give voice to subaltern subject positions and allowed for a discursive questioning of the dominant order, even though the design of a "more perfect" place from the perspective of the oppressed remains unstable. As a heterotope of both crisis and compensation, then, the pirate ship in *Emmanuel Appadocca* is a site of instability as well as potential.

Works Cited

Birkle, Carmen, and Nicole Waller, eds. *"The Sea Is History": Exploring the Atlantic*. Heidelberg: Winter, 2009.

Bolster, W. Jeffrey. *Black Jacks: African American Seamen in the Age of Sail*. Cambridge: Harvard UP, 1997.

Cain, William E. "Introduction: Emmanuel Appadocca in Its American Context." *Emmanuel Appadocca; or, Blighted Life. A Tale of the Boucaneers*. Ed. Selwyn R. Cudjoe. Amherst: U of Massachusetts P, 1997. xv-lv.

Casey, Edward S. *The Fate of Place: A Philosophical History*. Berkeley: U of California P, 1997.

Cudjoe, Selwyn R. "Preface." *Emmanuel Appadocca; or, Blighted Life. A Tale of the Boucaneers*. Ed. Selvwyn. R. Cudjoe. Amherst: U of Massachusetts P, 1997. ix-xiv.

---. "Afterword: Emmanuel Appadocca, the First Anglo-Caribbean Novel." *Emmanuel Appadocca; or, Blighted Life. A Tale of the Boucaneers*. Ed. Selwyn. R. Cudjoe. Amherst: U of Massachusetts P, 1997. 249-75.

---. *Beyond Boundaries. The Intellectual Tradition of Trinidad and Tobago in the Nineteenth Century*. Amherst: U of Massachusetts P, 2003.

Foucault, Michel. "Of Other Spaces." Trans. Jay Miskowiec. *Diacritics* 1 (1986): 22-27.

---. *The Order of Things: An Archaeology of the Human Sciences*. 1966/1970. New York: Vintage, 1994.

Ganser, Alexandra. "'That the Enchantments of the Sea, may not have too strong and quick a Force upon some': Seafaring Mobilities in Transatlantic Narratives of Piracy Around 1700." *Figures of Mobility: Pirates, Drifters, Fugitives in the U.S. and Beyond*. Eds. A. Ganser, Katharina Gerund, and Heike Paul. Heidelberg: Winter. Forthcoming.

Gilroy, Paul. *The Black Atlantic: Modernity and Double Consciousness*. London: Verso, 1993.

Harvey, David. *Cosmopolitanism and the Geographies of Freedom*. New York: Columbia UP, 2009.

Heller-Roazen, Daniel. *The Enemy of All: Piracy and the Law of Nations*. New York: Zone Books, 2009.

James, C.L.R. "Michel Maxwell Philip: 1829-1888." *The Beacon* 1.6 (Sep. 1931). Repr. in *From Trinidad: An Anthology of Early West Indian Writing*. Ed. Reinhard W. Sander. London: Hodder and Stoughton, 1978. 253-69.

James, Cynthia. *The Maroon Narrative: Caribbean Literature in English Across Boundaries, Ethnicities, and Centuries*. Portsmouth: Heinemann, 2002.

Kazanjian, David. *National Culture and the Colonizing Trick: Imperial Citizenship in Early America*. Minneapolis: U of Minnesota P, 2003.

Klein, Bernhard, and Gesa Mackenthun, eds. *Sea Changes: Historicizing the Ocean*. New York: Routledge, 2004.

Lefebvre, Henri. *The Urban Revolution*. 1970. Trans. Robert Bononno. Minneapolis: U of Minnesota P, 2003.

Lewis, Gordon K. *Main Currents in Caribbean Thought. The Historical Evolution of Caribbean Society in Its Ideological Aspects, 1492-1900*. 1983. Lincoln: U of Nebraska P, 2004.

Linebaugh, Peter, and Marcus Rediker. *The Many-Headed Hydra: Sailors, Slaves, Commoners, and the Hidden History of the Revolutionary Atlantic*. Boston: Beacon P, 2000.

Mackenthun, Gesa. *Fictions of the Black Atlantic in American Foundational Literature*. London: Routledge, 2004.

Nielsen, Aldon Lynn. *C.L.R. James: A Critical Introduction*. Jackson: UP of Mississippi, 1997.

Pedersen, Carl. "Sea Change: The Middle Passage and the Transatlantic Imagination." *The Black Columbiad: Defining Moments in African*

American Literature and Culture. Eds. Werner Sollors and Maria Diedrich. Cambridge: Harvard UP, 1994. 42-51.

Philip, Michel Maxwell. *Emmanuel Appadocca; or, Blighted Life. A Tale of the Boucaneers*. 1854. Ed. Selwyn R. Cudjoe. Amherst: U of Massachusetts P, 1997.

Pratt, Mary Louise. *Imperial Eyes: Travel Writing and Transculturation*. London: Routledge, 1992.

Procter, James. "Diaspora." *The Routledge Companion to Postcolonial Studies*. Ed. John McLeod. London: Routledge, 2007. 151-57.

Rediker, Marcus. "The Red Atlantic; or: 'a terrible blast swept over the heaving sea'." *Sea Changes: Historicizing the Ocean*. Eds. Bernhard Klein and Gesa Mackenthun. New York: Routledge, 2004. 111-30.

---. *Villains of All Nations: Atlantic Pirates in the Golden Age*. Boston: Beacon Press, 2004.

Smith, Faith. "Beautiful Indians, Troublesome Negroes, and Nice White Men: Caribbean Romances and the Invention of Trinidad." *Caribbean Romances: The Politics of Regional Representation*. Ed. Belinda J. Edmondson. Charlottesville: UP of Virginia, 1999. 163-82.

Walcott, Derek. "The Muse of History." *Is Massa Day Dead? Black Moods in the Caribbean*. Ed. Orde Coombs. New York: Anchor, 1974. 1-27.

Wilson, Gregory. "Between Piracy and Justice: Liminality in Maxwell Philip's Emmanuel Appadocca." *Postcolonial Text* 1.1 (2004). http://postcolonial.org/index.php/pct/article/view/260/769 (accessed 10 October 2010).

SUPERNAFTA and the Language of Global Excess: Trade Zone Encounters in Karen Tei Yamashita's *Tropic of Orange*

Susanne Wegener

Susanne Wegner focuses on the unequal global power relationships in the wake of NAFTA. In her reading of Karen Tei Yamashita's novel Tropic of Orange *(1997), Wegener highlights the discursive and paradoxical dynamics that Yamashita's Asian American protagonists negotiate in their own struggle for visibility and economical survival only to realize that in their own L.A. local contexts, the free trade motto NAFTA cast over the Pacific Rim constitutes a complex entanglement into economies that prosper on the free movement of capital.*

The victory of NAFTA is neither silent nor subtle. On the contrary, corresponding to the official broadcasting of its birth, this victory is a loud and shrill affair, a media performance that significantly takes place before tens of thousands of spectators in the Pacific Rim Auditorium of L.A. Admittedly, it is the fictitious Los Angeles of Karen Tei Yamashita's novel *Tropic of Orange* (1997)where the spectacular fight of "SUPERNAFTA" against his opponent "El Gran Mojado" is staged in a "self-consciously melodramatic" (Rody 146) scene towards the end of the novel. The highly allegoric dramatization of the encounter between a heroic personification of the North American Free Trade Agreement and the wrestling-superstar incarnation of the archetypal Pan-American trickster figure Arcangel, who is one of the seven focalizing protagonists in *Tropic of Orange,* is the culmination of a critical discourse that throughout the novel deconstructs the language of global excess, which marks the official rhetoric of contemporary global capitalism.

Presented in an original, cross-generic, hybrid, and fragmented narrative that blends the sober language of cultural criticism with a lyrical magical realism, the novel's discourse re-works the lingo of a homogenizing narrative of globalization and the pervasive, neoliberal rhetoric of contemporary capitalist free market ideology. Yamashita's fictional representation of L.A., the U.S. and Mexico in globalization thus evokes, interrogates and often ridicules the language of global excess and the cultural concepts this purely economic language has absorbed and stripped of its emancipatory agency.

The Freedom in "Free Trade"

Although a "de facto absorption of Mexico into the US economy" (Smorkaloff 88) has been going on for quite some time *before* the North American Free Trade Agreement among Canada, the U.S. and Mexico was legally codified and signed on 12 August 1992, NAFTA's official implementation by a 2000-page legal document (Wallace 146) has locked up provisions for a lopsided distribution of economic and political power in favor of the U.S. for decades to come. Noam Chomsky points to the rhetoric of freedom and transnational convergence in the official promotion of NAFTA that only thinly veils the de facto imposition of "a mixture of liberalization and protection, designed to keep the wealth and power firmly in the hands of the masters of the 'new imperial age'" (14). Identifying private, U.S.-based and state-subsidized 'transnational' corporations (TNCs)[1] as the true beneficiaries of NAFTA, Chomsky quotes the Labor Advisory Committee's[2] critical report on NAFTA in order to reveal a downside, which the agreement's free market rhetoric obscures. According to the 1992 LAC report the treaty

> will have the effect of prohibiting democratically elected bodies at [all] levels of government from enacting measures deemed inconsistent with the provisions of the agreement, ... including those of the environment, workers'

1 On the problematic distinction between "multi*national*" and "*trans*national" corporations see Miyoshi 1993, 736ff. Miyoshi defines a' truly' transnational corporation as "no longer tied to its nation of origin" but "adrift and mobile, ready to settle anywhere and exploit any state including its own, as long as the affiliation serves its own interest" ("A Borderless World" 736).

2 Significantly, according to Chomsky, the Labor Advisory Committee (LAC), "established by the Trade Act of 1974 to advise the executive branch on any trade agreement" and "based in the unions," was provided with the text of NAFTA only one day before its report on the treaty was due in order to preclude critical debate (14-17).

> rights, and health and safety, all open to challenge as 'unfair restraint of trade.' (19)

Only a few years after the implementation of NAFTA a soaring number of *maquiladoras*[3] in North Mexico and the desperate reality of their employees vigorously corroborate this somber prediction. Despite the poor working conditions and mere survival wages maquiladora workers, although working on Mexican soil, must be considered an indirect export of workforce, which in conjunction with direct labor export in the form of Mexican migration to the U.S., drain Mexico of the resources necessary for its economic reproduction (Wise and Breña 35). NAFTA thus secures the "contraction of part of the Mexican economy, which is compelled to serve as a labor reserve for foreign capital" (ibid.).

At the same time, paradoxically, a highly racialized anti-immigration discourse has urged the invigoration of rigid U.S. American immigration restriction laws. It has led to the criminalization of immigrants, who risk their lives crossing an intensely policed U.S-Mexican border in the hope of improving their own and their families' economic situation. As I intend to show in this essay, *Tropic of Orange* picks up and comments on these complex discursive and paradox migratory dynamics in the wake of NAFTA; Yamashita's novel reinterprets the concept of a deterritorializing transnationalism while leaving no doubt that the freedom in "free trade" essentially designates the free movement of capital.

Yet, contrary to what the reference to NAFTA might suggest, the drawing of "analogies between narrative space and discursive field" that Yamashita's work promotes (Chuh 309), does not limit a reading of *Tropic of Orange* to a hemispheric perspective. To be sure, Mexico and the U.S./Mexican borderlands of post-NAFTA America are an obvious choice as a setting for a fictional story on the unpopular effects of the neoliberal politics of NAFTA as they reflect its hemispheric North-South

3 Maquiladoras, also known as "maquilas," are manufacturing or export assembly plants situated in North Mexico in close proximity of the US-Mexico border. Taking advantage of inexpensive Mexican labor as well as low taxes and custom fees, maquiladoras produce parts and products for the United States. Maquiladora workers are notoriously underpaid and their rights are not represented by unions. After the implementation of NAFTA the number of maquiladoras has almost doubled. For more detailed information see Alejandro Lugo, *Fragmented Lives/Assembled Parts: Culture, Capitalism and Conquest at the US-Mexico Border* (Austin: University of Texas Press, 2008).

axis. The novel's depiction of L.A.'s unique urbanism, however, adds another, less conspicuous spatial dimension to this critique. It is a depiction that by far exceeds Edward Soja's observation that "[i]t all comes together in Los Angeles" (*Postmodern Geographies* 190). Rather than just negotiating a "synekism" (Soja *Postmetropolis* 12) of economic, political, social and cultural currents that might circulate in any hegemonic global city at the end of the twentieth century, Yamashita emphasizes the particular 'situatedness' of L.A. as a Pacific Rim city by investing three of the novel's seven focalizing protagonists with the complex histories and the multiple subject positionalities of contemporary Asian American Angelenos.

Contrary to Claudia Sadowski-Smith, who argues that "[i]n Yamashita's novel, the Japanese and Chinese Americans are not necessarily the most important protagonists "(61), and who foregrounds Yamashita's negotiation of Asian American pan-ethnicity in this context, I claim that it is the economic subtext underlying the novel's representation of its Asian American characters that not only endows them with equal importance as its Latin American protagonists but also suggests a reading of the text along the lines of neoliberal trade politics. The Asian American protagonists and their economic connotations inscribe the transnational imaginary of an economic "Asia Pacific" discourse into Yamashita's representation of the local and implicitly point to a West-East axis established by America's "incursions across the Pacific" (Palumbo Liu) as well as Asian migration onto American national soil.

Tropic of Orange thus displays the immensely productive crossing of hemispheric and Asia Pacific trajectories that Kandice Chuh has identified as the hallmark of Yamashita's prose work in general. Yet, while acknowledging that a reading of Yamashita might promote a call for the establishment of Asian Americanist Hemispheric Studies as a new critical framework that takes "as a critical point of departure the radical diversity of the United States" (Chuh 296), I want to locate *Tropic of Orange* within the spatial imaginaries of economic globalization and focus on the novel's critique of the neoliberalist ideology of free trade. This critique, too, addresses "the falsity of the homogeneity" (ibid.) not only of the nation but of the transnational trade zone as advertised by the neoliberal language of global excess. It exposes the double standard beneath an exuberant advertising of "a common utopianized marketplace" (Woodside 24) that masks "the coexistence of different regimes for the movements of capital and people" (Palumbo-Liu 263) to be a signature feature of this language, regardless of its specific manifestation, be it in the official promotion of NAFTA, or the economic Asia Pacific discourse.

Excessively Economic

The novel's most obvious negotiation of an economic transpacific imaginary takes place in the seven chapters that are focalized on Bobby Ngu, with the chapter headings blatantly signaling the primacy of money in the prevailing U.S. American value-system: "Benefits," "Car Payment Due," "Second Mortgage," "Life Insurance," "Visa Card," "Social Security," and "American Express." On the one hand these headings signal that the immigrant Bobby Ngu has 'made it,' because he has successfully crossed the "new line of hegemony" as Hans Ulrich Gumbrecht has termed "the absolute line of social division between those … who have a Social Security number and those who don't" (255). On the other hand they seem to reduce Bobby to a mere economic factor as they emphasize his absorption into a powerful finance and insurance system which produces dependency as a form of subjection and implies the possibility of ubiquitous surveillance and control. While this form of neoliberal governance applies to contemporary first world subjects regardless of nationality, race and/or ethnicity, the chapters focalized on Bobby foreground "the ways that global capitalism has inexorably and powerfully defined the Asian American subject"(So 32).

Accordingly, Bobby's history is shown to be economically motivated from scratch and simultaneously provides various instances of "America's incursions across the Pacific" (Palumbo Liu's cover blub). As the narrative gradually reveals, Bobby's real name is Li Kwan Yu, and he is not, as the pseudonym he has cunningly chosen suggests, a Vietnamese but a Chinese immigrant from Singapore. After his father's small Singaporean bicycle plant has been ousted by a globally expanding U.S. venture and the family's basis of existence has thus been destroyed, Bobby becomes an economic refugee at the age of twelve. As a victim of U.S. capitalist expansionism he pretends to be a Vietnamese war refugee and manages to emigrate to the U.S. under this label.

By investing Bobby's story with this twist of fraudulent mimicry, Yamashita skillfully contextualizes the racializing Western construction of 'the Asian' as shrewdly and excessively economic with the dubious principles of a hegemonic moral economy which grants immigration permits as compensation for U.S. military transgressions in Vietnam. Implicitly this representation of U.S. imperialism, political-economic entanglement and arbitrary immigration policy also negotiates the calculatedly produced yet deceptive illusion that immigration grants access to the economic abundance of wealthy first world nations (Wegener 168-69). Most importantly, however, it casts serious doubt on the assumption that access and excess stand as signs of social equality (So 27).

In keeping with this dense transpacific backstory, Yamashita sketches Bobby's life in the U.S. as an instance of perfect assimilation to American consumerism. Contrary to his Mexican wife Rafaela, a community college student whose term paper titles clearly signal her heightened political awareness, he is not dissatisfied with this life, although he and his wife "remain at the bottom of the U.S. socioeconomic hierarchy" (Sadowski-Smith 63). As the owner of a small service enterprise Bobby works tirelessly never minding the long hours or the primitive nature of his janitor job. He considers this job simply a means to achieve a better life for himself and his family, and it is in perfect conformity with the all-American notion of consumption as the key to happiness that his dream of a better life is one of affluence with little or no monetary limitations. "Gotta make money" is the mantra that makes Bobby tick, a mantra, though, that not only pushes him to work harder and harder, but one that forces him to replace enjoyment of life and vitality with self-destructing indulgence in liquor and cigarettes. A Kung-Fu fighting, hard-working, law-abiding and apolitical citizen, Bobby perfectly combines the excessive features ascribed to a stereotypical "Asianness" (including those attributed to Asian Americans as the well-assimilated model minority) with neoliberal practices of interminable self-improvement , at least until the shock of his wife and son leaving him induces a gradual process of change (Wegener 168-69).

Yamashita's novel seems to contradict this total integration into the world of American consumerism and fiat money only at first glance when the narrator, in the chapter entitled "American Express," dryly sums up Bobby's existence by stating "Bobby's a cash-man" (266). In fact, it is characteristic of the bold symbolism that Yamashita uses in her depiction of neoliberal politics when Bobby gains access to the spectacular wrestling match between SUPERNAFTA and his Mexican opponent in the climactic scene toward the novel's ending only by giving up his habit of paying cash and using his American Express card instead. While the label "cash-man" once again caters to the long-standing, racializing Western tradition of casting "the Asian" as excessively, yet primitively, economic, Bobby's acquisition of privileged access by his use of the credit card—"American Express gets him the best" (266)—reflects the equally threatening stereotype that constructs Asians and Asian Americans as embodying an excessive "economic overachievement and adaptability" (So 11). The scene thus ironically amalgamates the worn-out "Yellow-Peril" clichés of the first half of the twentieth century with the less obvious anxieties that underlie both the cultural construction of Asian Americans as model minority as well as the economic Pacific Rim discourse at the end of the century.

Although enthusiastically greeting the 21st century as the "Pacific Century" and embracing Asian 'miracle economies' as models of capitalist success, the U.S. American authors of the utopianist Pacific Rim discourse[4] can hardly conceal their fear in view of "the possibility of Asia's economic expansion (more often characterized as domination) and the specter of billions of Asian buyers, laborers, and sellers" (So 8), or gloss over their hegemonic agenda in a climate of stiff economic competition. Using the trope of the Pacific Rim to evoke connotations of physical boundaries, totality, and coherence (Dirlik 19-20) their rhetoric of free trade, transnational convergence and border-free economic spaces in the Pacific region is targeted at disguising the fact that the Pacific has become "a site of contestation between the United States and various East Asian competitors" (Dirlik 5).

In this struggle for hegemony over the region language plays a crucial role, as Alexander Woodside points out: "The language of the Asia-Pacific myth, with its invocations of 'Third Wave' civilizations and its focus upon the 'basic commonalities' of economic prosperity, rhetorically reconciles the tensely coexisting multiple rival capitalisms and usefully blurs potential battle lines among them" (24). It is important to note that this rhetorical suppression of differences and tensions *invents* and *constructs* the homogenous and borderless space it pretends to describe. In fact, the "newly invented space of the Asia Pacific" (Palumbo-Liu 343) is

4 See for example Staffan Burenstam Linder, *The Pacific Century: Economic and Political consequences of Asian-Pacific Dynamism* (Stanford: Stanford University Press, 1986); Robert Elegant, *Pacific Destiny: Inside Asia Today* (New York: Crown, 1989); John Naisbitt, *Megatrends 2000: Ten New Directions for the 1990s* (New York: Morrow, 1990).

a product of "rimspeak," as Bruce Cumings has trenchantly termed this very specific manifestation of the language of global excess (53).

Rimspeak Reloaded

Tropic of Orange most distinctly alludes to "rimspeak" in "Lane Change," one of the chapters focalized on Manzanar Murakami, the Japanese American protagonist, whose speaking pseudonym encodes some of the complex spatial, historical and cultural entanglements of twentieth century Japanese American relations. Between recollections of his childhood in a "relocation" camp for Japanese Americans during World War II (presumably the eponymous "Manzanar") and his hypersensitive perception of a moment of stasis interrupting the perpetual roar of traffic in L.A. Manzanar suddenly envisions the topography of the Pacific Rim:

> *Encroaching* on this vision [of his past] was a larger one: the great Pacific stretching along its great rim, *brimming over* long coastal shores from one hemisphere to the other. *And there were the names of places he had never seen,* from the southernmost tip of Chile to the Galapagos, skirting the tiny waist of land at Panama, up Baja to Big Sur to Vancouver, around the Aleutians to the Bering Strait. From the North, that peaceful ocean swept from Vladivostok around the Japan Isles and the Korean Peninsula, to Shanghai, Taipei, Ho Chi Minh City, through a thousand islands of the Philippines, Malaysia, Indonesia, and Micronesia, sweeping about that giant named Australia and her sister, New Zealand. Manzanar looked out on this strange end and beginning: *the very last point West, and after that it was all East.* (170, my italics)

Revealing in this passage is the seemingly random remark, which indicates that Manzanar's Pacific Rim vision is informed by "names of places he had never seen" (ibid.). It points to the fact that what is announced as a "larger vision" is actually the product of a representational strategy, the traditions and conventions of which are aptly reflected by the ensuing recital of places: both the lyrical rhythm, which echoes the pathos of national anthems, and the rhetorical gesture of an all-encompassing enumeration, which evokes the impression of abundance and a picturesque yet containable diversity, are telltale features of a hegemonic Pacific Rim discourse traceable as far back as to the appropriative storytelling and mapmaking of sixteenth century European travel accounts.[5]

Especially against this background of a traditional discursive imperialism it seems significant that Manzanar's Pacific vision is represented as "encroaching" on the bitter reminiscence of his childhood in Manzanar and thus on his recollection of an infamous instance of racist U.S. politics against Japanese Americans. With its connotations of stealth and transgression, the verb in this context conveys the idea of a subtle repression of even the most painful experience of racialization, a repression by an ideological narrative apparatus that has been collaborative in the shaping of the Asia-Pacific imaginary and its inherent racializing regulation of migrant flows. Pointing to the complicity of the academy in this process of discursive "encroaching," Rob Wilson emphasizes the role of "the hegemonic everyday spread of Anglo American culture in English, and English departments spreading 'the literature of the Pacific' as something written primarily by James Michener, Jack London and the white gaze of exoticizing representation" (397).

While it is obvious that Manzanar's vision of the Pacific region must be engendered by this hegemonic Western discourse because it conspicuously mimics its conventional topographical rhetoric, its image of the "great Pacific ... brimming over" (Yamashita 129) simultaneously inscribes an instance of resistance into "rimspeak" and forcefully confirms Rob Wilson's observation that "[m]etaphors matter and can materialize into compelling social forms and transformed pedagogies" (396). Doubly coded and profoundly ambiguous this metaphor conveys a moment of impending dread, the idea of an excessive and uncontainable 'natural' force, threatening to overturn the existing symbolic order represented by the topos of the "Rim." Yet, at the same time, while this dreadful aspect

5 For a brief overview of the origins, the history, and the conventional topographic rhetoric of the Pacific discourse see M. Consuelo León. David Palumbo-Liu's reference to Australia's prime minister Bob Hawke and his 1989 call for the creation of the Asia Pacific Economic Group (APEC) provides a contemporary instance of 'rimspeak' (343), which is strikingly analogous to Manzanar's Pacific vision. The strategic function of a rimspeak rhetoric in the promotion of APEC fully unfolds when contextualized with a 2007 radio interview in which Hawke admits: "The tactic there, this was a diplomatic tactic, was not to mention the United States upfront because you wanted to make sure that you had the ASEAN (Association of South-East Asian Nations) countries in and not feel that this was something which was bringing in the United States."

mirrors the hegemonic anxieties in view of "Asian economic excess," the metaphor also appropriates and reinterprets the prophetic promise of a "Pacific Rising," and invests it with a subtext of subversion and revolution.

Variations of this subversive symbolism are present throughout the chapters focalized on Manzanar, and it is not incidental that it is this Japanese American protagonist whom Yamashita invests with a symbolical leadership in the "materializing" of metaphoric subversion "into social form" at the end of the novel. In fact, Yamashita's depiction of Manzanar as the conductor of a programmatic "Lane Change" more than affirms David Palumbo-Liu's identification of Asian Americans as "Pacific Rim subject[s] par excellence," as "cultural translators," an ideal embodiment of "the shifting identities of Asian transnational diasporas," endowed with a " particularly productive, post-industrial subjectivity" (343). The novel casts Manzanar as an artist who has given up his bourgeois existence in order to become a freeway conductor of urban symphonies which only he can hear, a freak and a social dropout: "The Japanese American community had apologized profusely for this blight on their image as the Model Minority" (36-37). He is not only a Pacific Rim subject *par excellence* but also an "expert" Angeleno: "No one was more at home in L.A. than this man" (36).

Yamashita illustrates this intimate knowledge of L.A. with an imagery that is clearly indebted to the pictorial language that marks the philosophy of Gilles Deleuze and Felix Guattari. Drawing on the French philosophers' metaphors of layers, mapmaking, multiplicity, and, above all, the rhizome, she depicts L.A. not as the epitome of postmodern space *per se* (although there is a host of ironic allusions to this and other L.A. clichés throughout the text), but as a multi-layered, rhizomatic Pacific Rim city, a city that is characteristic of the rhizomatic American West, as Deleuze and Guattari have defined it in their introduction to *A Thousand Plateaus* (19).

The result is a form of rimspeak that celebrates the differences, contradictions and tensions, in short, the multi-layered complexity that the hegemonic discourse aims to suppress. The following passage from one of the novel's expository chapters provides an instance of this alternative rimspeak. It shows how Yamashita furnishes Manzanar's complex Pacific Rim subjectivity with an extraordinary synaesthetic sensitivity, thus enabling him to unearth the specific spatial and temporal complexity of L.A. She thereby links his "particularly productive" art of conducting to a resistant form of mapmaking that seems to exceed any (re-)appropriating functions of the map:

> *There are maps and there are maps and there are maps.* The uncanny thing was that he could see all of them at once, filter some, pick them out like transparent windows and place them even delicately and consecutively in a complex grid of pattern, spatial discernment, body politic. ... But what were these mapping layers? ... On the surface, the complexity of layers could drown out any ordinary person, but ordinary persons never bother to notice the prehistoric grid of plant and fauna and human behavior, nor the historic grid of land usage and property, the great overlays of transport—sidewalks, bicycle paths, roads, freeways, systems of transit both ground and air, a thousand natural and man-made divisions, variations both dynamic and stagnant, patterns and connections by every conceivable definition from the distribution of wealth to race, from patterns of climate to the curious blueprint of the skies. (56-57)

Manzanar's extraordinary ability to perceive and to handle the fluid spatio-temporal phenomena that constitute the city, his artful musical arranging of mapping layers clearly corresponds to Deleuze's and Guattari's concept of a de-territorializing, rhizomatic "mapmaking," a concept that favors principles of connectivity, heterogeneity, multiplicity, and 'becoming' over the binary logic, the dichotomies, and the hierarchies imposed by "the law of the One" that have characterized Western thinking since Enlightenment. What Manzanar seems to conduct, then, is a transformation of L.A. into a de-territorializing rhizome, a body politic deteriorating into a body without organs, a symphony of global flows climaxing into a chaotic crescendo of intensities (Wegener).

It is striking how enticingly this version of rimspeak projects an image of a utopian de-territorialization that appears to subvert the dominant capitalist discourse. However, a closer look at Deleuze's and Guattari's work reveals that the authors show capitalism to be "a fluid spatial economy" that "mimics flows of becoming and un-becoming" (West-Pavlov 185) a fluid spatial economy, in which the need to expand the market propels the dissolving of territories and codes, a process that is deceptively similar to rhizomatic mapmaking. Accordingly, their use of the terms fluidity and deterritorialization can, depending on the context, signify a liberatory, final disruption of codes or a transitional stage between different forms of capitalist codification. In drawing on Deleuze's and Guattari's spatio-temporal imagery Yamashita, then, introduces a double coding to her narrative discourse that reflects the ambiguity and the flexibility of the language of global excess.

An Asian Myth?

Representative of Yamashita's more subtle allusions to the deceptive character of this rhetoric is a scene that takes place long before the conspicuous wrestling match at the novel's end. Set in a trendy L.A. sushi bar, the scene presents Emi, another one of the novel's Japanese American protagonists and not incidentally the granddaughter of the excentric Manzanar, having a conversation with her Chicano lover Gabriel. By provocatively telling Gabriel "Cultural diversity is bullshit" and "I hate being multicultural" Emi in effect addresses a white woman sitting next to her, whose japanophile demeanor annoys her. Responding to the attack , the woman answers:

> I happen to adore the Japanese culture. What can I say? I adore different cultures. I've traveled all over the world. I love living in L.A. because I can find anything in the world to eat, right here. It's such a meeting place for all sorts of people. A true celebration of an international world. It just makes me sick to hear people speak so cynically about something so positive and to make assumptions about people based on their color. Really, I'm sorry. I can't understand your attitude at all. ... Emi sighed. She noticed the woman's hair was held together miraculously by two ornately-lacquered chopsticks. Maybe there was some precedent for this hair-do. Gabriel later remembered something about Oedipus blinding himself with his mother's hairpins. Not an Asian myth, however. Emi said:"Hiro, could we have two forks please?" Hiro quickly motioned and signaled for the occidental eating utensils. Emi examined the forks carefully and held them up for her neighbor. "Would you consider using these in your hair? Or would you consider that," Emi paused, "unsanitary?" (128-29)

By her quick-witted reaction Emi, who represents Yamashita's idea of the "anti-identitarian postmodern creature of the web" (Rody 146), unerringly unmasks an attitude of exoticist consumption of difference behind the woman's all embracing "globalism speak," while at the same time confronting her with one of the most pervasive stereotypes of Western racism, the cliché of Asian uncleanliness. She thus points to a function of the language of global excess that aligns the consumption of varieties of ethnic food with a general imperative of commodity consumption, which acknowledges and affirms not the difference of the ethnic other but the very concept of the speaker's own Americanness. Drawing on an argument of Christine So,[6] I contend that this is a representation of L.A. as a huge, if multi-ethnic, marketplace "in which Asian American identity can be assessed, valued, and made commensurate with other U.S. commodities," (So 34) and must therefore also be read as a self-reflexive comment on the consumption of ethnic literature.

Moreover, Yamashita in this passage very subtly, but unmistakably contextualizes the consumption of difference with the logic of capitalism by casually mentioning the myth of "Oedipus blinding himself with his mother's hairpins" (Yamashita 129). Gabriel's citation of a rather little known detail of the famous myth clearly alludes here to an aspect of psychoanalysis that Gilles Deleuze and Felix Guattari have critiqued in *Anti-Oedipus.* Deleuze and Guattari argue that the pattern of oedipal identification is not restricted to a process of psychological individuation but applies to processes of socialization in capitalist societies where the production of materialist desires substitutes the production of the unconscious. They claim that "within the framework of Oedipus ... the only real relationship, that of production [of the unconscious], has been done away with" (Deleuze and Guattari 24) and has been replaced by economic production and representation. The prevalence of the Oedipus-myth in psychoanalysis thus provides an ideological basis for capitalism and marks its representational space.

The Oedipus-myth is indeed, as Gabriel's seemingly casual remark states, not an Asian but a capitalist myth and the citation of the specific detail of "Oedipus blinding himself" simultaneously evokes notions of perpetual indebtedness and an inability to perceive the introduction of "lack into desire" (Cooper and Murphy 229) that is hidden behind the mask of capitalist representation. To put it more bluntly, that the invocation of Oedipus blinding himself in this scene serves to open the reader's eyes to a multiculturalism that designates nothing behind its conventionalized, 'excessive' trope of abundance. It exposes the multi-ethnic, global city of L.A., the economic and cultural meeting point of global flows from East, West, North and South, as the marketplace of a

6 Referring to readers of assimilationist Chinese American literature, So speaks here of "the mainstream reader's consumption of Chinese American difference" (34).

racialized economy which is firmly embedded in the representational space of capitalism.

Spectacular Speculations

While conjoining her Asian American and Latin American protagonists in interracial relationships, Yamashita leaves no doubt that it is the paradigm of the trade zone that defines the conditions of their encounter within that representational space. In the melodramatic wrestling match of "El Contrato con América" (256) her criticism of this racialized economy and its representational strategies loses all subtlety when applied to the context of the trade zone, which SUPERNAFTA so conspicuously exemplifies. By depicting SUPERNAFTA's pretentious, mawkish address to the "multicultural rainbow of kids out there," (257) and his pithy invitation to "get a piece of the action" as well as his prophetic promise of a golden economic future propelled by technological progress (ibid.) Yamashita mimics and points to the blatant advertising strategies by which an official U.S. policy has marketed NAFTA, while concealing the darker side of its neoliberal agenda: as the free trade zone protects and caters to the interests of transnational corporations by granting money and commodities to flow unimpeded by national laws, the immigration restriction by state law keeps up appearances of national sovereignty, and, at the same time, mobilizes and navigates the transnational migration of subaltern social groups and classes according to the varying needs of capitalist boom and bust cycles (see Miyoshi 1993, 1995, 2001).

This subaltern aspect of "global flows" that the futurologist rhetoric of the trade zone glosses over is embodied and represented by El Gran Mojado, who has already dragged the tropic of cancer, i.e. the North-South divide of the hemisphere, into L.A., and has brought with him tens of thousands of illegal Mexican migrants. As with her depiction of SUPERNAFTA, Yamashita does not save on symbolic excess in her representation of his challenger. The trickster's somewhat ridiculous outfit—he is wearing a "ski-mask of camouflage nylon, blue cape with the magic image of Guadalupe in an aura of gold feathers and blood roses, leopard bicycle tights and blue boots" (258)—and his ironic American superhero posture—he "stood, arms crossed and legs spread like a Power Ranger or a Ninja Turtle or Zorro" (ibid.)—satirically display both the officially required process of Americanization and a self-mockingly Hispanic interpretation of it. In addition, as Mojado appeals to a transnational, pan-American resistance against the policy of NAFTA in his speech, he also ironically and playfully invokes the stereotype of a lascivious Latin-American *machismo*, thus winning his audience's sympathy and laughter.

However, while this self-ironic parody of the Northern stereotype of Latin-American masculinity contrasts SUPERNAFTA's humorless, self-important, and pompous performance, Yamashita makes it clear that the migrant diasporas and the global flows that he leads and represents are not just an urban carnival: what the masses in the audience—and the readers—witness is, instead, a life and death fight, in which the fate of thousands of 'wetbacks' and maquiladora workers is at stake.

Predictably, the pathos of this archaic encounter of good and evil climaxes when SUPERNAFTA, true to his reputation, manages to kill El Gran Mojado with a secret weapon. Yamashita's excessive symbolism, however, does not allow the scene to end with the folk hero's melodramatic death after a "highly stylized match" (Wallace 157). Instead, the chapter ends with the remark that "somewhere the profits from the ticket sales were being divided" (263), thus accomplishing its purpose as a comment on the function of a discursive propaganda machine that is targeted on concealing the sheer economic rationality of its agenda.

Against this background, the victory of SUPERNAFTA over El Gran Mojado in the Pacific Rim Auditorium comes as no surprise. Always oscillating between counter-narrative and parody, its excessively symbolic, at times almost cheesy, representation parallels the obvious strategies of the ideology it depicts, thus justifying the cautionary address to the reader that Yamashita has placed in front of her novel's beginning like a disclaimer: "No single imagination is wild or crass or cheesy enough to compete with the collective mindlessness that propels our fascination forward." It is, however, just Yamashita's imaginative use of puns and metaphors that highlights "the gap between the cultural and the economic" (Wallace 150) that non-fictional globalization discourse and its metaphors tend to efface.[7] Taking the homogenizing

7 According to Molly Wallace's analysis the deceptive conflation of the economic and the cultural marks not only the official rhetoric of the neoliberal free market ideology but is also characteristic of a critical discourse that often perceives globalization in the oversimplifying terms of "David-Goliath archetypes," which the wrestling match

metaphors of the official language of global excess literally and unmasking their conflation of the cultural and the economic, Yamashita taps the full metaphoric potential of the fictional text "to figure the operation of language without committing to a referent" (ibid.).

In the past decade there has been a striking emergence of fictional texts[8] on the cultural scene of post-NAFTA North-America, which, like *Tropic of Orange*, creatively transform the tropes and metaphors of the pervasive neoliberal language of global excess. As spectacular speculations on the futures of migrant subjects these texts make ample use of the almost unlimited possibilities inherent to the genre of speculative fiction thus exposing and commenting on the speculative quality of this rhetoric on more than one level. In so doing these literary deconstructions of the trade zone not only raise the fundamental question of literature's capacity of political intervention but also call for a closer investigation of their own embeddedness in a globalized literary market.

Works Cited

Chomsky, Noam. "Notes on NAFTA: The Masters of Mankind." *Juárez: The Laboratory of Our Future*. Ed. Charles Bowden. New York: Aperture, 1998. 13-20.

Chuh, Kandice. "Of Hemispheres and Other Spheres: Navigating Karen Tei Yamashita's Literary World." *Hemispheric American Studies*. Eds. Caroline F. Levander and Robert S. Levine. New Brunswick, New Jersey, and London: Rutgers UP, 2008. 294-312.

Cumings, Bruce. "Rimspeak; or, The Discourse of the 'Pacific Rim'." *What Is In A Rim: Critical Perspectives on the Pacific Region Idea*. Ed. Arif Dirlik. Lanham/ New York/ Oxford: Rowman and Littlefield, 1998. 53-72.

Cooper, Brian P. and Margueritte S. Murphy. "Libidinal Economics: Lyotard and Accounting for the Unaccountable." *The New Economic Criticism: Studies at the Intersection of Literature and Economics*.

between SUPERNAFTA and El Gran Mojado simultaneously reproduces and parodies.(156).

8 See for example Jim Munroe, *Everyone in Silico* (2002); Donna McMahon, *Dance of Knives* (2003) Larissa Lai, *Salt Fish Girl* (2004); Margret Atwood, *Oryx and Crake* (2004); *The Year of the Flood* (2010). Earlier examples would include Octavia E. Butler, *Parable of the Sower* (2000) or Kim Stanley Robinson, *The Gold Coast (1988)*; *Pacific Edge* (1995); *Wild Shore* (1996) (Three Californias Series).

Eds. Martha Woodmansee and Mark Osteen. London: Routledge, 1999. 229-41.

Deleuze, Gilles, and Felix Guattari. *Anti-Oedipus: Capitalism and Schizophrenia.* Minneapolis: U of Minnesota P, 1998.

---. *A Thousand Plateaus: Capitalism and Schizophrenia.* Minneapolis: U of Minnesota P, 1987.

Dirlik, Arif. "The Asia Pacific Idea: Reality and Representation in the Invention of a Regional Stucture." *What Is In A Rim: Critical Perspective on the Pacific Region Idea.* Ed. Arif Dirlik. Lanham/ New York/ Oxford: Rowman and Littlefield, 1998. 15-36.

Gumbrecht, Hans Ulrich. "Epilogue: Untenable Positions." *Streams of Cultural Capital.* Eds. David Palumbo-Liu and Hans Ulrich Gumbrecht. Stanford: Stanford UP, 1993. 249-62.

Hawke, Bob. "APEC meeting its Potential: Bob Hawke." Interview conducted by Graeme Dobell, 9 Sept, 2007. 28 July 2010. <http://www.abc.net.au/correspondents/content/2007/s2027517.htm>

León W., M. Consuelo. "Foundations of the American Image of the Pacific." *boundary 2* 21.1 (1994): 17-29.

Lugo, Alejandro. *Fragmented Lives/Assembled Parts: Culture, Capitalism and Conquest at the US-Mexico Border.* Austin: University of Texas Press, 2008.

Miyoshi, Masao."A Borderless World: From Colonialism to Transnationalism and the Decline of the Nationstate." *Critical Inquiry* 19.4 (1993): 726-751.

---. "Sites of Resistance in the Global Economy." *boundary 2* 22.1 (1995): 61-84.

---."Turn to the Planet: Literature, Diversity and Totality." *Comparative Literature* 53.4 (2001): 283-87.

Palumbo-Liu, David. *Asian/American: Historical Crossings of a Racial Frontier.* Stanford: Stanford UP, 1999.

Rody, Caroline. "The Transnational Imagination: Karen Tei Yamashita's *Tropic of Orange.*" *Asian American Identities Beyond the Hyphen.* Eds. Eleanor Ty and Donald C. Goellnicht. Bloomington: Indiana UP, 2004. 130-48.

Sadowski-Smith, Claudia. *Border Fictions: Globalization, Empire, and Writing at the Boundaries of the United States.* Charlottesville and London: U of Virginia P, 2008.

Smorkaloff, Pamela Maria. "Shifting Borders, Free Trade, and Frontier Narratives: US, Canada, and Mexico." *American Literary History* 6.1 (1994): 88-102.

So, Christine. *Economic Citizens: A Narrative of Asian American Visibility.* Philadelphia: Temple UP, 2007.

Soja, Edward. *Postmodern Geographies: The Reassertion of Space in Critical Social Theory*. London: Verso, 1989.

---. *Postmetropolis: Critical Studies of Cities and Regions*. Malden, MA: Blackwell, 2000.

Wallace, Molly. "Tropics of Globalization: Reading the New North America." *symploké* 9.1-2 (2001): 145-60.

Wegener, Susanne. "Lines and Layers, Grids and Maps. Das Konzept des Rhizoms als Ausdruck postkolonialer Hybridität in Karen Tei Yamashitas *Tropic of Orange*."*LiLi: Zeitschrift für Literaturwissenschaft und Linguistik* 37.147 (2007): 164-77.

West-Pavlov, Russell. *Space in Theory: Kristéva, Foucault, Deleuze*. Amsterdam, New York: Rodopi, 2009.

Wise, Raúl Delgado and Mariana Ortega Breña. "Migration and Imperialism: The Mexican Workforce in the Context of NAFTA." *Latin American Perspectives* 33.2 (2006): 33-45.

Wilson, Rob. "Doing Cultural Studies inside APEC: Literature, Cultural Identity, and Global/Local Dynamics in the American Pacific." *Comparative Literature* 53.4 (2001): 389-403.

Woodside, Alexander. "The Asia-Pacific Idea as a Mobilization Myth." *What Is In A Rim: Critical Perspective on the Pacific Region Idea*. Ed. Arif Dirlik. Lanham: Rowman and Littlefield, 1998. 37-52.

Yamashita, Karen Tei. *Tropic of Orange*. Minneapolis: Coffee House Press, 1997.

The Camp as Matrix: "The Visitor," "Babel," and a "Repeating District 9"

Ana Mª Manzanas Calvo

Ana Mª Manzanas Calvo analyzes three recent films for their representations of the camp as a spatial metaphor which represents the marginal status of the Other. Manzanas extends the spatial metaphor issued by the Bush administration in the aftermath of 9/11, namely, the emergence of an "axis of evil" which separates the patriotic American self from the terrorist Other, and applies this notion to Tom MacCarthy's "The Visitor" (2007), Alejandro González Iñárritu's "Babel" (2006), and Neill Blomkamp's "District 9" (2009). The heterotopic spaces in these films, so Manzanas' contention, are transnational and highly stylized in their cinematographic realization.

> The topics of human rights, democracy, rule of law, and so on, are ultimately reduced to a deceptive mask for the disciplinary mechanisms of 'biopower' whose ultimate expression is the twentieth-century concentration camps.
>
> Slavoj Žižek, *Welcome to the Desert of the Real*

Explicitly or implicitly, encounters and collisions between self and Other tend to be conceived of in spatial metaphors. The Other might be welcomed or turned away, but is most often characterized as one who has been spatially mobilized or relocated (Dikeç, Clark, Barnett 4), for he/she is the bearer of an inescapable "exteriority" (Levinas 1987, 84). The destabilizing effect of the Other is stated at the outset of *Totality and Infinity*, where Emmanuel Levinas introduces the "Stranger [*l'Etranger*] … who disturbs the being at home with oneself [*le chez soi*]" (39). "The Other as Other," Levinas explains in *Time and the Other*, "is not only an alter ego: the Other is what I myself am not" (83). This otherness or strangeness of the other manifests itself not as something given or intended, but "as a certain disquietude, as a *derangement* which puts us out of our common tracks" (Waldenfels 63). The interpellation of the Other, and our coming to self-awareness in relation to the Other has been sublimated to an unprecedented degree in the aftermath of 9/11 and the rhetoric of a global state of exception. Just one day after the attacks on the Pentagon and the World Trade Center and the forceful downing of the fourth plane in rural Pennsylvania, writes Paul Virilio,

> George Bush declared that his country was the champion of *good*, and that the battle against terrorism would be 'a monumental struggle of *good* versus *evil*,' and '*good* will prevail.' He was speaking the same language as his father in 1991, itself copied from the language of the 'just war' fought by the United States against Nazism half a century before! (36)

The pronouncement immediately split the world into black and white, into an ontological frontier that the Republican administration termed "the axis of evil." This axis confronted the United States with an uneasy feeling of homelessness stemming from a violated home. If the home is the space that for Derrida represents a site of recollection, or a "coming-to-oneself, a retreat home with oneself as in a land of asylum or refuge" (38), not being able to come to oneself, not being able to recollect oneself in the home as a result of the threat from the stranger equals being homeless, being an exile in one's own home. Suddenly, the home felt inhospitable. An undefined part of the world turned inhospitable too, for it came within the elusive coordinates of the axis of evil, the threatening home of the Other. The axis could be a straight line marked in the sky, but also a tropic, a parallel or a zig-zag fracturing the world. And fracture it is, a supra-line that divides ontological and ethical categories; a preview of the final judgment, the perfect separation of the good and the bad, the self and the Other in the new global order. This state of emergency legitimizes more and more suspensions of legal and other rights (Žižek 107). The ultimate expression of these disciplinary mechanisms for Žižek, as the heading reflects, is twentieth-century concentration camps. In this essay, I explore such spaces of detention in three movies: Tom MacCarthy's 2007 movie "The Visitor" (2007), Alejandro González Iñárritu's "Babel" (2006), and Neill Blomkamp's "District 9" (2009). The analysis of these cultural artifacts illustrates the fact that the encounter with the Other, especially in the aftermath of 9/11, tends to be conceived within the spatial and ideological parameters of the camp.

I: The Camp as Matrix

> Matrix: Latin, female animal used for breeding, parent plant, from *matr-*, *mater*
>
> Webster's Dictionary

Žižek is by no means the first to link state of emergency and camps. In *Homo Sacer*, Giorgio Agamben underlines the "constitutive nexus" between the sate of exception and the concentration camp (168). The camp, Agamben claims, "is the space that is opened when the state of exception begins to become the rule" (*Homo* 168-89). As a place of exception, the camp is a *locus classicus* in the history of the United States. We only need to recall the "Praying Indians," the slave quarters, the reservation system, and the Japanese internment in concentration camps during WWII, as well as the rigid and invisible lines that secure urban ghettoes. In wider hemispheric terms, Agamben mentions the *campos de concentraciones* created by the Spanish in Cuba in 1896, the concentration camps into which the English herded the Boers at the turn of the 20th century, the camps created by the Social-Democratic governments, which interned thousands of communist militants in 1923 on the bases of *Schutzhaft* [literally, protective custody], also the *Konzentrationslager für Ausländer*, which housed mainly Eastern European refugees, as well as the concentration and extermination camps that harbored Jews, among other contingents, during WWII (*Homo* 166, 167). This camp logic can be traced in the 1991 herding of all presumably illegal immigrants by the Italian police at the stadium in Bari (*Homo* 174). In the history of the United States, the philosopher argues, the Patriot Act issued by the U.S. Senate on October 26, 2002, whereby any alien suspected of activities that endangered national security can be taken into "custody," stands as another instance of the rounding up of the different. "What is new about President Bush's order," Agamben claims, "is that it radically erases any legal status of the individual, thus producing a legally unnamable and unclassifiable being." Detainees are the object of a *de facto* rule and held in a total void, for their detention is "indefinite not only in the temporal sense but in its very nature as well, since it is entirely removed from the law and from judicial oversight" (*State* 4). The closest thing to which it could possibly be compared, the philosopher continues, "is the legal situation of the Jews in the Nazi *Lager* [camps], who, along with their citizenship, had lost every legal identity" (*State* 3-4). Following the Greeks' articulation of the word "life" into *zoe* (the simple fact of living common to all living beings), and *bios* (the form of living proper to an individual), the inmates of the concentration camps are mere *zoe.* The contemporary version of these *Lager* harboring life as *zoe* is Guantánamo, an open air prison that has turned into a legal black hole, a legal limbo, a prison beyond the law (Kaplan 831).

This logic of displacement and emplacement, which is transnational and cuts across time and space, allows Agamben to establish the camp as matrix or nomos[1] of the political space in which we are still living (*Homo* 166). The matrix or womb is a network, a fossil-bearing rock, a principal metal in an alloy, a point of ceaseless input and output, a web of intersecting impulses that signals the multidirectionality of the juncture or crossing (Baker 3-7). The camp as matrix is always open and manifests itself in a variety of spatial and temporal coordinates. This does not mean that camps are all the same, but rather that they respond to the same oxymoronic logic of dislocating localization (*Homo* 175). It is this structure, Agamben cautions, that we must learn to recognize in all its metamorphoses, into the *zones d'attentes* of our airports and certain outskirts of our cities.

> [I]f the essence of the camp consists of the materialization of the state of exception and in the subsequent creation of a space in which bare life and the juridical rule enter into a threshold of indistinction, then we must admit that we find ourselves virtually in the presence of a camp every time such a structure is created, independent of the kinds of crime that are committed there and whatever its denomination and specific topography. (*Homo* 174).

Identifying the generic geography of the camp implies detecting the anatomy of its inmate, the *homo sacer*. The bare life of the *homo sacer*, Agamben reasons, concerns us in a special way: "Sacredness is a line of flight still present in contemporary politics, a line that is as such moving into zones increasingly vast and dark" (*Homo* 115). This line of flight makes the distinction between *zoe* and *bios* irrelevant. "If today there is no longer any one clear figure of the sacred man," Agamben concludes, "it is perhaps because we are all virtually *homines sacri*" (*Homo* 115).

---

1 The meaning of nomos is law, and can more broadly apply to any custom, usage or tradition, contract or convention. In early usage the word was firmly anchored in the religious sphere (Bromiley 646-648).

If we flatten out the time and space dimensions, what is, then, the common denominator to camps and *homines sacri*? The camps, in Agamben's argument, are born out of a state of exception. The juridical regime for internment was not common law but *Schutzhaft*, "a juridical institution of Prussian origin that allowed individuals to be 'taken into custody' independently of any criminal behavior, solely to avoid danger to the security of the state" (*Homo* 167). *Schutzhaft*, in turn, was based on the proclamation of the state of siege or exception, and the corresponding suspension of the articles of the German constitution. As the state of exception begins to become the rule, the camp opens as a space (*Homo* 169). The question is what kind of place the camp creates and who are its inmates. The premises of the camp physically and ideologically overlay the nation, and can offer a heterotopic location, a spatial palimpsest of former occupations and uses, as in "Babel," or they can be an inverted sanctuary created *ad hoc* to contain the Other, as in "The Visitor" and "District 9." The inmates, in either case, are literally "bandits" in the sense that they have a ban imposed on them (Cautier and Dehaene 97). These "bandits" are individuals "whose behaviour is deviant in relation to the mean or required norm" (Foucault 1977, 18). Deviance meets not the habitual workings of the nation, but what can be termed as the "anti-nation" that strips the inmates of every political status and reduces them to bare life, to the status of *homo sacer*. In the camp, Agamben reasons, "power confronts nothing but pure life without any mediation" (*Homo* 171). A new time dimension opens for the *homo sacer*, one in which he/she is severed from traditional time and enters a heterochrony. If, as Foucault claims, there are heterotopias associated to the accumulation of time, such as libraries and museums, and others that are linked to time in its most futile, most transitory, most precarious aspect, such as fairgrounds ("Of Other Spaces" 20), the camp is not linked to the accumulation of time, nor to the absence of it; it is instead associated with the annihilation of time, for the internees are taken out of their specific time coordinates.

III: Visitors: *Homo Sacer* and *Homo* Sucker

Globalization, we might say, is the predicament in which some of us enjoy the benefits of easy connection and extensive mobility, while others are locked in place or coerced into motion by dire economic and political pressures. It is the condition in which globe-trotting business people, aesthetes, academics, holiday-makers and medical tourists take advantage of an international 'hospitality' industry, while economic migrants, guest-workers, asylum seekers and refugees find themselves up against regulation and infrastructures that can be described as best as inhospitable.

> Mustafa Dikeç, Nigel Clark, Clive Barnett "Extending Hospitality: Giving Space, Taking Time"

Literature, popular culture, and the news have familiarized viewers and readers with diverse manifestations of spatial black holes: visitors who are literally trapped in viscose areas or inspection areas, where travelers are required to provide a unified vision of themselves.[2] If they do not manage to do so, they might turn into different degrees of *homo sacer*. Stephen Spielberg's "The Terminal" makes a point in case as it introduces Viktor Navorski, a native of a fictional European country, Krakozhia. Dressed as a global traveler, Navorski seems to enjoy the benefits "of easy connection and extensive mobility." Yet upon arrival to JFK in New York, he is informed of the fact that, as a result of a successful coup, the country he departed from only hours ago no longer exists. With his passport legally void, he is a citizen of nowhere. Although he is not an economic migrant, a guest-worker, an asylum seekers or a refugee, he is suddenly unacceptable bare life. While his legal situation clears up or something happens in Krakozhia, he is to remain in the vast in-between area of the "International Transit Lounge," a fairy-tale camp of neon lights, fast food, and designer clothes. As the movie evolves, however, the viewer witnesses how Navorski, in spite of his deluxe incarceration, is capable of creating a narrative of spatial and national belonging. Yet, he "belonged" to "America" even before he flew to the country. Like his late father, he is an aesthete and a consumer of American music, that liberating language that possibly made the political upheavals of Krakozhia more bearable. It is jazz that makes Viktor a speaker of a supra language of cultural and political freedom. Thus the movie illustrates to what extent the United States carried out the double task of Americanizing the

---

2 See, for example, Dagoberto Gilb's *The Magic of Blood*, Thomas King's "Borders," Joyce Carol Oates' *Crossing the Border*. For an analysis of these encounters see Ana Mª Manzanas and Jesús Benito *Cities, Borders and Spaces in Intercultural American Literature and Film*.

immigrant and Americanizing Europe.[3] In his pilgrimage to New York, Viktor illustrates the fruits of the cultural campaign that has converted Europe to American cultural trends. He is *homo sacer* but also *homo* sucker,[4] irresistibly attracted by jazz. His sentimental mission consists in securing that last signature of the jazz musician that completes his father's collection. This is Spielberg's way of softening the encounter with the Other. Yet there is a lot that the movie silences, such as the 1996 Illegal Immigration Reform and Immigrant Responsibility Act, and the 2009 Patriot Act, which allow for non-revisable indefinite detention both at Guantánamo and at facilities that have been termed "little Guantánamos" near airports and border-spaces within the United States (Feldman 339, 340).

This is the kind of detention facility that is fully exposed in Tom McCarthy's "The Visitor." During the first ten minutes of footage, however, the viewer remains uncertain as to who the visitor is, and where he is visiting. The main character, Walter, a university professor in Connecticut, behaves as if he was a fleeting occupier of his own house, a non-place that does not shelter the individual. Similarly, Walter is shown in his office, in a classroom, and at the university cafeteria, yet the impression is that a stranger is going through routine places without any sense of attachment. Into this dreaded routine erupts a colleague who announces to Walter that he has to present a paper (one he has not even written) at a conference on Middle Eastern politics in New York. From the trodden pathways of a university town in Connecticut McCarthy takes us to the panoramic city of New York. Walter appears transplanted onto new soil, and opening the door to an apartment in New York City. Surprisingly, Walter's apartment is inhabited, and there is light in the bathroom. For those within, Walter is the trespasser and unexpected visitor and is treated accordingly. After the first confusing minutes, Walter learns that a couple had sublet his apartment, which he had not occupied for years, from someone he does not know. Confronted with the alien Other, Walter does not feel the need to defend his turf. When the undesired guests apologetically leave, he walks out, catches up with them, returns the photo they left behind, and invites the couple, Tarek, from Syria, and Zainab, from

3 I am indebted to Rob Kroes's seminar on the American city (Salamanca, Spain, April 2010).

4 I am taking this juxtaposition of terms from Slavoj Zizek in *Welcome to the Desert of the Real*.

Senegal, to stay for the night until they find a place of their own. It is a conditional and temporal hospitality, yet the gesture is an investment in the "futurity"[5] of the Other. As Levinas postulates, "Relationship with the future, the presence of the future in the present, seems all the same accomplished in the face-to-face with the Other" (Time 79). For Walter the interaction with the Other triggers the future into the present. Walter does not seek a return on his act of hospitality, and hence he breaks out of the closed circuit of what can be worked out and weighed in advance when looking at the couple. His gesture opens the realm of "perhaps" (Dikeç, Clark and Barnett 6).

This "perhapsness" is implicit in the very notion of the word "hospitality" and its uneasy relation to personal and national identity. Significantly, the Latin *hospes* is made up of the elements hosti-pet-s, where two different roots—*hostis*, meaning "guests" or "host," and pet, meaning "master"—converge. The master who offers hospitality must be the master *chez soi*, thus implying the importance of location for the exercise of power and identity (McNulty x). Hence the oxymoronic nature of hospitality, a term that implies the union of two contradictory notions: one defined by reciprocity and exchange, the other by despotic power, mastery, and personal identity. Two fundamental directions emerge from these colliding terms, Tracy McNulty enunciates: "One can result in a feeling of recognition and respect between host and guest;" the linking can also turn into "a source of anxiety, rivalry, or hostility, in which the host's power over the guest is conceived in a threatening manner, or in which the guest threatens to overtake the host's place as master by usurping his home, personal property, or social position" (xi). The latter possibility bespeaks the semantic transformation of *hostis* from a reciprocal and compensating guest to a threatening enemy that must be excluded.[6] The change refashions the position of master, the pet, who now becomes a figure constantly menaced by dispossession, one who must constantly defend his or her rightful proprietorship (McNulty xiii) and who, in so doing, constitutes him- or herself in the gesture of turning to address the outside.

In *The Visitor*, Walter embraces hospitality as reciprocity and exchange within the limits of the apartment, while the nation will uphold

---

5 I am taking the concept of the "the Other as a figure of futurity" from Dikeç, Clark and Barnett's revision of Levinas and Derrida (6)

6 This transformation also explains how *hostis* became the root of "hostility."

hostis as the stranger or foreigner, as the potential-threat-to-national-identity that needs to be expelled. Walter opens the home to the stranger and in the process redefines his identity and his space. Although boundaries form an inherent part of the notion of welcoming the Other, hospitality "is about opening, without abolishing, those boundaries and giving spaces to the stranger where recognition on both sides would be possible. Hospitality, in this sense, implies the *mutuality of recognition*" (Dikeç 229). This mutuality is staged in the apartment, the location of the I, the site of enunciation, which does not become *unheimlich* in the process of encountering the Other, nor is it dispossessed of its identity; instead it opens to a new conceptualization of interpersonal space.

McCarthy stages this brave new world in a variety of premises. The official forum of the conference at NYU where Middle Eastern politics is discussed finds an echo in the microcosm of the apartment, where a new middle ground of complicities and transcultural alliances develops. Yet Tarek introduces another stop between the two locales: Washington Square and its improvised drumming. Walter, unable to play the piano that his late wife, a concert pianist, mastered, is fascinated by Tarek's playing and his sense of rhythm. When Tarek gives Walter his first formal lesson on drumming, he admonishes his student, unsurprisingly, to think in threes: it is McCarthy's particular spatial, aural, and ideological thirding. Totally open to the advent of the Other, Walter is literally nudged out of his familiar patterns and is given the prospects of a future undetermined by the past (Dikeç, Clark, Barnett 6). A whole different city unfolds for Walter under Tarek's instruction. It is a city of vendors and musicians, lining the sidewalks of Astor Place, and gathering in Washington Square under the summonings of the drum. Yet the rituals of hospitality as performed by a welcoming Walter come to a halt when Tarek, drum slung over his shoulder, gets stuck in the rotating gate at the subway. The exterior perimeter turns inward and repeats itself in the policed urban landscape, for the national perimeter now connotes the imaginary line between safety and terrorism, host and *xenos*. Since he fits the profile and does not have any papers with him, Tarek is arrested by undercover agents, taken away, turned over to immigration, and kept at a detention center in Queens. When it comes to the national stage, the host's power over the guest is conceived in a threatening manner. Tarek is simply an asylum seeker, not a visitor; he is just the *hostis*, the stranger or foreigner, the potential-threat-to-national-identity that is expeditiously incarcerated. If there is a process of depersonalization inherent to incarceration, the detention center effects a further process of subtraction. Here migrants are divested of their Americanness, the layer of nationhood represented in the movie by language, geography, and music, and are severed from the nation-state. Transformed into mere *zoe*, they face the anti-nation. Whatever they were, and whatever facts could justify their belonging to the country, are of no avail. Identities are flattened out and become paper-thin, cut off from specific time coordinates, especially in the aftermath of 9/11 and the nation's exclusionary logic: either you belong or you don't. And Tarek, who never heard about his deportation hearing, is surgically removed from the United States.

III: Outsourcing the Camp: "Babel"

> Once completed, the Tower would be large enough to hold every inhabitant of the New World. There would be a room for each person, and once he entered that room, he would forget everything he knew. After forty days and forty nights, he would emerge a new man, speaking God's language, prepared to inhabit the second, everlasting paradise.
>
> Paul Auster, *City of Glass*

In *City of Glass*, Paul Auster overlays the semi-transparent texture of the city with two metaphors of place: the Garden of Eden and the Tower of Babel. The two utopian locations, if we listen to the predictions of the deranged Peter Stillman Sr., were to crystallize in America, where a tower would be created around 1960. Once completed, the new tower would be the locus of a regained paradise, of a new *tabula rasa* that reconnects fragments into a new whole. The subtle engineering of a similar global texture is the subtext of Alejandro González Iñárritu's "Babel." González's re-creation appears as an engaging revision of the double place Auster describes, with each story showing vistas into each of the rooms of this ascending tower. The four stories that make up the movie, the Moroccan shepherd family, the American couple made up of Susan and Richard on vacation in Morocco, the Mexican nanny in charge of their kids in San Diego, and the ramblings of a motherless deaf and mute Japanese teenager whose father gave a rifle to his guide in Morocco, represent a show case of each room. It is the two Moroccan boys who trigger the tragedy when they test the range of that very rifle on a bus making its way on the winding desert road. Silent and practically imperceptible in its trajectory, the bullet appears as a violent invasion that literally creates a hole. Susan's body becomes a ground zero, understood here as the center or origin of rapid, intense, or violent activity or change.

Automatically, and as if responding to a default mechanism, the shooting is represented by the American media as an act of terrorism. The children and their spartan home in the Moroccan desert become part of the new demarcation of the axis of evil. Yet the viewer, who has been privy to Yussef and Ahmed's testing of the rifle, knows that the incident responds to no pattern; it is just a "contingent encounter" (McGowan 407). The viewer finds him/herself reconstructing the narrative of contingency in retrospect: if the Japanese businessman had not given the rifle as a gift to his guide, and the latter had not sold it to the family of shepherds, the shot would have never reached Susan. If she had not been injured, the limits and dimensions of the axis of evil would not have been activated. The kids would have returned home like on any other day, they would not have attempted a desperate escape with their father, and the younger boy would not have been shot by the police. The shepherd's house would not have become a sleeper cell, a rhizomatic place-without-a-place in the unmarked geography of global terrorism. Susan and Richard, in turn, would have returned safely to their California home to take care of their children, and Amelia, the nanny, could have attended her son's wedding without the couple's children, which, in turn, would have kept her out of the spotlight of the border patrol. Finally, she would not have been sent back to Mexico.

But all these wrong turns do happen, and the movie deals out its implacable justice: "illegals" are repatriated south of the border; those suspected of terrorism face the stern face of anti-terrorist forces, even if they happen to be children. The movie is about connections, as the producer Jon Kilik notes (McGowan 408), and it does manage to unite Richard and Susan while they desperately wait for an ambulance in a remote Moroccan village. It also shows Chieko, the Japanese deaf and mute young woman holding hands with the detective who has come to investigate the selling of her father's rifle. Yet it is also about the firm separation between visitors and asylum seekers, between characters that enjoy the pleasures of globalization, and those who suffer its consequences. In "Babel," as in "The Visitor," hospitality is understood not as reciprocity but as personal identity. Yet "Babel" shows a further refinement of this reduction of meaning. While Amelia embodies the semantic transformation of *hostis* from a reciprocal and compensating guest to a threatening Other that must be excluded south of the border, the Moroccan father and his two children become exiles in their own home. The family is no longer *chez soi*, for the land hosts a global demarcation that automatically transforms them into hostiles, into threatening enemies. Their humble house is not a site of enunciation, is no longer the location of the I, but has become *unheimlich* in a new camp-like conceptualization of global space. As portrayed in "Babel," the global tower is another locus of a lost paradise that is more akin to Foucault's vision of the panoptic tower in *Discipline and Punish*. It is a tower where everyone is enclosed in a cell isolated from other inmates. Directly watched by the inspector, those inside are seen but cannot see outside their cells. With no need for a physical keeper, the new global watcher and seer-of-it-all is the media, the global structure that provides the measure of all things, as well as the structural parameters to interpret the world. Functional, efficient, almost invisible and apparently harmless, the media turns into the perfect Panopticon that has the power to delineate the net-web of coercions for a society of the future (Foucault 201, 209).

IV: A Global Camp: "District 9"

> La première reaction, spontanée, à l'égard de l'étranger est de l'imaginer inférieur, puisque different de nous: ce n'est meme pas un homme, ou s'il l'est, c'est un barbare inférieur
>
> Tzvetan Todorov, *La conquête de l'Amérique, la question de l'autre*

Neill Blomkamp's "District 9" can be described as an action movie, an alien story, sci-fi adventure, racial allegory and horror movie that blends "Robocop," the "Terminator" series, and "Transformers" all into one. The title plays on District 6, a vibrant, mixed race area of Cape Town that was declared whites-only in 1966, after which 60,000 of its residents were forcibly removed (Corliss and Grossman). This revamped district illustrates once again how the topics of human rights and rule of law, as illustrated in the *faux* interviews with researchers and academics, are just a mask for the machinery of "biopower" in the face of the encounter with the Other, literally an alien coming from an unknown origin. More than twenty years ago, a massive alien ship, rendered inoperable for unknown reasons, hovered above Johannesburg with no apparent purpose and became part of the sky line of the city, providing a visual and ideological split that accompanies the narrative. When special forces make their way into the space ship, thus making a historical "first contact," and having the whole world as an audience, the vision is dismal: over a million of malnourished and unhealthy insect-like aliens inhabited the ship. The term "first contact" signals Blomkamp and co-writer Terri Tatchel's intent on describing the encounter as an instance of colonial interaction, of a "contact zone" of unequal forces that brings back into focus previous accounts, from Columbus's journals to John Smith's and William Bradford's renditions, to contemporary cultural representations such as James Cameron's 2009 "Avatar." The aliens, pejoratively called "prawns" by the South Africans because of their crustacean-like appearance, embody the set of ineradicable physical differences that are frequently attributed to the Other. For our encounter with the Other is always marked by that hierarchization of difference, as Todorov has clairvoyantly stated. In the movie, these inferior barbarians are skinny cyborgs with insect-like faces. Without much certainty as to what to do with them, the creatures are ferried to a camp that is immediately fenced in, then militarized. There is no state of exception to speak of, just the protective custody of the different. The aliens are "bandits," individuals whose behavior is deviant in relation to the required form. The camp finally morphs into a slum where the aliens survive in utter squalor scavenging on dumps, or selling their weapons to Nigerian gangsters in return for cat food and prostitutes, thus awaking the ghost of miscegenation. The correlation between the alien Other and his location in precise spatial coordinates is clear. The moment the "prawns" are isolated, it becomes much easier to dehumanize them, then harm them, then kill and exterminate them (Pacate 20), or use them for genetic research programs. The movie portrays these metamorphoses of inmates and their spatiality in a series of sketches taken from the news. The images also exemplify the conceptual and spatial continuity between trash and aliens, for both are rendered as the unwanted residue of society. District 9 embodies the abject, and its inhabitants represent the "ejected beyond the scope of the possible, the tolerable, the thinkable" (Kristeva 1). Though there is evidence that they represent an advanced civilization, as their superior space-age-looking weaponry indicates, there are theories that the stranded aliens belong to a working class. Harboring no initiative or leadership, the aliens are apparently happy to survive as *homo sacer* but also as *homo* sucker, as social and spatial parasites. There is no investment in the "futurity" of the aliens. No opening of the realm of the perhapsness of the newcomer. In "District 9" the ineradicable difference of the aliens redefines the triangulation of self, Other, and time. For the aliens, detained and relocated, the future is already the past. To rewrite Levinas's sentence, the presence of the past in the present seems all the same accomplished in the face-to-face with the Other. The aliens merely embody the anteriority and exteriority automatically attributable to the Other.

As the number of crimes attributed to the "prawns" peak, violent riots ensue. Snatches of documentaries acquaint the viewer with an apartheid regime that clear-cuts the human from the alien, and that openly evokes the apartheid era in South Africa, but also in the United States. Unsurprisingly, South African natives no longer want to live with the camp in sight, an "open wound," to use Gloria Anzaldúa's metaphor, which constantly hemorrhages next to the city. Expedite solutions to the alien problem are put forward, such as a selective virus that only affects the "prawns." Due to international pressure, however, the government comes up with a humane option that implies the relocation of the 1.8 million aliens to a prawn city, allegedly a better and safer location away from humans, or more specifically, as the images indicate, where humans are not allowed to loiter outside the fence. As Christopher Johnson, one of the aliens, is later warned, the new city is even worse than District 9, with tents smaller than the shacks, and more like a concentration camp. Yet in the promotional leaflets the relocation is carried out in the spirit, as Agamben would remark, of *Schutzhaft*, of a protective custody that makes sure that the aliens are taken care of in another case of dislocating localization.

To carry out this relocation, a private firm, MNU, gets a government contract, and appoints overexcited and under-intelligent Wikus Van DeMerwe. Overjoyed by his new responsibility, and happy to narrate the development of the operation to a camera, Wikus and his entourage are escorted by MNU especial forces in what seems a military operation, and enter the forbidden area. The ground forces are given very specific instructions: "When dealing with an alien, be always polite but firm. Remember that a smile is always cheaper than a bullet." The messages conveyed from the loudspeakers, however, emphasize the humanitarian aspect of the deployment. As he goes from shack to shack Wikus is visibly more focused on confiscating the alien's weapons—It is no coincidence that MNU is a weapon manufacturer—, and on aborting the "prawns' eggs," humorously poping "like popcorn" when set on fire, than on "assisting" the aliens. "There is kids everywhere," he remarks, "that's why we need to get rid of them." As he serves eviction notices, he encounters Christopher Johnson, an alien that has managed to reassemble a space ship aided by scraps scavenged from the dump. Christopher's name, a play on the explorer, alleged discoverer of the New World, and representative of a superior civilization, is another instance of the colonial overtones of the story. In a direct reversal of Columbus's account, the movie unfolds the process of incarceration of the superior culture, even if, in a humorous turn, Christopher Johnson, like Christopher Columbus, is supposed to have come from heaven.[7] Johnson is also at the center of the messianic subplot of the movie. Christopher means Christ bearer, and Johnson means son of John, the writer of Apocalypse (Pacate 20). As the action of the movie moves from Mary Louise Pratt's concept of "the contact zone" into a war zone, the narration of Wikus's last three days as a human becomes apocalyptic in tone. Christopher, in turn, becomes the martyr who turns into a potential liberator of aliens and humans alike. His shack, a sanctuary of stolen computer parts, according to Wikus, has turned into a workshop where he has distilled a fluid that contains alien DNA. When Wikus comes upon it and manipulates it to show it to the ever-present camera, he is spattered with it. This incident, regarded as minor by Wikus, will change his life, for he becomes infected with prawn DNA and starts his metamorphosis into an alien. In becoming an alien, however, he becomes more human, and will be privy to the genocidal agenda of the MNU. It is a painful process of self-discovery, not unlike the one undertaken by Neo in "The Matrix" (1999), which will allow him to uncover the other side of the barbed wire, the side supposedly free. The *chez soi* will reveal itself intimately fettered to a particular view of reality based on multinationals and corporate agendas. His metamorphosis makes him the target of MNU, for which his liminal state as human-alien grants them the right to carry out all kinds of medical experiments on him. Wikus is shuttled to the MNU building and the messy dungeons of biopower: laboratories that harbor aliens' body parts. Wikus's body, the perfect balance between alien and human DNAs, is clinically assessed in the terms of a global *raison d'état*. Like a conquered land, Wikus becomes a "specimen" automatically plundered and fragmented into body parts: tissue, bone marrow, blood, all of them precious items in the global market. He is also the coveted post-human that, in the Nigerians' view,

7 See "Journal of the First Voyage to America, 1492-1493."

harbors a special power. As a hybrid fugitive, Wikus flees to the only place where he can be safe among the kind he has contributed to subjugate. District 9 becomes his sanctuary, the contact area now transmuted into war zone between dehumanized humans and humanized aliens. Wikus will undergo a full transformation, but before he does so, he manages to escort Christopher to the ship he has assembled so that he can return to the mother ship. After more than twenty years, the mother ship, that fixture suspended in the sky, restarts engines again. It is a historic time, and the crowds cheer in awe. The closing credits of the movie inform the viewer that "District 9 was demolished after the alien resettlement operation was completed," and that "District 10 now houses 2.5 million aliens and continues to grow."

V: District X

> … It is our mark, our cross, our X, our sign of never Ceasing being born at the point of two arrows colliding, X, And the gentle laying of one line over the other …
>
> Alfred Arteaga, "X Antecanto: The Xicano Sign"

The new digit for the new camp situates the incarceration experience in different spatial and temporal coordinates, for there will always be a district 11, 12, 13, etc. It also places the X, the Roman numeral, at the heart of a double transformation: the X is the matrix, the crossing that assures the breeding of similar places of incarceration, from *matr-*, *mater*; it also marks the X of the hybrid, for in the eyes of those who carry out or witness the incarceration, there is frequently something less than human about the *homo sacer*, as Blomkamp illustrates in his digitalized version of difference. The X is also the sign of the discarded, of the abject that constitutes the "place where I am not and which permits me to be" (Kristeva 3); the X is the crossing of space and time, of a repeating heterotopia and a recurrent heterochrony. It is this possibility of endless metamorphosis and replacement that opens the political overtones of the movie; they move back into the past as they delineate the future. "District 9" thus creates its own anteriority and futurity: It engages the South African apartheid, but also South African's xenophobic reaction to the massive influx of refugees from Zimbabwe, Somalia, and other African nations.[8] Its exploration of detention and removal outlines the pattern I have traced through "The Terminal," "The Visitor" and "Babel," and spreads outward, according to its *matr*-like quality, to encompass similar experiences of incarceration. The plight of the aliens, detained, evicted, and relocated seems comparable to that of the Japanese Americans during WWII, to that of the Palestinians in Gaza, the detainees in Guantánamo (Corliss and Grossman) and little Guantánamos. But it is also reminiscent of the so-called "illegal aliens" that, in spite of facing a variety of provisions or laws, are allegedly carrying out a silent invasion of the United States, and need to be secured behind barbed wire. These different contingents provide instances of the anatomy of the *homo sacer* and the changing and expanding geography of contemporary camps.

Works Cited

Agamben, Giorgio. *Homo Sacer: Sovereign Power and Bare Life*. 1995. Translated by Daniel Heller-Roazen. Stanford: Stanford UP, 1998.

---. *State of Exception*. Tanslated by Kevin Attel. Chicago: U of Chicago P, 2005.

Arteaga, Alfred. *Cantos*. San José: Chusma House Publications, 1991.

Auster, Paul. *City of Glass*. London: Faber, 1985.

"Babel," DVD, dir. Alejandro González Inárritu (Paramount Vantage, 2006).

Baker, Houston, Jr. *Blues, Ideology, and Afro-American Literature*. Chicago: U of Chicago P, 1984.

Bromiley, Geoffrey William. *Theological Dictionary of The New Testament*. William B. Eerdmans Publishing Company, 1985.

Columbus, Christopher. "Journal of the First Voyage to America, 1492-1493." *The Heath Anthology of American Literature* vol. 1. 3rd Edition. Ed. Paul Lauter. Boston & New York: Houghton Mifflin Co., 1998.

Corliss, Richard and Lev Grossman. "Space Invaders." *Time* 174: 7 (2009).

De Cautier, Lieven, and Michiel Dehaene. "Towards a General Theory of Heterotopia." *Heterotopia and the City: Public Space in a Postcivil*

8 While the movie was being filmed in the Chiawelo section of Soweto, other townships were ravaged by outbursts of xenophobic violence perpetrated by indigenous South Africans upon illegal immigrants from other African countries.

Society. Eds. Michiel Dehaene and Lieven De Cuter. London and New York: Routledge, 2008. 87-102.

Dikeç, Mustafa. "Pera Peras Poros: Longings for Spaces of Hospitality." Theory, Culture & Society 19: 1-2 (2002): 227-47.

Dikeç, Mustafa, Nigel Clark and Clive Barnett. "Extending Hospitality: Giving Space, Taking Time." *Paragraph* 32: 1 (2009): 1-14.

Derrida, Jacques. *Adieu to Emmanuel Levinas*. Stanford: Stanford UP, 1999.

"District 9," DVD, dir. Neill Blomkamp (Sonny, 2009).

Feldman, Leonard C. "Terminal Exceptions: Law and Sovereignty at the Airport." *Law, Culture and the Humanities* 3 (2007): 320-44.

Foucault, Michel. *Discipline and Punish*. Translated by Alan Sheridan. London: Penguin, 1977.

---. "Of Other Spaces." *Heterotopia and the City: Public Space in a Post-civil Society*. Eds. Michiel Dehaene and Lieven De Cuter. London and New York: Routledge, 2008. 13-29.

Kaplan, Amy. "Where is Guantánamo?" *American Quarterly* 57.3 (2005): 831-57.

Kristeva, Julia. *Powers of Horror*. New York: Columbia UP, 1982.

Levinas, Emmanuel. *Time and the Other*. Pittsburgh, Pennsylvania: Duquesne UP, 1987.

---. *Totality and Infinity: An Essay on Exteriority*. Dordrecht: Kluwer Academic Publishers, 1991.

McGowan, Todd. "The Contingency of Connection: The Path to Politization in 'Babel.'" *Discourse* 30.3 (2008): 401-18.

McNulty, Tracy. *The Hostess: Hospitality, Femininity, and the Expropriation of Identity*. Minneapolis: U of Minnesota P, 2007.

Pacate, Rose. "'District 9': Gritti, Violent, Brilliant." *National Catholic Reporter*. 4 September 2009, p. 20.

"The Terminal," DVD, dir. Steven Spielberg (Dreamworks, 2004).

"The Visitor," DVD, dir. Tom MacCarthy (Unanimous, 2008).

Todorov, T. La conquête de l'Amérique, la question de l'autre. Paris: Editions du Seuil, 1982.

Virilio, Paul. *Ground Zero*. Translated by Chris Turner. London: Verso 2002.

Waldenfels, Benhard. "Levinas and the Face of the Other." *The Cambridge Companion to Levinas*. Eds. Simon Critchley and Robert Bernasconi. Cambridge: Cambridge UP, 2001. 63-81.

Žižek, Slavoj. *Welcome to the Desert of the Real*. London: Verso, 2002.

From Conflict Spaces to Contact Zones: The Contested Landscapes of Gentrification in the American Inner City

Eric C. Erbacher

Eric C. Erbacher investigates the sharing of neighborhood space in the currently gentrifying neighborhood of Williamsburg in Brooklyn, NYC. The process of transforming a marginalized ethnic and working-class neighborhood into a 'hipster' residential area has made Williamsburg a complex site of contact offering both possibilities for genuine interaction, exchange, and meaning but also opportunities for economic exploitation and hegemonic domination. By analyzing print media representations of Williamsburg's gentrified community, Erbacher also sheds light on how marketing strategies serve to exert hegemonic control over both the meaning of place and the actions of its population.

Introduction: Contact Zones of the Contemporary Inner City

> The mile-long stretch of Bedford Avenue is lined with art galleries, bars, and secondhand boutiques that have made Williamsburg so popular with the hipster set. Off the main strip, visitors will find the area is rich in ethnic diversity, comprised of Italians, Latinos, and a large Hasidic Jewish community. ("Williamsburg and Greenpoint")

With these two simple sentences, readers of the real estate and travel section of *New York Magazine*'s 2009 online edition are introduced to the Brooklyn neighborhood of Williamsburg and to its attractions. It might seem odd, even for a lifestyle magazine, to collapse the social, cultural, and economic complexities of a multiethnic neighborhood of over 100,000 inhabitants[1] into such ostensibly harmoniously co-existing

1 Determining Williamsburg's exact and current population size is difficult as the data available from the U.S. Census Bureau do neither correspond precisely to the

groups. Yet for all its reductionism, the quote is symptomatic of a strategy in which the media represents and constructs gentrifying neighborhoods like Williamsburg as exciting and congenial "bourgeois playgrounds" (Smith and LeFaivre 60) in order to promote them to a "creative class" clientele (Florida). Such an image, however, is very much in contrast to predominant descriptions of gentrification, both in popular and academic publications, which emphasize issues of class antagonism, conflict, and displacement. Urban planning scholar Peter Marcuse, for instance, defines gentrification as "the movement into a previously working-class area by upper-income households, generally professionals, managers, technicians, the new gentry, resulting in the displacement of the former lower-income residents" (Marcuse 790-791). Ensuing from such definitions is a notion of gentrifying space that is occupied by two seemingly fundamentally opposed factions, the gentrifiers and the displaced, whose only contact can be conflictual. Such a view, however, is prone to a similarly ideologically narrow conception of the transformations connected to gentrification as is a celebratory perspective.

Using Mary Louise Pratt's concept of the "contact zone," this article attempts to broaden the conventional conceptualization of gentrification in going beyond the dichotomy of seeing affected neighborhoods as either bourgeois playgrounds or conflict spaces. This is to be done in a comparative study that simultaneously looks at gentrification in other American neighborhoods as well as at processes of transformation in Brooklyn Williamsburg. The first part of this study is concerned with the notion of gentrifying neighborhoods as conflict spaces, discussing its theoretical roots and some case studies. The second part, in taking the cue from Pratt's concept of "contact zones," examines opportunities for interaction and cooperation within gentrifying neighborhoods, thereby creat-

neighborhood's boundaries nor are they available for the relevant date. The number given here is therefore an estimate based on a reduction of the figure (146,856) provided by the U.S. Census Bureau in the "American Community Survey 2006-2008" for the Brooklyn Community District 1, which also includes the neighborhood of Greenpoint, and an extrapolation of the figure (85,089) given by the U.S. Census Bureau in the census of 2000 for the ZIP code area 11211, which is smaller than Williamsburg's established boundaries (U.S. Census Bureau, "11211—Fact Sheet."). These boundaries, however, are not officially set and have thus been subject to a continual discursive extension by the real estate industry and the media over the course of Williamsburg's gentrification. New York Magazine's 2010 real estate profile of Williamsburg specifies a neighborhood population of 125,000 ("Williamsburg, Brooklyn—New York City Neighborhood").

ing the potential of a meaning-making contact zone for all neighborhood groups. In the third part, the concept of the "packaged contact space" will be introduced. This is to describe various media strategies that aim to counter the increasing sociocultural homogeneity of the neighborhoods effected by gentrification. Mass media thus create an imagined "packaged contact space" by a narrative (re-)construction and representation of that space as one still offering possibilities for heterogeneous interaction and diverse contacts.

Disciplinary Contacts: Notes on Methodology

Due to the multifaceted nature of urban phenomena like gentrification, their study necessitates an equally multifaceted inter- and transdisciplinary approach that draws on studies from economics, sociology, geography, anthropology and cultural studies. While thus being informed by a broad base of research, the field of cultural studies provides the major lens through which to read the cognitively powerful medial constructions of such a contested place as gentrifying Williamsburg. Based on a critical reading of local print media texts as discourse, the present analysis will center on the gentrifying processes that took place in Williamsburg between 1985 and 2010. Within this socio-economic frame, Williamsburg is seen as a complex contact zone that spurs both occasional conflict due to spatial exploitation, domination, and resistance thereof, as well as mutually productive interactions and exchange. While such a contact zone is always a physically defined and grounded place of real-life and every-day interactions, it is also a medially represented relational place constituted by a network of various diachronic and translocal connections (Massey). Through their power of representation, framing, and agenda setting (McCombs and Shaw), local print media such as the *New York Times* and *New York Magazine* thus play a pivotal role in the discursive construction of a neighborhood's image as conflict or contact space. By focusing on the diversity and the ambiguous positions of the social groups involved in gentrification and by searching for expressions of their interests, it is possible to acknowledge both the co-operative as well as the conflictual sharing of neighborhood space among them. Moreover, through their medial representation, the power relations determining these often ambivalent relationships can be conceptualized and uncovered. These power relations, however, are not negotiated in a self-contained space but are highly contingent on larger socioeconomic and political processes often subsumed under the labels post-Fordism and neoliberalism. Gentrifying neighborhoods, particularly in global cities[2] such as New York City, are thus places of convergence where global forces intertwine and directly intersect with the daily lives of diverse local populations creating situations of contact and conflict.

Williamsburg Clashing: Conflict Spaces of Gentrification

Much of the academic research devoted to gentrification is based on conjectures of a binary opposition between gentrifiers on the one side and existing neighborhood populations[3] on the other side (Glass). Rooted in the statistical findings of sociological and geographical case studies, most explanatory theories of gentrification, otherwise as divergent as Marxist structuralist and cultural liberalist, thus revolve around assumptions of fundamental class differences between both groups (Lees, Slater and Wyly 39-126). As one of the most prominent scholars of gentrification, Marxist geographer Neil Smith contends in *The New Urban Frontier* that gentrification "has become the leading residential edge of a much larger endeavor: the class remake of the central urban landscape" (39). In this view, the gentrifying inner city has become a socially contested and dichotomic space characterized by mutually excluding interests, little direct interaction except for occasional clashes, and the increasing marginaliza-

---

2 Throughout this paper, the term "global city" will be used in reference to Manuel Castells' and Saskia Sassen's concept of certain cities, including New York, acting as informational and financial hubs for the global economy, resulting in an increasing socioeconomic polarization of its populations.

3 A note on terminology: The term "gentrifiers" is a definitionally problematic one as over the course of a neighborhood's gentrification people of diverse sociocultural, economic, and ethnic backgrounds move to the neighborhood for different reasons, many of whom, however, contribute to its social and economic revaluation. In this paper, the term refers to various sociocultural groups moving into inner-city neighborhoods during the revaluation process by their own choice for reasons of building style, lifestyle, or financial incentives. It thus includes both "pioneer" gentrifiers such as artists as well as "fourth-stage" gentrifiers like professionals and managers. For a discussion of stage models of gentrification see Lees, Slater, and Wyly 30-34. The phrase "existing neighborhood populations" or "long-term residents" is not intended to imply that neighborhoods are to be considered socially static entities. It is used to refer to groups living in a neighborhood prior to its gentrification, often due to historic spatial attachment, financial restrictions, and cultural and ethnic bonds.

tion and eventual displacement of long-term populations—all part of a "revanchist" urban strategy to "take the city back" from the "poor and the homeless" (Smith, *New Urban Frontier* 210-12).

According to this trajectory, increasing housing demand in gentrifying neighborhoods, encouraged by governmental or corporate actors such as banks or real estate developers, leads to the rising of real estate prices and property taxes, both of which eventually result in the direct displacement of residents as well as in "neighborhood resource displacement" (Hackworth and Smith; Davidson 2392)—the loss of important community institutions. Although studies on the extent of direct displacement are disputed and methodologically difficult to obtain, most scholars agree on its salience and recognize it as the most traumatic effect of gentrification (Atkinson). The threat of being displaced is thus a frequently cited reason for conflict between existing residents and gentrifiers. Reminiscent of tensions between social groups in nineteenth century cities (Boyer), other issues typically pitting gentrifiers against existing population groups include diverging views on affordable and public housing, on public order and morality, and the quality and quantity of neighborhood services and amenities (Muñiz; Lees, Slater, and Wyly 217-21).

Since the 1980s, gentrification processes have repeatedly been accompanied by open conflicts, such as the partly violent anti-gentrification protests in the Mission District of San Francisco around the turn of the millennium (Rinaldo 156-57) or in Vancouver's Downtown Eastside in the early 2000s (Lees, Slater, and Wyly 263-71). Most notorious, however, was the protracted struggle over Tompkins Square Park in the Lower East Side of Manhattan which culminated in August of 1988 when riots broke out as "a diverse mix of anti-gentrification protesters, punks, housing activists, park inhabitants, artists ... and Lower East Side residents" (Smith, *New Urban Frontier* 3) were attacked by police supposedly aiming at cleansing the park of its homeless population, its youths playing loud music, and its drug trade. As Smith convincingly argues, however, these harsh measures accompanied wider "revanchist" municipal attempts to rid the Lower East Side of its oppositional groups and make it ready for full-scale gentrification (*New Urban Frontier* 3-29).

The neighborhood of Williamsburg in Brooklyn has not experienced similar riots or violence during its gentrification. Williamsburg was settled in the early nineteenth century as a suburban neighborhood for

Brooklyn's economic elite. By the middle of the century, however, its location on the East River had turned it into one of the most densely populated and diverse industrial neighborhoods of Brooklyn and, after Brooklyn's merger with New York in 1898, of the whole city. In the first half of the twentieth century, it became home to a large Orthodox Jewish population, a Polish-American, an Italian-American community, and, since the 1960s, to growing numbers of Hispanics, mostly Puerto Ricans (Curran, "Nature of Work" 1247). By that time, its architecture was mainly characterized by plain wood-frame houses and industrial lofts. As deindustrialization started in the 1960s, however, many industrial employers, such as the nearby Brooklyn Navy Yard, relocated or closed down. Williamsburg's social and economic fabric was hit hard, thus conforming to the predominant narrative of American inner cities of the 1970s as places of decline (Beauregard). The increasing influx of Hispanics as well as the high birthrate of the Orthodox Jewish community put additional pressure on the employment and housing situation. This was exacerbated by cultural misunderstandings and charges of the Jewish community's preferential treatment by municipal agencies. As described by the *New York Times* in October 1990, these tensions periodically erupted in public disputes over scarce housing, making Williamsburg a far from harmonious place even before gentrifiers moved to the area in noticeable numbers:

> A square city block in Williamsburg, overgrown with tall grass and wild shrubs, has become a battleground between Hasidic Jews and Hispanic residents in a struggle for control in the deeply split Brooklyn neighborhood. The largest Hasidic sect in the area, the Satmar, which bought the land from the city, has drawn up plans to build what they believe will be the nation's largest synagogue, with 6,000 seats. ... But a coalition of Hispanic groups, claiming that their constitutional rights have been violated, has gone to Federal court to permanently block the construction. The coalition ... claims that New York City, in collusion with the Satmar, circumvented standard legal procedures in selling the land. The development, they say, will tip the area's ethnic balance and lead to Hispanic residents being forced out." (Goldman)

Through the choice of vocabulary ("battleground," "struggle," "deeply split," "forced out") and an emphasis on dichotomies, Williamsburg is here presented as the stereotypical urban place of inter-ethnic conflict, recalling films like Spike Lee's *Do the Right Thing* (1989), set in the nearby Brooklyn neighborhood of Bedford Stuyvesant. In the medially represented inner city, ethnic rifts even seem to have become inscribed in the urban landscape, as evidenced by a quote from the *New York Times* in February 1992: "In Williamsburg, the battle over the grant application [to convert public housing to market rate co-operatives] shows how sharp are the resentments and misunderstandings between the largely Hasidic northern Williamsburg and the mostly Hispanic South Side, which are separated by the aptly named Division Avenue" (Mitchell).

By the time its gentrification becomes noticeable in the early 1990s, Williamsburg's status as a conflict space is thus firmly established as increasing numbers of artists, students, and professionals turn Williamsburg into a poster child for contemporary gentrification. The influx of this neo-bohemia (Lloyd) adds another element to the uneasy situation by putting even more pressure on the housing situation. In 1999, the *New York Times* covers a protest of Hispanic community groups against proposed zoning changes because they "would price poor, working Hispanic residents out of the area" and replace them with "Hasidic residents and Manhattan yuppies, who are already driving up rents" (Waldman 8). While fears of displacement are certainly not unfounded around the turn of the millennium, and the coverage of the *New York Times* does stress that repeatedly, ethnic and social oppositions continue to be presented in clear-cut and stereotypical terms.

In contrast to many Hispanics, members of the close-knit and frequently real-estate owning Hasidic community seem more concerned about the newcomers' lifestyle. Presented as an insular and dogmatically orthodox community, it apparently feels provoked and threatened by the young gentrifiers' supposed permissiveness, complaining about their loud nightlife, drinking, and generally licentious behavior and looks. The objections are expressed quite vehemently on flyers distributed in 2004 declaring the incoming gentrifiers a "bitter decree from Heaven" (qtd. in Weiss) and comparing their invasion into Williamsburg to the 9/11 attacks on the World Trade Center: "'How long did it take the Twin Towers to fall? Eight seconds. How long will it take for Williamsburg??? God Forbid" (qtd. in Bahrampour, "Plague"). These denunciations are seconded by pleas to the "Master of the Universe" to "remove from upon us the plague of the artists, so that we shall not drown in evil waters, and that they shall not come to our residence to ruin it" (qtd. in Bahrampour, "Plague"). Yet, far from attempting to dampen the passions, the newspaper also provides a forum for the newcomers' prejudices against their Orthodox neighbors: "When you willingly have ten-plus children based on your religious beliefs, feed most of them on food stamps, and displace everyone else in the neighborhood, there's hardly any sympathy to be had" (qtd. in Weiss).

As the gentrification of the blocks surrounding the Hasidic enclave has continued despite the real estate and financial crisis of the "Great Recession" (Krugman), tensions over bike lanes leading through the Hasidic enclave flared in 2009. Members of the Orthodox community have complained about Williamsburg's hipsters riding through their part of the neighborhood wearing inappropriately tight and short-cut clothes, upsetting the adults and morally endangering the youth. After the bike lanes were removed—a reaction that followed the demands by Hasidic rabbis before New York City's municipal election in November 2009—the hipsters fought back by repainting the lanes (Olshan and Schram).

Yet, the fault lines in Williamsburg do not only seem to run between ethnicities and religions or between younger gentrifiers and pre-existing population groups, but also between earlier gentrifiers and more recent newcomers, as indicated by numerous reports on disputes about the noise and drunken behavior associated with the opening of new bars (Barnes), the replacement of older community stores with chic boutiques and cafes (Bahrampour, "Neighborhood"), and the requisite anti-gentrification graffiti advising "Yuppie Go Home!" (Hevesi). Williamsburg thus appears to be the highly charged and contested place of opposition, struggle, and mutually excluding interests pertinent to conventional gentrification wisdom.

Common Grounds: Shared Community Interests in a Gentrification Contact Zone

Yet, upon closer look, each group sharing space in Williamsburg is far less homogenous internally and less antagonistic externally than presented, and their interests therefore show significant amounts of intersection. The resulting complexity of the various groups' interactions might best be theorized within the framework of Mary Louise Pratt's concept of the "contact zone." Among other points, Pratt stresses the "interactive, improvisational dimensions" of the contact while maintaining that they take place in a "space of imperial encounters, the space in which peoples geographically and historically separated come into contact with each other and establish ongoing relations usually involving conditions of coercion, radical inequality, and intractable conflict" (8).

Such an approach, while originally rooted in a critique of colonialism, seems highly pertinent to the analysis of the uneven landscape of the gentrified American inner city. In particular, it promises to be methodologically valuable for the present study on the diversity and the ambiguous positions of the people involved in and affected by Williamsburg's gentrification as it offers the opportunity to capture both the potential for conflict as well as for cooperative forms of interaction, while also recognizing the power relations governing these interactions. This is not intended to gloss over the problematic aspects of gentrification, particularly the socially disruptive and destructive issue of displacement. Rather, it is an attempt to move away from binary oppositions to open up a more nuanced view of gentrification as a spatial process that is also offering opportunities for communication and cooperation.

Little specific research has been done on the diversity and range of productive interactions within gentrifying neighborhoods. In their attempts to explain gentrification, however, scholars associated with demand-side explanatory theories have focused on the socio-cultural characteristics of gentrifiers and stressed the positive connotations that older and diverse inner-city neighborhoods have for many gentrifiers. Referring to notions of the "emancipatory city" (Caulfield 18), Canadian geographer David Ley argues that at least for early gentrifiers, inner-city neighborhoods were "oppositional spaces: socially diverse, welcoming difference, tolerant, creative, valuing the old, the hand-crafted, the personalized, countering hierarchical lines of authority" (210). From such a white middle-class perspective, living in the inner city and everyday interaction with its inhabitants promised liberation from oppressing homogeneity.

Studying the impact of gentrification on a neighborhood's long-term residents, urban planning scholar Lance Freeman has been met with heavy criticism for his analysis of the New York City neighborhoods Harlem and Clinton Hill which showed displacement to be far less directly tied to gentrification than generally assumed. In their study on Harlem, Freeman and Braconi also found that while long-term inhabitants are often suspect of the gentrifiers and their lifestyle, they also welcome and profit from the various changes to the neighborhood, including a broader variety of retail and services as well as rising real estate values:

> As neighborhoods gentrify, they also improve in many ways that may be appreciated as much by their disadvantaged residents as by their more affluent ones. To the extent that gentrification is associated not only with an influx of higher-income households but also with better retail and public services, safer streets, more job opportunities, and improvements in the built environment, disadvantaged households may have less reason to change residences in search of a better living environment. (48)

Moreover, gentrifiers, with their own diverse backgrounds, often make valuable contributions to community groups aiming to slow further gentrification or mitigate its effects. One example of such a common ground between some gentrifiers and long-term population groups where common grassroots community activism was able to effect changes in an urban pro-growth climate is the Tenderloin district in San Francisco: "Tenderloin activism in fact reveals the potential for neighborhood political activism to exercise significant proactive influence over the localized impact of postindustrial world transformations" (Robinson 506).

Gentrifying neighborhoods can thus be conceptualized as complex contact zones where, for the incoming populations, the encounter with the gentrifying 'Other' is not necessarily conflictual but can lead to common grounds of various kinds. The intersections of interests as well as hegemonic aspects of gentrification can also be found in Brooklyn Williamsburg. Due to Williamsburg's ethnic and social diversity, gentrifiers are offered ample opportunities for interaction with and experiences of difference along the lines of the emancipatory city discourse, even if their predominantly acquisitive and appropriatory nature points to the asymmetrical relation. This is exemplified in by an article in the *New York Times* from 1986, where it says:

> Restaurants on Lee Avenue serve either dairy or meat, and kosher delicacies such as herring and baked salmon salad are a favorite of Hasidim and non-Hasidim alike at Flaum's Smoked Fish at the corner of Lee and Wilson Streets. Shopping offers bodegas, Italian bakeries that make fresh bread daily, and, further north, Polish specialty shops. Residents of the northern waterfront area enjoy shopping on Bedford Avenue, where they can buy produce, fish, meat, eggs and bread from wholesalers. (Dorian)

While the contact zone here seems to be rather dominated or conceptualized by the culinary desires of the incoming population, there are several examples of long-term residents welcoming, profiting from, and appropriating the influx of gentrifiers and the attendant changes. These range from a trendy new hipster bar offering Bingo nights for elderly Italian-American women (Christian), a Hispanic supermarket entrepreneur catering to the newcomer's tastes by stocking Ben and Jerry's ice cream (Sexton), to residents appreciative of population growth, as in the following quote from a *New York Times* article: "'I welcome the people coming in because I think they bring positive change,' Mr. Webster said. 'They insure the neighborhood isn't going to deteriorate and become vacant and abandoned'" (Cohen).

Whereas this form of interaction is largely one-directional, gentrification in Williamsburg has also created spaces for shared interests uniting all major population groups. Particularly cases in which the neighborhood as a whole is perceived to be negatively affected by outside forces help to unite its residents, thus contributing to the establishment of a common ground. Among these cases was the 1992 formation of a collective organization called *Williamsburg Organized for the Walkway* aimed at pressuring the municipal authorities to reopen the walkway of the Williamsburg Bridge, a connection to Manhattan deemed important across community lines:

> The groups—Hispanic residents, a Hasidic community and a newer population of young artists—are frequently at odds over issues of housing, police protection and race. But after the city closed the walkway last summer, each realized its interest in a reopening. Many Hispanic residents work and have relatives on the Lower East Side. Hasidim use the walkway to visit hospitals on the Sabbath, when they cannot drive or take subways. And the artists—some poor, some avid bike riders—wanted an alternative to the subway. They formed Williamsburg Organized for the Walkway, and demanded that City Hall restore the passageway quickly. After some wrangling late last summer, they won. "They wanted to be sure that it didn't seem too cozy, but individuals from all parts of the community did come together," said Anna West, a 36-year-old photographer who organized the effort. "It will go a long way toward smoothing the path to peace among the groups" (Fisher).

Other issues of cooperation include the opposition against a garbage incinerator, which was only successful after the involvement of gentrifiers (Berger, *Metro*) and against the closing of a neighborhood firehouse (Kilgannon). Significantly, also the 2005 plans for the rezoning of Williamsburg's waterfront to allow high-rise real estate development, which many, including many gentrifiers, felt would threaten the character of the neighborhood, was able to at least temporarily unite most neighborhood groups (Bleyer). Long-term residents and newcomers thus share common concerns primarily relating to general neighborhood improvements that benefit most communities. However, the common ground thus established is an uneven one: While the long-term population groups might profit from many of the changes, gentrifiers are clearly its agents and are thus also governing its direction. Moreover, this dominant position of the newcomers is discursively reinforced by the media, since it is usually the gentrifiers' voices that comment on, and thus hegemonically interpret, projects of shared community interests.

A Packaged Contact Space: Medial Constructions of a Diverse and Safe Williamsburg

Gentrification has become a pervasive phenomenon, a "global urban strategy" (Smith, *Antipode*) closely connected to neoliberal processes in which cities vie for members of a "creative class" as supposed guarantors of a city's competitiveness in the global information economy. Particularly the media are not disinterested parties in this process but an integral part of the "urban growth regime" (Wyly and Hammel 2647), and are thus susceptible to a boosterist and euphoric coverage of the neighborhood and its changes, especially in light of the financial and reputational promises of advancing gentrification. Gentrifying neighborhoods in global cities and their medial promotion play an integral part in the Postfordist inter-urban competition as they promise to attract "creative classes" by providing the services that this social group supposedly yearns for: proximity to employment, transportation, and lifestyle amenities centering around a diversity of people and experiences, as well as a unique sense of place. Such a place can fittingly be described along the lines of Pratt's concept of the contact zone, as it acknowledges the complexity, multiplicity, and the intersections of the various interests within gentrifying neighborhoods, allowing for a recognition of both the harmful and productive as well as the hegemonic ramifications of gentrification.

However, with intensifying gentrification the precarious and uneven balance of the (mediated and real) contact zone is threatened. As neighborhoods gentrify, they progressively lose some of the lifestyle qualities making them attractive to gentrifiers and start to run the danger of becoming generic. Even though these neighborhoods once were unique places due to their historically contingent social, cultural, and functional diversity, such distinctiveness tends to be more and more erased through the influx of more affluent, middle-class people with an increasingly similar socio-economic and cultural background as well as exclusive and security-minded notions of an inner-city lifestyle. The resulting changes effectively act as socio-economic barriers restricting access to certain populations and uses. While this process is essential to the gentrification logic, it also threatens to undermine the credibility of the neighborhood's representation and marketability as a contact zone for diverse experiences and thus its success in attracting the "creative classes."

In attempts to counter this trend, gentrifying neighborhoods are increasingly being constructed and marketed, particularly in and by the media, as, what I term, "packaged contact spaces." These are mediated spaces that promise the desired qualities of both social and ethnic diversity and difference, as well as intercultural interaction and experiences, while also being represented in a way that carefully avoids any undue disturbance of middle-class expectations of harmonious multiculturalism and safety. Whereas they are thus cleansed of their problematic or conflictual aspects such as interethnic tensions or issues of displacement, some socio-cultural characteristics of the old neighborhood are thus discursively preserved, ready to be experienced, consumed, and appropriated by "creative class" consumers. Particularly for audiences without first-hand knowledge of the respective neighborhood, these discursive representations become encompassing and the primary means to imagine and evaluate gentrifying urban spaces (Soja 13; Mele 14). Gentrifying neighborhoods are thus medially constructed, exploited, and packaged as exciting and diverse spaces for the safe experience of and interaction with the urban 'Other.'

As Williamsburg's gentrification advances and many parts of the neighborhood are becoming socially and ethnically more homogeneous, it is also being medially represented as a packaged contact space, ready to be marketed to "creative class" hipsters and professionals. At least since Williamsburg was declared to be the third hippest place in America by the *Utne Reader* in 1997 (Walljasper and Kraker), the neighborhood and its real estate have been heavily promoted in the news media and by the municipal authorities—successfully so as the approval of the 2005 zoning changes enabling high-rise condominium construction on the Williamsburg waterfront shows. Increasingly, and especially in articles showcasing the neighborhood's real estate opportunities, Williamsburg's older ethnic and social groups are represented as adding little more than local color, history, and consumable experiences:

> There are the streets filled with Yiddish-speaking Hasidim branching off clamorous Lee Avenue, the awning-shaded row houses and indolent cannoli cafes in the Italian enclave to the north, the domino players and Technicolor murals of the Puerto Rican Southside, the garage art galleries of the bohemian quarter along Bedford Avenue. (Berger, *Other*)

Here, Williamsburg's main population groups are not only presented with their clichéd attributes ("clamorous" Hasidim; "indolent" Italians; Puerto Rican domino players; "bohemian" gentrifiers) but the article also provides the exact locations to experience these clichés. The selection of these details is a decisive factor in the medially packaged construction of Williamsburg as contact space: On the one hand, they prepare the readers, and thus the potential visitors or residents, for their experiences, thus eliminating the risk of unpleasant surprise. On the other hand, they represent these social places as static, fixed, and removed, thus inhibiting the possibility of personal interaction, except maybe for the appropriating consumption of stereotypical products of the 'Other,' be they cannoli or art. Interestingly, just like the still present older community groups, the early, more bohemian gentrifiers have also become part of Williamsburg's diverse socio-cultural attraction. Together, these groups are increasingly coming to act as mere background to an acquisitive middle-class lifestyle with little to no regard for or interest in the lives of the previous inhabitants, as the following report about a gentrifier couple from the 2004 *New York Times* exemplifies:

> Old Williamsburg, the one with the Latin flavor, is still here: the vacant lot opposite Mr. Oceguera and Mr. Koveleskie's living room terrace is filled with pumpkin vines. The "artists" are represented too: a juice bar around the corner has a street sign with the words Haight-Ashbury painted on its galvanized steel walls (there's even a VW bus emblazoned with peace signs). But this couple mostly ignores such signage on their walks to emporiums like Uva's Wines and Bedford Cheese down the block; both men love to cook. (Green)

As Green makes clear, the few and arbitrarily selected remnants of "old" Williamsburg's more diverse past ("the Latin flavor"; the "'artists'") have little relevance for the portrayed couple. Their inclusion in this passage thus points to the fact that they are directed at the readers, who are once again given advice for what to experience and how to interpret it, in this case as colorful signs of Williamsburg's thoroughly gentrified contact zone. Indeed, it is precisely the superficiality and arbitrariness of these symbols drained of conflict and vitality that makes them so suitable for their inclusion in medial constructions of Williamsburg as a packaged contact zone.

Conclusion

Brooklyn Williamsburg can be considered one of the best known examples of the most recent wave of gentrification, so-called "third wave" gentrification[4]. The most prominent features of this "third wave" are the heavy promotion of the neighborhood's real estate and quality of life issues as well as the relative lack of resistance movements (Lees, Slater, and Wyly 173-185). As such, "third wave" gentrification processes lend themselves readily to being medially represented and marketed as what I have termed a packaged contact space: A largely medially constructed space offering seemingly unrestricted opportunities for different socioeconomic and cultural groups to come into contact and to negotiate their interests ostensibly free from interference. This space, however, is cleansed of most controversial, problematic, or threatening aspects of that encounter, initially primarily discursively but increasingly also in real and daily life. It is also a represented space that is deeply inscribed with power relations in which the incoming population groups are able to exert their hegemony over both the meaning of place as well as the actions of its population. What is largely lost in such a packaged contact space, however, are the various opportunities for genuine interaction, challenge, and co-operation. Yet, dissecting gentrifying spaces with Pratt's contact zone approach can help to overcome the strong ontological dichotomy of seeing gentrification as either conflictual or harmonious. A conceptualization of gentrification and its specific spatial manifestations as an open contact zone stresses the complexities, ambiguities, and contingencies of gentrification itself and especially of its actors. It thus allows for a greater recognition of both the various experiences of gentrification as well as of the subtlety and the range of its medial representations.

4 On the wave theory of gentrification, identifying four chronological phases of the process since the 1960s, see Lee, Slater, and Wyly 173-87.

Works Cited

Atkinson, Rowland. "The Evidence on the Impact of Gentrification: New Lessons for the Urban Renaissance?" *European Journal of Housing Policy* 4.1 (2004): 107-131.

Bahrampour, Tara. "Neighborhood Report: New York Up Close: In Williamsburg, a Club Tests Tolerance for the Hip." *New York Times* 23 July 2000: 14.8.

Bahrampour, Tara. "'Plague of Artists' a Battle Cry for Brooklyn Hasidim." *New York Times* 17 February 2004: B1.

Barnes, Julian. "Neighborhood Report: Williamsburg: Manhattan Night Life Creeps South, to Mixed Reviews." *New York Times* 19 September 1999: 14.8.

Beauregard, Robert A. *Voices of Decline: The Postwar Fate of US Cities*. New York: Routledge, 2003.

Berger, Joseph. "Metro Matters: Fear Builds a Bridge Across Gulf of Cultures." *New York Times* 31 August 1992: B3.

---. "The Other Bridge, but all Brooklyn: Over 100 Years, the Williamsburg Has Diversified a Borough." *New York Times* 22 June 2003: 25.

Bleyer, Jennifer. "To the Ramparts, Hipsters, and Hold the Latte." *New York Times* 6 March 2005. 20 January 2010 <http://www.nytimes.com/2005/03/06/nyregion/thecity/06warr.html>.

Boyer, Paul. *Urban Masses and Moral Order in America: 1820-1920*. Cambridge, Mass.: Harvard UP, 1992.

Caulfield, Jon. *City Form and Everyday Life: Toronto's Gentrification and Critical Social Practice*. Toronto: U of Toronto P, 1994.

Christian, Nichole M. "Women's Social Club Bridges Generations on the Stoop." *New York Times* 10 August 2001: B7.

Cohen, Joyce. "Trendy Ambiance and Manhattan Views." *New York Times* 6 October 1996: 9.5.

Curran, Winifred. "Gentrification and the Nature of Work: Exploring the Links in Williamsburg, Brooklyn." *Environment and Planning* A 36 (2004): 1243-1258.

Davidson, Mark. "Spoiled Mixture: Where Does State-led 'Positive' Gentrification End?" *Urban Studies* 45.12 (November 2008): 2385-2405.

Dorian, David. "If You're Thinking of Living in: Williamsburg." *New York Times* 15 June 1986.

Fisher, Ian. "Williamsburg Bridge Journal: For Brooklyn Neighborhood, at Long Last, the Way Is Clear." *New York Times* 9 March 1992: B3.

Florida, Richard. *Cities and the Creative Class*. New York and London: Routledge, 2005.

Freeman, Lance. *There Goes the Hood: Views of Gentrification from the Ground Up*. Philadelphia: Temple UP, 2006.

Freeman, Lance, and Frank Braconi. "Gentrification and Displacement: New York in the 1990s." *Journal of the American Planning Association*. 70.1 (2004): 39-52.

Glass, Ruth, ed. *London: Aspects of Change.* London: MacGibbon and Kee, 1964.

Goldman, Ari L. "Brooklyn Project Shakes Hispanic-Hasidic Peace." *New York Times* 1 October 1990: B1.

Green, Penelope. "Living in the New Suburbia, With Plans for Children." *New York Times* 10 October 2004. 20 January 2010 <http://travel.nytimes.com/2004/10/10/realestate/ 10HABI.html>.

Hackworth, Jason. "Post recession gentrification in New York City." *Urban Affairs Review* 37 (2002): 815–843.

Hackworth, Jason, and Neil Smith. "The Changing State of Gentrification." *Tijdschrift voor Economische en Sociale Geografie* 92.4 (2001): 464-77.

Hevesi, Dennis. "Prices Send Loft Pioneers in Search of New Frontiers." *New York Times* 21 February 1999: 11.1.

Kilgannon, Corey. "Some Firehouses Go Quietly, Some With Rage." *New York Times* 26 May 2003: A1.

Krugman, Paul. "How Did Economists Get It So Wrong?" *New York Times* 6 September 2009: MM36.

Lees, Loretta, Tom Slater, and Elvin Wyly. *Gentrification*. New York and London: Routledge, 2008.

Ley, David. *The New Middle Class and the Remaking of the Central City.* Oxford: Oxford UP, 1996.

Lloyd, Richard. *Neo-Bohemia. Art and Commerce in the Postindustrial City*. New York and London: Routledge, 2006.

Marcuse, Peter. "Comment on Elvin K. Wyly and Daniel J. Hammel's 'Islands of Decay in Seas of Renewal: Housing Policy and the Resurgence of Gentrification.'" *Housing Policy Debate* 10.4 (1999): 789–797.

Massey, Doreen. *For Space*. London: Sage, 2005.

McCombs, Maxwell E., and Donald L. Shaw. "The Evolution of Agenda-Setting Research: Twenty-Five Years in the Marketplace of Ideas." *Journal of Communication* 43.2 (1993): 58 - 67.

Mele, Christopher. *Selling the Lower East Side. Culture, Real Estate, and Resistance in New York City.* Minneapolis and London: U of Minnesota P, 2000.

Mitchell, Alison. "Co-op Effort Worsens a Rift in Williamsburg." *New York Times* 7 May 1992: B3.

Muñiz, Vicky. *Resisting Gentrification and Displacement: Voices of Puerto Rican Women of the Barrio*. New York: Routledge, 1998.

Olshan, Jeremy, and Jamie Schram. "Hipsters Repaint Bike Lanes in Brush Off to Hasids." *New York Post* 9 December 2009. 20 January 2010 <http://www.nypost.com/p/news/local/brooklyn/bike_war_paint_g7EizkFEZktV3IlNUJosQM>.

Pratt, Mary Louise. *Imperial Eyes: Travel Writing and Transculturation.* 2nd ed. London and New York: Routledge, 2007.

Rinaldo, Rachel. "Space of Resistance: The Puerto Rican Cultural Center and Humboldt Park." *Cultural Critique* 50 (2002): 135-174.

Robinson, Tony. "Gentrification and Grassroots Resistance in San Francisco's Tenderloin." *Urban Affairs Review* 30 (1995): 483-513.

Sassen, Saskia. *The Global City: New York, London, Tokyo*. Princeton: Princeton UP, 1992.

Sexton, Joe. "Welfare Cuts Don't Dash the Optimism of Store Owners." *New York Times* 19 July 1997: 1.21.

Smith, Neil. *The New Urban Frontier. Gentrification and the Revanchist City.* London and New York: Routledge, 1996.

---. "New Globalism, New Urbanism: Gentrification as Global Urban Strategy." *Antipode* 34.3 (2002): 434-457.

Smith, Neil, and Michele LeFaivre. "A Class Analysis of Gentrification." *Gentrification, Displacement, and Neighborhood Revitalization.* Eds. J. John Palen and Bruce London. Albany: State U of New York P, 1984. 43-64.

Soja, Edward. *Thirdspace. Journeys to Los Angeles and Other Real-and-Imagined Places.* Malden, Mass.: Blackwell, 1998.

U.S. Census Bureau. "American Community Survey 2006-2008." *Population Division – New York City Department of City Planning.* November 2009. 27 September 2010 <http://www.nyc.gov/html/dcp/pdf/census/puma_demo_06to08_acs.pdf#bk1>.

---. "11211 – Fact Sheet." *American FactFinder*. 2000. 22 September 2009 <http://factfinder.census.gov/>.

Waldman, Amy. "Neighborhood Report: Williamsburgh: A Slight Hint of Progress, Maybe, on Needed Housing." *New York Times* 22 February 1998: 14.8.

Walljasper, J., and D. Kraker. "Hip hot spots." *Utne Reader* November/December 1997: 57–59.

Weiss, Steven. "Hasidim vs. Hipsters." *New York Magazine* 19 January 2004. 15 September 2009 <http://www.nymag.com/nymetro/news/people/columns/intelligencer/n_9756>.

"Williamsburg and Greenpoint Travel Planner." *New York Magazine* 2009. 22 September 2009 <http://nymag.com/visitorsguide/neighborhoods/williamsburg/>.

"Williamsburg, Brooklyn – New York City Neighborhood." *New York Magazine* 2010. 27 September 2010 <http://nymag.com/realestate/articles/neighborhoods/williamsburg.htm>.

Wyly, Elvin, and Daniel Hammel. "Commentary: Urban Policy Frontiers." *Urban Studies* 45.12 (2008): 2643-2648.

Forging a "Common Life" in the Ghetto: The Settlement House as Contact Space

Laura R. Fisher

Taking Katie Donovan's fictional description of the settlement house as its main premise, Laura R. Fisher's essay shows how the settlement house emerged as a paradigmatic contact space at the turn of the twentieth century. As a site in which the global phenomena of immigration and subsequent Americanization are processed on a local level, the settlement house, Fisher argues, is an institutional space that is both wildly unequal and practically advantageous. Thus, the settlement house's cultural pedagogy illuminates questions of acculturation and cross-class relations, while also offering a unique vantage point from which to understand the literary culture of early twentieth-century America.

Vida Dutton Scudder's 1903 novel, *A Listener in Babel*, explores the inner life of an educated and inquisitive young woman who has moved into a settlement house in the fictional American town of Brenton. Scudder's semi-autobiographical heroine, Hilda Lathrop, moves into the Langley House social settlement in search of resolution to some of her life's most profound questions: the limits of art's transformative potential, the meaning of social service, and the seemingly irreconcilable conflict between her keenness for beauty and her desire to help people whose lives are bound up with ugliness and struggle. Midway through the novel, Hilda comes to feel that she has failed in this endeavor: the settlement house movement, she worries, has done little to suppress the poverty, labor disputes, and industrial crises that mark turn-of-the-century American cities. Noting her disillusionment, a young, Irish settlement client and laundress named Katie Donovan reminds Hilda that the institution has had a powerful impact on the lives of workers and immigrants: "[T]hink how much you're doing to help [our poverty]," Katie implores Hilda. "Not the hunger of the body—that you can't help, I know—but the other worse kind. Now you've come, we've not got no call to feel that any more" (235). Katie proceeds to describe exactly how the settlement has changed the lives of its working class clients:

> All the girls that come to the House, you'd ought to know how different it is with them. Why, they used to talk all the time of silliness ... and now it's all books and pictures an' poetry. Annie Cronan, she's going to be married soon, and she said to me, "Ain't it luck I didn't get engaged before I knew the Langley House? I'd have got me a set of plush furniture sure, an' now I'm going to have a wood floor and a rug, and wicker furniture stained green, and those plaster angels on my walls." (ibid.)

While Katie's reassurance does little to quell Hilda's doubt within the context of Scudder's scarcely-known novel, this brief dialogue resonates with the pedagogical imaginary of the settlement house movement as it existed at the turn of the twentieth century. To Katie, and to the real life reformers who founded, lived in, and chronicled the hundreds of social settlements that cropped up in urban centers throughout the United States in the late nineteenth and early twentieth centuries, the settlement house was an important space of identity formation that acculturated immigrants and the working classes through a complex fusion of literacy and aesthetics ("to talk all the time" not of "silliness" but of "books and pictures an' poetry"), knowledge of bourgeois domestic norms ("a wood floor and a rug, and wicker furniture [and] plaster angels"), and personal contact between affluent reformer and underprivileged beneficiary ("Now you've come, we've not got no call to feel that any more").

In addition to being a novelist and educator, Vida Scudder was an influential settlement worker at Boston's Denison House, and she is correct in suggesting that this reform movement was less concerned with material poverty than with "the worse kind" of cultural impoverishment. After all, the mission of Scudder's fictional surrogate Hilda was not to raise industrial wages or end the class system, but rather "to be able to meet [her] fellows in the region of the common life"—a decidedly more abstract and humanistic goal (104). In her career as a social worker, Scudder shared with her reformist colleagues a vision of the settlement house as just that "common life" for immigrants, workers, and members of the middle and upper classes, who otherwise lacked a space in which to forge a communal cultural and social experience.

The settlement house was an important Progressive reform institution with roots in late-Victorian England. The first settlement, Toynbee Hall, was built in 1884 in London's East End by a group of Oxford graduates, and in 1886 the first U.S. settlement was founded in New York City's densely populated Lower East Side. The settlement house movement found a ready client base in the United States among the waves of "new immigrants" who passed through the gates of Castle Garden and Ellis Island between 1881 and 1924, the majority of these twenty million migrants hailing from Southern and Eastern Europe.[1] The number and influence of settlement houses escalated around the turn of the century as immigration rates continued to climb; there were 74 settlements across the United States by 1897, 200 by 1905, and over 400 in 1910.[2] The settlement house became an important social service organization, providing English lessons, vocational training, legal aid, libraries and public baths, as well as a range of recreational and educational offerings such as kindergartens, dances, literary circles and drama clubs. Through these means, settlement reformers aimed to de-factionalize American social and cultural life, to create a microcosm of "common life" for the privileged and disadvantaged alike.

The settlement movement was founded on the belief that the social, cultural, and physical separation of the working class and the middle and upper classes, and of immigrants and native-born Americans, made it impossible to resolve the social problems that fractured U.S. society.[3] Aiming to eradicate that distance, idealistic college graduates built their institutions in the heart of working class neighborhoods, moving into settlement houses in order to work closely with the poor on what they hoped would be neutral ground. As Paul Boyer has argued, these social

---

1 The period of the "new immigration" is bounded by two significant events: the 1881 assassination of the Czar Alexander II and subsequent wave of anti-Jewish pogroms in eastern Europe, and the passage of the Johnson-Reed Immigration Act in 1924, which limited the number of immigrants from any given country to a tiny fraction of the number of immigrants from that country residing in the U.S. in 1890 (thus practically eliminating eastern and southern European immigration), and eliminated all Asian immigration. U.S. Bureau of the Census, *Historical Statistics of the United States, Colonial Times to 1970* (Washington DC, 1975).

2 Allen F. Davis, *Spearheads for Reform* (New York: Oxford UP, 1968) 12.

3 African and Asian Americans were mostly ignored by the mainstream, white settlement movement, though a few white-run settlements were built to serve these communities in the early twentieth century. There were several important settlements run and patronized by African Americans on a self-help model; such institutions were conducted at a remove from white settlements and were often connected to a specific church. The relative absence of institutions serving people of color illustrates the movement's investment in preserving and endorsing a vision of white American identity. For more on the African American settlement movement, see Elizabeth Lasch-Quinn's *Black Neighbors: Race and the Limits of Reform in the American Settlement Movement, 1890-1945* (Chapel Hill: UNC Press, 1993).

reformers learned from the example of earlier moral reform campaigns that had floundered because physical and therefore personal distances kept them at a remove from those they wished to help. In this new movement, the motivation to be of service to the community would be more than an abstraction; it had to be personal, and it had to change the reformer's life in addition to the beneficiary's (Boyer 56). Therefore, while settlement workers aimed to acculturate immigrants and their first-generation children through various means, including clubs, classes and cross-class relationships, the more liberal reformers among them also believed that this cultural interaction would rejuvenate individual settlement workers and enrich U.S. society. Settlement workers insisted on the broadly reformist potential of this new social space.

Katie Donovan's spontaneous paean to the settlement house crystallizes the role of this institution as a historical contact space of American culture, a site in which the phenomena of immigration, Americanization, and upward mobility were processed at a local level. In Mary Louise Pratt's schema, a "contact zone" refers to a specific historical, material place as well as a mode of interaction and a way of viewing the social world in terms of "how subjects are constituted in and by their relations to each other" (7). Pratt's conception of the contact zone as a site of encounter with difference offers a useful critical perspective on the turn-of-the-century social settlement. This reform organization's spatial organization brought people from wildly unequal social locations and positions of power into physical proximity, as Eastern European factory workers, Italian anarchists, and earnest, college-educated men and women born in the United States mingled in its classrooms and parlors. Moreover, the philosophy supporting the settlement movement depended upon, and indeed celebrated, asymmetrical personal relations: the opportunity to mingle across the social boundaries that usually kept communities far apart was a centerpiece of its reform methodology. A vast archive of novels, memoirs, plays, periodical and institutional literature written within and about the settlement house constitutes a kind of "arts of the contact zone," as Pratt puts it, and comments at every turn on the movement's unique approach to reform. Taking the fictional Katie Donovan's description of the settlement as its main premise, this essay shows how the settlement house emerged as an important contact space at the turn of the twentieth century by organizing a reform methodology around the logic of contact with refined interior space and bourgeois mentors. This cross-class contact, settlement workers believed, could uplift the disadvantaged and resolve the social problems that plagued the nation. Understanding the settlement house as a contact space sheds light on the spatial and interpersonal dimensions of turn-of-the-century efforts to forge a "common life" out of the diverse populations that comprised the United States, and shows how American literature participated in this reformist project.

Mary Louise Pratt's notion of the contact zone describes an explicitly colonial situation, and indeed, many reformers used their era's available vocabulary for describing cross-class, cross-cultural experience by coding the reform encounter in discourses of imperialism. As evidenced by institutional documents and journalistic accounts of the movement, the first generation of settlement workers called themselves "pioneers" or "settlers" on an "urban frontier" and referred to the area's working class denizens benignly as "neighbors," employing colonial metaphors that carried associations of "settling" as a missionary activity. This language of imperial encounter was the rhetorical vehicle through which reformers brought necessary attention to neighborhoods that desperately lacked effective infrastructure and social services. But despite reformers' best intentions, interactions between affluent social workers and working class clients, many of them Catholic and Jewish immigrants, occurred within a space that was fundamentally unequal. Settlement workers imagined social reform as a process of translating social asymmetry into a "common life": that is, it was precisely the inequality between giver and receiver of aid that supported the work of the settlement house.

As a physical and social space that engendered insufficient contact with native born, affluent Americans and *too much* proximity among working class, ethnic, and immigrant Americans, the ethnic ghetto emerged as a central concern of the movement. Settlement workers were committed to eliminating the urban ghetto by social, cultural, and legal means: they joined other Progressives in petitioning the municipal government to address the congested streets, dangerous tenements, and unregulated labor conditions of the urban ghetto, and won a series of legislative victories in the early twentieth century. Beyond the physical and environmental problems posed by the ghetto, reformers worried that the ever-renewing pockets of foreigners within major cities threatened the nation's identity as a fundamentally Anglo-American, English-speaking community. The ghetto, they believed, was filled with "social dynamite" (Strong 78), incubating the most pernicious social tendencies of their time: radicalism, vice and crime, religious orthodoxy, and ignorance of the social norms, democratic conventions, language and culture of American life. Settlement workers were convinced that the ghetto hindered immigrants' social development by segregating them from representative Americans who would model the language, behavior, and customs of their new land, and organized programs around what they perceived to be essential compensatory experiences.

Settlement Pedagogy: Contact, Space, Culture

From the beginning, the settlement's primary goal was to Americanize immigrants and their first-generation offspring in order to ease their adjustment into U.S. society and facilitate their upward mobility. As a trustee from New York City's Educational Alliance, a Jewish settlement, put it, "the ultimate aim of all club and social work is the development of character, [and] literary work, dramatic, athletics, etc. are but the means to this ultimate end."[4] For settlement workers, Americanization named the process by which immigrants came to identify with the nation and its democratic tenets and exhibit the manners and behaviors associated with American life. Reformers believed that Americanization would enable immigrants and their first-generation children to succeed socially and financially by blunting obvious signs of difference. Jewish reformers had further reasons for encouraging their Eastern European Jewish clients to acculturate: they were acutely aware of the social and political repression that followed from European ghettoization and urged their clients to Americanize in part to ensure that unofficial ethnic ghettos in U.S. cities did not become permanent fixtures.[5] Though settlement workers were not without prejudices and maintained a fundamentally hierarchical view of cultural value in which Anglo-America enjoyed a privileged position,

4 Ludwig B. Bernstein to Allen Davis, 1910, Box 2 of 2, Folder "The Work of the Educational Alliance: Allan Davis 1910," *Educational Alliance Collection,* AJHS.

5 It is important at this point to note the distinctions among the terms Americanization, acculturation, and assimilation. "Acculturation" denotes the cultural adaptation of minority groups, whereas "assimilation" suggests the deeper and more intractable structural adjustment of minority communities to the ways of the majority. "Americanization" was the most commonly used term at the turn of the century for settlements' acculturation practices; the concept began to assume overtly political connotations when the approach of WW1 made any enduring allegiance to a foreign nation suspect. For a recent re-evaluation of the language of assimilation, see Sarah Wilson, *Melting-Pot Modernism*, Cornell University Press, 2010.

they understood Americanization to mean an equalization of opportunities.

The ideal of contact—with high ideas, artistic riches, refined interiors, and cultivated individuals—was at the root of the settlement's Americanization practices during the Gilded Age and Progressive Era. Becoming an "American" first meant adapting to the spatial codes of middle class domesticity, a process that began the minute a client passed through any given settlement's front door. Reformers worried that the physical constraints of immigrant families' cramped tenement homes would drive young people into the streets and dance halls in search of freedom and recreation. They therefore constructed a literary and artistic curriculum intended to substitute for baser pleasures and designed the institution's interior as the setting for reading, aiming to offer working class visitors a quiet place for cultural engagement.

From the first, the settlement movement described itself in domestic terms, identifying as a "home among other homes" (Carson 59).[6] As Shannon Jackson has argued, the urban working class home and the settlement house had distinct and often oppositional spatial legacies. Many settlement workers had lived most of their lives in spacious homes with the parlors, drawing rooms, and privatizing subdivisions that were the markers of Victorian comfort. They sought to reproduce key elements of bourgeois domesticity within settlements, which typically began inside small buildings indistinguishable from others on surrounding blocks and then expanded into larger structures to accommodate institutional growth. As Jackson notes, the mere experience of navigating different rooms and domestic objects inside the settlement familiarized patrons with the spatial and behavioral conventions of middle class American domesticity (153). Moreover, reformers believed that this setting would support the social instruction received in classrooms, clubs, and through casual interaction. Vida Scudder's *A Listener in Babel* displays this kind of spatio-social thinking when its young laundress suggests that the greatest proof of the settlement's social power lies in her knowledge that the "wood floor and a rug, and wicker furniture stained green, [and] plaster angels" of middle class America surpasses the "set of plush furniture" of a socially inferior housewife (235).

6 This self-identity as fundamentally a home above all else would lessen after 1910, as the settlement movement became increasingly bureaucratic and linked to larger municipal reform projects.

Settlement workers drew on the Victorian conviction that décor helped to create character and linked this idea to a broader institutional mandate of cultivation, assimilation, and reform. Despite the fact that settlements often scrambled to maintain basic economic solvency, institutional records from the movement's early years consistently emphasize the importance of fresh flowers, attractive divans, framed pictures of important personages, and a generally genial atmosphere. New York City's Christodora House, for example, aimed to have "the order of a well-appointed home—the order which grew into beauty. Flowers graced the office desk, tables, pianos" (Steiner). A journalist's report on a neighboring institution, the female College Settlement, adds more detail to this description.

> Although the exterior of the building is dingy and unattractive, the interior is all 'sweetness and light.' The visitor upon entering the parlor is impressed with the air of refinement which pervades the apartment as his eye makes note of the really fine engravings on the delicately-tinted walls, the well-bound books on the cabinet shelves, and the objects of *virtu* scattered about with the careless grace that suggests the presence of cultivated women. (Richardson 785-786)

This account describes an emblematic Victorian parlor through the eyes of an imagined male visitor. Importantly, this (female) journalist advertises the project of settlement reform, still in its infancy in 1891, by describing the parlor, a room conspicuously *not* made for use. As Katherine C. Grier has argued, the parlor was the "'comfortable theater' for middle-class self-presentation" (3) in Victorian America, the site for the display and cultivation of the public self that set the tone for the rest of the home (64). The objects strewn about the room do not belong to working class clients, but are "objects of *virtu*"—art objects or antiques—that suggest "the presence of cultivated women" (786). The domestic orbit of affluent female reformers set the terms of the settlement's spatial organization and decoration. Moreover, the settlement's physical structure emerges as a metaphor for the ideal recipient of its philanthropy: a rough and uninviting exterior gives way to a pleasant interior suffused with the "sweetness and light" that cultivation, education, and cross-cultural contact produce. This physical model of dingy surface and cultured depth matches the image of an immigrant, working class subject transformed by her time spent inside the contact space.

Commentators and social workers continued to emphasize the physical setting of reform even as the domestic symbols of Victorian affluence gave way to a more stripped-down aesthetic. By the early twentieth century, as Gilded Age Victorianism waned and Progressivism's increasingly scientific standards melded with the emergent Arts and Crafts Movement, clean lines, bare furnishings, and a functional aesthetic replaced parlor refinement as reformers attempted to integrate art with labor, accentuate the dignity of simple living, and highlight the serious work that was undertaken within the spaces of settlement reform. For example, when settlement leader Mary McDowell was planning the appearance of the University of Chicago Settlement's new building in 1904, she avoided motifs and decorative objects that suggested feminine refinement. Instead, she chose a community-themed mural that illustrated the cultural origins of settlement clients rather than those of residents or volunteers (Bachin 5). Even as design philosophies changed, then, reformers from all corners of the movement imbued physical space with enormous pedagogical value. They expected settlement visitors to "paraphrase" aspects of its layout, furnishing, and design, re-creating those ideals in their own homes as much as was financially feasible. Even more importantly, settlement workers expected their clients to absorb the social lessons embedded in those design choices as they would from a conversation, book or dramatic performance.[7]

Reform writers regularly linked the settlement's spatial and domestic organization to the project of spreading English literacy and high culture. One writer boasts of the "double work" performed by the Girls' Home Culture Club at Chicago's Maxwell Street Settlement, frequented by Jewish "working girls" with a special interest in reading:

> About twenty working-girls from seventeen to twenty-two years old are being directed in their reading by an able teacher, who gives informal talks on the choice of books, and aids in the interpretation of the best English novels [...] A taste for good literature once formed, there is little danger of relapsing into trifling enjoyments. The Home Culture Club does a double work. Meetings are held at the homes of the members, who take great delight in making their humble living-rooms bright for the occasion. Home-making comes to be a part of the educative processes of the club, with its resultants of neatness, friendliness and hospitality. (Raymond 68-69)

7 Grier argues that Victorian Americans "paraphrased" the examples of interior space they observed in hotels, photographers' studios, world's fairs, and elsewhere (16-17).

In this text, reading and home-making operate along a single axis. Their aesthetic and pedagogical value is presumed to be the same, as book selection becomes home decoration, and literary interpretation becomes cheerful hospitality. Along similar lines, a drama coach at Chicago's Hull-House argued that the aesthetic impact of literary and drama classes should be judged not by the artistic results themselves, but by the way settlement clients adapted cultural refinement into their everyday lives: "One has only to go to [immigrant] homes to see the effects. You would be amazed at the charming apartments that ... most of the older young people have" (qtd. in Jackson 240). Certainly one of the ways that reformers aligned cultural expression and domesticity was through the logic of gender socialization, in which a penchant for the arts was commensurate with good taste in furnishing "charming apartments." More importantly, these quotations exemplify the settlement movement's larger practice of linking aesthetics with the eradication of tenement domesticity, of tying cultural value to measurable social progress. The settlement's pedagogical orientation measured cultural enrichment less by its intellectual benefits than by its potential for acculturation, its ability to transform slum apartments into "bright" and "charming" homes modeled on the settlement's interior. In turn, reformers hoped the physical environment of the contact space would function as a preparatory exercise in middle class American domesticity.

The settlement movement's archive of imaginative literature betrays a similar inclination to describe the reformist powers of the institution's interior. Zoe Beckley's 1918 novel *A Chance to Live* evokes settlement space in terms that mirror journalistic and institutional accounts. Beckley's young heroine steps tentatively into a New York City settlement house and instantly takes note of its genteel physical appearance:

> Her first impression was of unbelievable spaciousness and cleanness [...] She got a quick picture of gray-blue walls and hangings, and golden lamplight glowing upon a long table, at which girls were reading. Without examining the furnishings in detail, she felt the quality of everything. She knew that the pictures hanging in discreet spaces were good pictures, well framed. That the tables and chairs and bookcases were of artistic rightness, though very plain. All was quiet, orderly, warm, and handsome. So much so that Annie felt vaguely uncomfortable and afraid of it. (80)

"Very plain" but also spacious, clean, and supported by all-encompassing "artistic rightness," the settlement house emerges here as an eminently respectable and cultured setting. Another reform novel, Isaac K. Friedman's 1901 *By Bread Alone,* describes how the settlement interior was organized around the imperatives of culture: "A portrait of Shakespeare, another of Tennyson, one of Dickens ... smiled literature down on the room; a revolving book-case was ready to turn under a Braun's copy of Burne-Jones' 'Golden Stairs,' which faced that artist's 'Venus' Mirror'" (278). As these brief excerpts suggest, the idea of the settlement's physical space as a force for upward mobility and Americanization—as, indeed, a symbol of culture itself—was well established in the early twentieth century, appearing not only in institutional writing but also in reform novels.

If the settlement's reform methodology depended upon a specific physical setting, it also required that its beneficiaries maintain close personal contact with educated benefactors and volunteers. Settlements sought to put people from different class locations—and frequently, religious and ethnic backgrounds—into close association under the guiding assumption that proximity to the white elite was essential to the socialization of immigrants and the working class. The belief that "coming into close personal contact with refined young [Americans is] of inestimable value to the young immigrant" united otherwise distinct factions of the settlement movement.[8] An 1889 editorial on the College Settlement explained that "[settlement] ladies fully believe with Tolstoy that 'Enlightenment is not propagated by pictures,' not 'chiefly' by the spoken word, or the medium of print, but by the infectious example of the whole life of men" (Porter). When a college-educated woman met with a group of young adults for a weekly meeting of their literary circle, that interpersonal contact—conversation, mutual affection, the example of the club leader's wardrobe, accent, and comportment—was understood to be reformist praxis.

Clubs, whether of a literary, dramatic, athletic, political, or purely social nature, proved an ideal context in which to cultivate relationships across social boundaries. Reformers considered clubs an important model of political organization and understood their formation in metaphorical terms as a political shift from ethnic mob to democratic citizenship, with each group's American leader as a representative guide. Institutional writing from the movement constantly affirms that the club was the nucleus

8 Minutes of the Woman's Auxiliary to the Educational Alliance, March 21, 1918, Box 1, Folder 15, Educational Alliance Papers, 312, YIVO, 91.

of settlement life. No matter what a club's theme or principal activity, the club room was the contact space in which "right ideas" were inculcated into young people's minds; where, as the Christodora House's 1910 Annual Report put it, reformers could "help [each patron] to become a well-rounded human being" by fostering close personal relations between staff workers and clients. Similarly, the Educational Alliance's 1899 Annual Report made the point that clubs were "the most feasible way of bringing culture home to the [clients] and of entering into intimate relationship with them in a way that ought to benefit everybody concerned ... of course, in work of this character, the emphasis is to be laid on the personal influence of the directors."[9] Clubs and circles were an important vehicle for the settlement's literary, artistic, and social curricula; it is therefore significant that the clubs' larger structural task was simply to bring working class immigrants and affluent Americans into a room together.

Cross-class proximity was essential to settlement workers' social and intellectual development as well. Importantly, reformers believed that contact with the immigrant working classes offered truths that could not be learned in books. An essay published in an 1893 collection on *The Literature of Philanthropy* argues that cultivating intimacy with the poor would make reformers more effective civic campaigners, equipping them "with certain individual facts and general truths regarding the character and lives of the young friends of the [settlement] that are most useful guides in the work" (Spahr and McLean 32). Both imaginative and institutional settlement literature makes clear that social reform was never merely a selfless gesture. Settlements certainly offered valuable educational advantages to their clients, for most of whom attending college was an unrealistic dream, but they were equally conceived as an intellectual project for the benefit of reformers in which the goal was to generate knowledge outside of but adjacent to the university.

Many American settlement houses were directly linked to institutions of higher education. The College Settlement was founded and staffed by graduates of four women's colleges (Smith, Vassar, Wellesley, and Bryn Mawr), the University Settlement was closely connected to Columbia University, and Hull-House maintained ties with the newly opened Uni-

9 Annual Report, 1899, 99-100, Box 1 of 2, Folder "Educational Alliance Annual Reports 1896 and 1899," Educational Alliance Collection, AJHS, 44. Annual Report, 1910, Box 6, Folder 4, "Annual Reports 1910-1911." Christodora House Records 1897-1991, Columbia University Rare Books and Manuscript Library.

versity of Chicago, to cite only a few examples. Such institutional relationships were an important source of funding, a means of validation, and provided a ready pool from which to draw volunteers, lecturers, and residents. At Christodora House, college students who donated $100 yearly to the settlement house formed Christodora chapters at their schools. Members of these chapters would then visit the settlement for a week or more during school holidays, strike up friendships with reformers, fellow volunteers, and attendees, and involve themselves in the life of the institution, all while furthering their own education.[10] When settlement theorists portrayed their institutions as "universities in the slums," then, they did not intend the revolutionary concept of a low-cost, local college for the immigrant poor. Rather, they described an organization that would "attempt to test the value of human knowledge by action, and realization, quite as the complete and ideal university would concern itself with the discovery of knowledge in all branches" (Addams, *On Education* 78). The settlement house would, in short, serve as a social laboratory offering pragmatic forms of knowledge to social workers.

On a personal level, many believed that institutionalizing cross-class relations at the settlement house would regenerate the "inauthentic" and over-privileged class of reformers, who had been "cultivated into unnourished, over-sensitive lives" (Addams, "The Subjective Necessity of Social Settlements" 16). The settlement movement coincided with a late nineteenth century structure of feeling specific to the white middle and upper classes: the sense that too much leisure and privilege rendered individual lives meaningless and caused depression. Beginning in the 1870s, a range of psychological, literary, and journalistic texts began reporting upon the problem of "neurasthenia" among affluent Americans, particularly women. Many diagnosed neurasthenics, including Jane Addams, turned to reform work as a means of recovery, believing that contact with social inferiors might re-introduce them to a lost 'reality' and rejuvenate their empty lives. Boston's Andover House founder Robert Woods argued that the settlement house was a natural solution to this problem: "The University Settlements are a message of life and hope to that increasing body of

10 The categorization of reform institutions as "university" or "college" settlements suggested the source of their funding and their general philosophical and reformist bearing. Alliance with a male university typically implied a political or social science orientation, whereas a college settlement was generally oriented toward women and the domestic and liberal arts.

men and women in these days who are stifled and crushed under the gifts of society become impediments through disuse" (Woods 93). Jane Addams went so far as to claim that the educated but idle American woman was "as pitiful as the other great mass of destitute lives" before discovering a vocation in settlement work (Addams, *Twenty Years at Hull-House* 21).

Reform novels like Vida Scudder's *A Listener in Babel* echo these institutional declarations, offering a fictional affirmation that cross-class contact simultaneously reformed working class beneficiaries and regenerated middle and upper class benefactors. Hilda Lathrop has always "stifles[d] in class isolation" (60), and moves into an urban settlement because "she had hoped that among those with whom primal experiences were more evident, the common ground of humanity would be easier to find" (85). Affluent Americans, Scudder suggests, will not find transcendence in books, religion, and social philosophies, but rather in their relationships with "real"—that is, underprivileged—people. The social equilibrium of upper class life is potentially as "stifling" as the too homogenously working class and ethnic urban ghetto. Only when Hilda enjoys a picnic lunch with three settlement clients does she come near enough to the human source to have a revelation:

> An impulse largely intellectual had sent her to live among the poor: now, she met at close range the problems of poverty, and bad as they had seemed when states in the mass, they choked her as she felt their pressure on three individuals she loved [...] her dry faith in democracy [was] renewed by the treasure of fellowship with the humble. The reality which she had sought in vain throughout her girlhood was hers at last. (238)

Elsewhere in *A Listener in Babel*, Scudder is more interested in her protagonist's emotional journey than in working class character development or even with the social problems that underlie poverty. In this moment, however, Hilda finally comes to have a sense of reality—she comes to see *herself* as real—through her brief intimacy with the immigrant poor. In Scudder, as in the writing of countless settlement workers and authors not directly involved with the movement, working class figures facilitate a social worker's breakthrough, just as tangible models such as tidy parlors and unaccented club leaders permit settlement clients to Americanize with ease. In the literature of this contact space, cross-class relations are mutually transforming. The social asymmetry of settlement space requires careful negotiation and produces revelation on both sides, and provides the narrative throughline for this contact space's literary archive.

The settlement house as museum: contemporary appropriations

Cultural geographer Doreen Massey suggests that places are not bounded or singular, but formed through the particular articulation of social interrelations at different historical moments (5). The turn-of-the-century settlement house makes clear that the social positions of different constituencies change the way spaces are perceived and used, and is thus an emblematic example of the interactivity and relationality that characterize contact zones. Reformers understood the institution to operate by a spatial logic of containment and substitution, whereby the settlement's refined interior would form a prototype for clients seeking to make their way out of the tenement and ghetto. The cross-class personal contact that occurred within this space made all social encounters potentially pedagogical in nature.

Although the densely populated neighborhoods of working class Jewish, Irish, Italian, and Slavic immigrants that dotted turn-of-the-century American cities have long since disappeared, interest in the history of the urban ghetto has not abated. Today, new built environments like New York City's Tenement Museum, founded in 1988, permit visitors to walk through an "authentic" urban tenement at 97 Orchard Street on the Lower East Side, whose apartments are preserved and decorated in period style. In one apartment, narrow beds are pushed against the stove; in another, a small bedroom is given over to a makeshift tailor shop. The Tenement Museum invites visitors to imagine immigrant life in the late nineteenth or early twentieth century. Literary representations of the turn-of-the-century tenement, ethnic ghetto, and surrounding community organizations are central to this process of imagining: the museum's bookstore sells a large selection of immigrant literature in reissued editions, much of which addresses the importance of the settlement house to the Lower East Side and to an immigrant generation that has disappeared forever. The bookstore shelves the autobiographies of settlement client Rose Cohen and Henry Street Settlement founder Lillian Wald alongside Irving Howe's encyclopedic rendering of Jewish American history; indeed, most of the Museum's recommended books deal to some degree with the settlement movement.[11]

In spite of the obvious deprivations that the tenement's original inhabitants suffered, and the vigorous efforts of reformers to abolish these structures and their surrounding milieus, the institutions of the turn-of-the-century ghetto are here the subject of intense nostalgia. The settlement house and adjacent ghetto institutions emerge as sites of cultural memory in the absence of any extant material place, functioning as a crucial node in the museum's narrative of immigrant mobility and acculturation. Interestingly, the museum's fond retrospection on overcrowded tenements, bustling multilingual streets, and unmelted ethnics precisely reverses the tenets of Progressive reform, which aimed to change the very aspects of the immigrant's urban experience that the contemporary Tenement Museum most treasures. Just as affiliation with working class and immigrant life once served as a balm for reformers in search of a "common life," here too direct contact with physical space and real historical figures—the tenements' former residents are explicitly named and described—constitutes the Tenement Museum's pedagogical method. Contemporary museum visitors reach out to the same historical milieu to rediscover the nation's roots, and possibly also their own, in working class urban space. Although nostalgia and social reform look very differently at the same cultural milieu, the museum's memorialization suggests that the settlement movement continues to galvanize new narratives into the twenty-first century.

Works Cited

Addams, Jane. *On Education*. Ed. Ellen Condliffe Lagemann. Piscataway, NJ: Transaction Publishers, 1994.

---. "The Subjective Necessity of Social Settlements." *Philanthropy and Social Progress*, 1893.

---. *Twenty Years at Hull-House*. 1910. New York: Penguin, 1998.

Addams, Jane, Robert Woods, et al. *Philanthropy and Social Progress*. New York: Thomas Y. Crowell, 1893.

Bachin, Robin Faith. *Building the South Side: Urban Space and Civic Culture in Chicago, 1890-1919*. Chicago: Chicago UP, 2004.

Beckley, Zoe. *A Chance to Live*. New York: The MacMillan Co., 1918.

11 See "Our Favorite Lower East Side Books," http://www.tenement.org/research.html

Bender, Daniel E. "Perils of Degeneration: Reform, the Savage Immigrant, and the Survival of the Unfit." *Journal of Social History* 42 (2008): 5-29.

Berger, Morris Isaiah. *The Settlement, the Immigrant, and the Public School*. New York: Arno Press, 1980.

Carson, Mina. *Settlement Folk: Social Thought and the American Settlement Movement, 1885-1930*. Chicago: Chicago UP, 1990.

Christodora House Records 1897-1991. Columbia University Rare Books and Manuscript Library.

Davis, Allen F. *Spearheads for Reform*. New York: Oxford UP, 1968.

Educational Alliance Collection. I-359, American Jewish Historical Society.

Educational Alliance Papers. 312, YIVO.

Friedman, Isaac K. *By Bread Alone*. New York: McClure and Co., 1901.

Grier, Katherine C. *Culture and Comfort: Parlor Making and Middle-Class Identity, 1850-1930*. Washington: Smithsonian Institution Press, 1997.

Holden, Arthur C. *The Settlement Idea: a Vision of Social Justice*. New York: MacMillan Co., 1922.

Horton, Isabelle. *The Burden of the City*. Chicago: Fleming H. Revell, 1904.

Jackson, Shannon. *Lines of Activity: Performance, Historiography, Hull-House Domesticity*. Ann Arbor: Michigan UP, 2001.

Lasch-Quinn, Elizabeth. *Black Neighbors: Race and the Limits of Reform in the American Settlement Movement, 1890-1945*. Chapel Hill: UNC Press, 1993.

Massey, Doreen. *Space, Place, and Gender*. Minneapolis: Minnesota UP, 1994.

Meyer, Annie Nathan. *Woman's Work in America*. New York: Henry Holt, 1891.

Porter, Mary H. "A Home on Halsted Street." *Advance* July 11 (1889): n.p.

Pratt, Mary Louise. "The Arts of the Contact Zone." *Ways of Reading*, ed. David Bartholomae and Anthony Petroksky. New York: St. Martin's, 1999.

---. *Imperial Eyes: Travel Writing and Transculturation*. New York: Routledge, 1992.

Raymond, Josephine Hunt. *The Social Settlement Movement in Chicago*. MA Thesis, University of Wisconsin, 1897.

Richardson, Hester Dorsey. "The College Settlement." *Lippincott's Monthly Magazine* 47 (1891): 785-790.

Scudder, Vida D. *A Listener in Babel.* Boston: Houghton, Mifflin and Company, 1903.

Spahr, Jean Fine and Fannie W. McLean. "The Tenement Neighbor Idea." *The Literature of Philanthropy,* ed. Frances A. Goodale. New York, Harper & Bros., 1893.

Steiner, Edward. "Christodora, 1897-1940." unpublished manuscript, n.d., *Christodora House Papers* (box 3, folder 3).

Strong, Josiah. *Our Country: Its Possible Future and Present Crisis.* New York City: Baker and Taylor, 1885.

U.S. Bureau of the Census. *Historical Statistics of the United States, Colonial Times to 1970.* Washington DC: 1975.

Woods, Robert. "The University Settlement Idea." *Philanthropy and Social Progress*, 1893.

"And One": Bruisers in the Paint and the Globalization of the N.B.A.

Louis J. Kern

Louis J.Kern reads the NBA basketball court as a contact space which facilitates the often violent encounter between the individual players. On a grander level, as Kern argues, the NBA itself is a contact space through its continuous integration of players from around the world and its adaptation to international situations and developments. And thirdly, U.S. basketball's heavy mediation also shapes basketball's popularity worldwide.

> The process of American amalgamation is not assimilation or simple surrender to the dominant type, as is popularly supposed, but an all-round give and take by which the final type may be enriched or impoverished.
>
> Israel Zangwill, *The Melting Pot*

> It's unfortunate when other teams take liberties with you. I get clubbed hard all the time, but if I get up swinging I would be in the wrong. It's ridiculous, man, ridiculous.
>
> Alonzo Mourning

We live, Michel Foucault has observed, in an "epoch of spaces," of "simultaneity," of "juxtaposition," an "epoch of the near and far, of the side-by-side, of the dispersed." Our experience of the world is of a "network that connects points and intersects with its own skin." The globalized, postmodern world is one in which "space takes for us the form of relations among sites" (Foucault). And those sites, as Mary Louise Pratt reminds us, are typically experienced as "contact zones," nodal crossroads where people from discrete geographical locales and of diverse historical experiences come into unmediated social and physical contact and interact with one another and through conflict or cooperation construct new trans-national relationships (34-35).

The N.B.A. as Post-Modern Contact Zone

The economic, cultural, and physical dimensions of American professional basketball as embodied in the National Basketball Association provide an intriguing expression of postmodern concepts of space and contact zones, combining Foucalult's notion of interlocking, dispersed networks of related sites and Pratt's vision of nodal sites of interaction where people from diverse cultures engage one another socially and physically. As an interesting and instructive expression of contemporary spatial consciousness, the N.B.A. philosophically conceives the idea of place not as anchored to any particular locale but rather as a network of places when considered from the perspective as an international sports organization, while conceding that experientially it functions more immediately in more particular and delimited spaces of conjunct physical contact, when viewed from the perspective of its players. In its globalization initiatives the N.B.A. has functioned within an international sports network to produce an enhanced international awareness and popularity of basketball and as a conduit to train and channel international talent into the contact space that is professional American basketball. In recruiting players abroad, the N.B.A. provides a proximate subset of contemporary immigration foreign-born basketball players migrating to the N.B.A., where a rich ethnic and cultural diversity is subject to enhanced physical and cultural contact and contestation.

The N.B.A.: From Exceptionalism and Exclusivity to Globalization

Historically, the United States virtually owned the sport of basketball in international competition.[1] It won Olympic gold medals from 1936 through 1968, lost a disputed one-point decision to the Soviet Union in 1972, and won gold in 1976 and 1984 ("U.S. Men's National Basketball Team"). Between 1936 and 1984, the United States had a total of one loss in Olympic play. But the seeming American athletic exceptionalism in this sport was belied by the U.S. record in F.I.B.A. World Championship

1 Basketball of all major sports played professionally in the United States is the only one demonstrably invented on American soil (Springfiled, MA 1891) albeit by Canadian physician James Naismith.

competition. Between 1950 and 2006, the United States placed first only three times and finished fifth in 1970 and sixth in 2002. The real wake-up call for American basketball was the third place finish in the 1988 Olympics by a team comprised of future N.B.A. stars (USA Senior National Team). Sixteen years later, after the F.I.B.A. allowed the United States to use professional players in Olympic competition (1989), the United States finished third, sustaining a 19-point defeat by Puerto Rico in the opening game, the greatest point spread for an American team in the history of international competition. At the same time, however, the participation of American professional players in international competition after 1992, especially the "Dream Team" in the Barcelona Olympics (1992) and the "Redeem Team" (2008 Olympics) meant increased contact between N.B.A. and international players and much broader exposure of American professionals to international spectators (U.S. Men's National Basketball Team).

The first international players entered the N.B.A. in the late 1970s, but all had played college basketball in the United States. Rolando Antonio Blackmon, drafted by the Dallas Mavericks in 1981, was the first foreign-born player who had not played at a U.S. college. There were only six foreign players in the N.B.A. in 1979. A key turning point in the recruitment of international players came in 1989-90 season. It was the result of three factors: the performance of high-profile international players drafted previously, like Hakeem Olajuwan (Nigeria) of the Houston Rockets and Detlef Schrempf (Germany) of the Dallas Mavericks; the third-place finish of the U.S. Olympic team in Seoul in 1988; and the third-place U.S. finish in the 1990 World Championship (only one American, Kenny Anderson, made the All-Tournament Team). While internationalization of the N.B.A. began haltingly—fewer than five foreign players were drafted by N.B.A. teams each year from 1989 to 1995, the beginning of a significant international presence in American professional basketball dates from this period. The most significant and sustained influx of foreign players (1996-2009) resulted not from competitive ranking or tournament results but from administrative and business decisions of the two most powerful basketball organizations in the world—the oldest, the F.I.B.A. (Fédération Internationale de Basketball Amateur, established in 1932), and the N.B.A., founded in 1946.

The F.I.B.A. revoked the distinction between amateur and professional players in 1989, paving the way for the exultant participation of the N.B.A. "Dream Team" in the 1992 Olympics. That participation provided international exposure of the best players in the world, contributing to the enhanced popularity of basketball worldwide and offering an opportunity for international players to play against the most challenging competition. What happened was dramatic. As Olivier Pheulpin of *L'Équipe*, France's leading sports periodical, put it, "after the Dream Team of 1992, many of our best athletes began playing basketball instead of soccer. Simple as that" (Monroe). Basketball became the second most popular sport in Europe.

Meanwhile, the N.B.A. Commissioner, David J. Stern (elected 1984), aggressively sought to internationalize the N.B.A. In 1987, Stern and Boris Stankovic, Secretary General of the F.I.B.A., agreed to establish a tournament, the McDonald's, that featured an N.B.A. and two European professional teams. Subsequent tournaments were held until 1999 under the name the McDonald's Championship. The first held outside the United States was in Spain in 1988. N.B.A. teams were undefeated during this period, but contact with N.B.A. stars raised the level of European competition and represented a significant N.B.A. contribution to international basketball ("McDonald's Championship").

The first overseas pre-season N.B.A. exhibition game was played in China in 1979, and in 1990 the N.B.A. became the first major American sports league to play regular season games outside the United States. Since 1990 selected regular-season N.B.A. games have been played in Japan. Since 1991 the league has conducted the N.B.A. World Clinic, featuring N.B.A. coaches and players, at various worldwide locations. Individual or small groups of players have conducted clinics and undertaken goodwill promotional tours of all regions of the globe, commencing in Africa (Kenya, Zaire, and South Africa) in 1993 and expanding dramatically since 1997. The first N.B.A. offices outside the United States were opened in 1992 (Hong Kong and Melbourne) and by 1996 had expanded to Europe, Latin America, and Japan. By 2008 there were twelve international offices. In 2010, a Moscow office and the first permanent N.B.A. office in Africa (Johannesburg, South Africa) were opened ("N.B.A. International Historic Timeline").

The N.B.A. experienced rapid and dynamic expansion between 1988 and 1997, growing by 30% from 23 teams (in four divisions) in 1984 to 30 in 1997. In a move befitting the game's origins and pursuant to globalization, two of the expansion teams (added in 1995)—the Toronto Raptors and the Vancouver Grizzlies were Canadian-based ("N.B.A. Growth

Table").[2] While much of N.B.A. expansion was market-driven, these overtures also brought greater global exposure of American professional basketball and significantly expanded contact between spectators, fans, and players worldwide. Not all of that contact was passive.

In 1995 the N.B.A. initiated a system of global balloting for selection of All-Star teams, and in 1996 the N.B.A. finals were televised in 169 countries. By the 1999-2000 season international television agreements provided N.B.A. game coverage to 205 countries, in 42 languages. At least in part for strictly commercial reasons, but also to connect more immediately with global affairs, the N.B.A. aired in 2000 six 30-second, televised, multi-lingual public service announcements by its international players that addressed current problems and concerns of their native countries ("N.B.A. International Historic Timeline").

Global engagement and the goodwill ambassadorial outreach of the N.B.A. was furthered by the initiation of its collaborative (with the F.I.B.A.) program, Basketball Without Borders, in 2001. It operated exclusively in Europe until 2004, but then expanded to three continents and is currently operating in four—Africa, Asia, Europe, and Latin America. Essentially, the program conducts a series of summer camps for youth to foster international comity and to develop educational and athletic skills. Current and former N.B.A. players and coaches coach the teams, which are comprised of promising players selected by their national associations, who play together on mixed-nationalities teams. Of particular note in this program has been its African outreach, that has conducted the Africa 100 camp since 2003. Since 2003 Basketball Without Borders has partnered with UNICEF to promote education and HIV/AIDS and drug abuse prevention programs ("Basketball Without Borders").

Furthering its commitment to social responsibility both nationally and internationally and building on the established foundation of ongoing concern of N.B.A. personnel to "give back" to the community, the N.B.A. launched the "N.B.A. Cares" program in 2005. Its primary areas of concern are education, youth services and family life, and health and wellness-related issues. By 2009 this program had raised $105 million and donated over 950,000 man-hours of volunteer service to communities worldwide. Two recent public health ventures were the "Vaccines for

2 The Grizzlies played in Vancouver for six seasons, but economic losses forced their relocation to Memphis for the 2000-2001 season. At present, Toronto remains the only N.B.A. team based outside the United States.

Teens" program to provide inoculation against life-threatening illnesses for American teenagers in communities at risk due to inadequate health counseling (in concert with the CDC), and the "Nothing But Nets" program (a collaboration with UNESCO) to raise awareness of the widespread threat of malaria and to deliver bed nets to those most at risk. Both these coadjutive programs were launched in 2009 ("N.B.A. Cares"; "Nothing But Nets"; "N.B.A. and W.N.B.A. Launch Vaccines for Teens"). Something easily overlooked when considering these programs from a global perspective is their effect on the relationships among the N.B.A. participants themselves. When asked about his motivations for establishing "N.B.A. Cares," David Stern responded that "our teams were doing so much individually, but we weren't feeling the connection to each other. We wanted to show the collective impact we were having (Bucher,"Why N.B.A. Cares").

These programs often bring together people who don't normally interact—coaches, GMs, players from different teams, referees, etc. Intraleague and international contact are both enhanced by these programs. Thus, while these programs project the image of the N.B.A. as an international goodwill ambassador that promotes health and education in areas like Asia and Africa, they also serve to promote opportunity for men from diverse cultures, whose skills, when properly trained, will qualify them for a professional basketball career. From the internal perspective of the league itself, they foster heightened contact among a diverse group of professionals both players and administrative officers.

Supplementing these broader, league-sponsored programs are developmental projects funded by private industry or conducted by individual N.B.A. players. Two examples of the former are: Adidas Nations, initiated in 2007 to foster the growth of international basketball in Africa, the Asian Pacific, Canada, China, Europe, Latin America, and the United States. Current and former N.B.A. coaches and players provide training and run drills, and the youth are provided "education and insight on off-court elements that are crucial to the success of a basketball career, such as nutrition, education, media training, and community outreach ("Addidis Nations"; "Fundamentals Stressed at Addidis Nations") and the SEEDS (Sports for Education and Economic Development Foundation) in Senegal, with the joint corporate sponsorship of Nike and the N.B.A.. Funded in 2002 as a non-profit organization by Senegalese athlete Amadou Gallo Fall, it provides an intensive 10-month program of academic and athletic instruction designed to prepare students for admission to U.S. colleges and to play Division I basketball. It seeks to "inspire, empower, and support the holistic development of promising African youth" by facilitating their "use of basketball as a ticket to education, a better life, and a chance to become a positive force for change back in Senegal ("Sports for Education and Economic Development").

Examples of player initiatives include: the "Big Man Camp" in Nigeria, founded by Masai Ujimi of the Toronto Raptors and Goodwin Owinje of the Phoenix Suns, designed to prepare players 6'8" and taller for competition in U.S. Div. I college basketball; and the "Darfur Dream Team" "Sister Schools Program," an internationalized service venture (in conjunction with the UNHCR) whose mission is to make a quality education available to every refugee child by linking Chadean camp schools with sister schools in the United States from middle-school to university level (McCormick, Basketball Devlopment in Africa).

As a result of these and similar developmental programs in the former Yugoslavia and Europe, there has been an increased presence of international players in the U.S. collegiate ranks and in the last few years in American high schools as well. International representation at the collegiate level has doubled in the last decade, and there has been a concerted effort to enroll foreign players in American secondary schools. As N.B.A. Director of Scouting, Marty Blake, reported during the 2008 season, 54 players from 35 countries, including 18 from Nigeria and 10 from former Yugoslavian states participated in Div. I programs, and hundreds of other international players in lower divisions. During the 2008-09 season, 170 African players participated in collegiate programs in the United States (Rhoden). My own institution, Hofstra University, is typical. Of thirteen players on the current roster, three are international—one from Hungary and two from Lithuania, comprising 23% of the team. On the high-school level, international sports clubs have come to view the United States as a kind of apprenticeship or "farm" system that "refines their less seasoned players, polishes the more advanced, and prepares them all for eventual professional and national team competition (Rhoden). The dramatic globalization of the N.B.A., embodying sustained contact with and integration of international players, coaches, and spectators, coupled with the extensive overseas developmental and charitable programs of the league, have made American professional basketball the most international of U.S. sports both in terms of integration of foreign players and worldwide media access. These efforts have facilitated the expanded participation of international players on N.B.A. teams, a more immediate form of player contact. Since 1997, no fewer than nine foreign players have been drafted in any year. In 1999 there were 37 international players, representing 25 countries in the league; in 2000 there were 48 from 28 countries; and in 2007 there were 87 from 37 countries. In 2008 there were 75 international players from 30 countries. In N.B.A. drafts from 2002-2006, 76 non-American players were selected for 240 slots (32%), 28 in the first round (23%). In the 2006 All-Star game, 6 of 24 players (25%) were foreign-born. In the 2009 draft 13 international players were selected out of 60 slots (22%). The percentage of foreign players on N.B.A. teams seems to have hovered statistically at just under 25%, despite the hyper-inflated claims of Nike's George Raveling, who predicted that international players would make up 50% of N.B.A. rosters by 2010 (N.B.A. Draft 2009).

The in-migration of international players, like historical immigration, is motivated by a quest for opportunity and economic mobility. It brings together a broad diversity of ethnicities and two very distinct cultures of basketball.[3] Americans have come up through the tradition of "in your face," "take-it-to-the rim," and "above-the-rim slam dunks" inner-city street ball, in which one-on-one athleticism is the most admired trait. International players, especially Europeans, are brought up in a tightly-organized system that tracks players as early as eight or nine years old, identifies top prospects by twelve, and signs them at sixteen to "under control" agreements with a professional team. This agreement is a kind of modern apprenticeship contract by which the controlling club provides all living, training, and educational expenses for the player. Players are schooled in the fundamentals of the game and all players, regardless of position, are trained in essential skills. The emphasis in international basketball is on teamwork and fundamentally sound five-on-five basketball (Boeck).

3 The N.B.A. has also been recognized as a leader in promoting racial and gender integration in its programs by the Institute for Diversity and Ethics in Sport. In the 2010-11 season, one-third of the league's coaches , 45% of assistant coaches, and 26% of general managers were men of color. In the league office, 36% of professional positions were held by men of color and 42% by women. Overall, the league was assigned a grade of "A" by the IDES (see Washburn).

Hip-Hop Culture and Race in the N.B.A.

Beyond styles of play, the N.B.A. brings distinctly different cultural forms into direct contact. Since David Stern's accession as Commissioner, the N.B.A. demographic has become preponderantly African American. Today 79% of its players are people of color and 75% are African American. The period from 1984 to the present that has recently been dubbed the "Dunkadelic Era," witnessed an exponential growth in the number of Black players in the league and a corresponding integration of hip-hop culture. African American players readily accepted the sartorial trappings of hip-hop—the loose baggy clothing, the razor cuts, the ostentatious "bling."[4] Attitude reigned supreme: a macho culture that tolerated no disrespect and that threatened immediate response to being "dissed" prevailed. "Two worlds of American entertainment intersected and overlapped. N.B.A. players like Shaquille O'Neal, Kobe Bryant, and Ron Artest essayed rap as an avocation, and pop stars Nelly and Jay-Z became major team investors (in the Charlotte Bobcats and the New Jersey Nets, respectively). Hip-hop became the theme music of the N.B.A.; both NBC and ESPN incorporated it into their t.v. coverage of games ("N.B.A. Criticisms and Controversies"; "National Baketball and Hip-Hop Culture Month"). In the wake of the Detroit brawl between players and fans in November 2004, Rush Limbaugh provided a racialist reading of the N.B.A., charging that it was "hip-hop culture on parade," that teams should be referred to as "gangs," and that the league should be re-named the T.B.A. (Thug Basketball Association). Phil Jackson, current coach of the L.A. Lakers, concurred: "The Players have been dressing in prison garb the last five or six years. All the stuff that goes on, it's like gangster, thuggery stuff" ("Limbaugh on the N.B.A."; "Is the N.B.A. Dress Policy for Racial Discrimination?"). Despite this white backlash, the N.B.A. remained closely allied with hip-hop culture,[5] its most visible manifesta-

4 "N.B.A. Street," Vol. 2, a current video game, marketed by Playstation 2 which blends N.B.A., street ball, and hip-hop culture. Vol. 2, the most popular version, is currently sold out.

5 Recent evidence suggests that the game of some foreign players has changed to accommodate N.B.A. style and thus made them less effective in international play. The perennially-contending Azzuri team was eliminated from qualification for the European championships, losing twice to France and once to Finland. La Gazetta Dello Sport reported that its two N.B.A. players, Andre Bargnani and Marco Belinelli, repeatedly tried to set up one-on-one and two-on-two situations, only to be consistently

tion being the explosion of tattoos on players' bodies since the late-1990s. League officials, after some attempts to draw back, decisively identified the N.B.A. with hip-hop in its current slogan, "Where Amazing Happens," featuring a promo with a soundtrack of Kanye West's hit "Amazing." June of 2009 was declared National Basketball and Hip-Hop Month. Since the late 1990s, urban street style has dominated American style in basketball in the proliferation of tattoos. Dennis Rodman was the first N.B.A. player to sport visible body art, but currently approximately 70% of N.B.A. players bear tattoos. Allen Iverson alone has over two dozen. Tattoos are seen exclusively on American players, overwhelmingly African American, leading critics to comment that the "two-bit punk attitudes, tattoos, and chest-beating . . . [have] made a great sport look like a thug convention" (Limbaugh). On 28 April 2009 the controversy continued when the Celtics' Paul Pierce and the Wizard's DeShawn Stevens were each fined $25,000 for making "menacing" hand gestures in post-season play that were interpreted, rightly or wrongly, as gang signs ("N.B.A. Criticisms; "Paul Pierce Gang Sign"; Murray).

For international players, adjusting to the N.B.A. is often a major culture shock. For many, assimilation, as for earlier groups of immigrants, is aggravated by language difficulties that impede communication with coaches and other players. Some players, like Germany's Dirk Nowitzki, are initially uncomfortable with their living situation, and with American culture generally. For others, like Georgi Glouchkov, diet is a problem; he was rumored to have developed an inordinate fondness for American fast food. Others experienced troubles with aggressive groupies and a seemingly ubiquitous availability of easy sex ("Basketball U on International Players"; "Inter Basketball Profiles: Glouchkov"). The hip-hop world so central to N.B.A. style was only a part, albeit a significant one, of the overall struggle for the "Americanization" of the international player. It was, inevitably, an aspect of American life and culture that was almost universally but partially and with great difficulty assimilated by foreign players.

In the decade 1985-95, Europeans who dressed more traditionally were seen as "foreign" and "out of it." In the period 1995-2005, after the institution of the N.B.A. dress code, Zaza Pachulia of the Atlantic Hawks observed that "Euro style used to be a bad thing. Now guys like it

---

thwarted by a typical match-up zone defense commonly employed in international play. See Frank Della'Appa. "Arrivedercii Italy," *Boston Globe*, 30 August 2009: D6.

(Bucher, "Above the Rim"). While the N.B.A. dress code (1985) banned chains, medallions, pendants, baseball caps, doo-rags, retro jerseys, sleeveless shirts, shorts, sunglasses (indoors), headphones, sneakers, sandals, and work boots, the hip-hop element of N.B.A. culture persisted. The dress code was a response of the league after the 1995 Detroit brawl and the subsequent decline in attendance, but international players, already accustomed to dressing more conservatively, served as models and helped their African-American teammates adjust to the new requirements for a more professional appearance (Vollrath).

Flagrant Fouls and Bruising Brawls: Hard Physical Contact in the N.B.A.

In terms of styles of play, international players also needed to make a major adjustment to the N.B.A. with its greater speed, bruising, overpowering dunks, and brutal physical contact, especially during the playoffs. But here, too, as with hip-hop style, the N.B.A. has been more of a mutual melting pot than a salad bowl of discrete cultural elements. International basketball is very different from the American version. Two distinctions are critical in terms of physical contact between players. The first is the difference in the lane or "key" running from the foul line to the end line. The American lane is a rectangle, 15' long by 12' wide. The international lane is trapezoidal, widening out from the foul line from 12' to 19'6" at the baseline. The international lane, therefore, keeps players further from the basket and consequently there is less muscling for position in the paint in international play. The second difference is in officiating and rule interpretation. In international play, defensive players are given the advantage on foul calls, and "offensive players are not rewarded with free throws if they initiate the contact; no pump fake and fling yourself into the defender and expect free throws, à la Kobe Bryant" (McCormick,"European Invasion). Player innovation, like LeBron James' stop-jump, or "crab dribble" move also can initiate more contact with defensive players (Pollakoff).

The American inside game is dominated by powerful men who contend for space around the basket by leaning back into the defender to push him out of the way, and who use arms and elbows to clear out defenders. For their part, the defenders establish a position "in the paint" to deny it to the offensive player, and use forearms and hands to shove and hold the offensive player as far from the basket as possible. As Orlando's Dwight Howard puts it: "[I]n the paint, basketball is very physical. You get elbows flying, bodies flying, crashing, and people fighting for position" Ron Culp, Miami Heat trainer, concurred: "Basketball is the most physical non-contact sport in the world (Abrams).

N.B.A. teams have always had enforcers or "goons" to put rough body checks on and commit hard fouls against opponents, players like Bill Laimbeer, Rick Mahorn, and Kermit Washington. Especially in key games of the playoffs, star players are targeted for particularly rough treatment to try to minimize their impact. Cleveland's LeBron James, for example, faced a rough-and-tumble, hard-banging Washington team in the 2008 Eastern Division playoffs. "Washington's plan from the outset was to be rough with King James, who has been knocked on his royal rear-end several times (Windhurst). James claimed the Wizards were deliberately trying to injure him, to which Brendon Haywood responded acerbically, calling James a whiner: "No one is trying to hurt him, everybody is trying to play basketball, trying to play tough. Play basketball and leave it alone ("Wiz's Haywood Says LeBron").

Indeed, that often seems to be the philosophy of officials as well, particularly in the final minutes of close or playoff games. It is not surprising, then, that there is a striking incidence of injury to key players, especially in the run-up to the playoffs.

> League priorities may determine the nature of officiating—"Let them play because this is a crucial game in the series, and we don't want to determine the outcome with our whistles ("Kery Playoff Trends").

Given these conditions, teams take counter-steps to protect key players. Two examples will suffice. In the late 1970s the L.A. Lakers used Kermit Washington to protect Kareem Abdul Jabbar. The recent acquisition by the Lakers of current bad boy Ron Artest is clearly designed in large part to protect Kobe Bryant (Wilson). This physical style of play and the attitudes towards roughness have filtered down from the professional to the pick-up playground game, where, since 1980, the mantra has been "no blood, no foul." Indeed, the N.B.A. did not introduce its "Blood Rule" until the 1991-92 season, fully a decade after the outbreak of the AIDS epidemic and did so solely in response to fears of HIV/AIDS infection. The official rules site lists this rule under the heading "Guidelines for Infection Control ("Official Rules").

Individual players have taken the initiative in recent years to protect themselves from the continual pounding of body contact. Many N.B.A. and college players wear thigh and chest pads in the form of padded compression shorts and tight-fitting V-neck undershirts under their loose-fitting uniforms. Shaquille O'Neal was the first player to adopt this under armor, and today top stars like LeBron James, Kobe Bryant, and Amare

> Stoudemire wear it. This gear, originally developed for football, has been adapted for what is realistically, as one manufacturer put it, a "full-contact sport requiring full-time protection." Basketball body armor is today a $15-20 million business, dominated by Underarmour's Modular Protection Zone protection equipment and McDavid's Hex Pad spandex system (Abrams).

The danger of hard physical contact to players' wellbeing was made painfully clear in a fight that erupted during an L.A. Lakers-Houston Rockets game on 9 December 1977. After several rebounding scuffles, Houston's Kevin Kunnert threw an elbow and hit Kemit Washington in the arm. L.A.'s Kareem Abdul Jabbar grabbed Kunnert's arms to pull him away and to defuse the situation, but Washington punched Kunnert, bringing him to his knees. In the meantime, Houston's Rudy Tomjanovich was running up to assist Kunnert. Washington, seeing him peripherally, turned and punched him full in the face. Unconscious, Tomjanovich hit the floor; his skull was fractured. The whole posterior portion of his face was misaligned and it took five operations to correct the damage. Though Tomjonovich was able to return to play in 1978, he was never the same, and he retired in 1981. Washington received a $10,000 fine and a 25-game suspension, the longest suspension for twenty years (Marlin).

The league drew no lesson from the Washington-Tomjanovich episode, and in 1989-90 the Detroit Pistons "Bad Boys" compiled a 63-19 record and won back-to-back championships in 1989 and 1990. They played hard, tough, and dirty. Some observers argued that Detroit "ushered in a bruising, over-the-top defense that brought rugby to the N.B.A., [and] lowered scores for decades (Shouler). It was clear from Detroit's success that excessive roughness paid off handsomely; hard contact translated into championships. It was not until 1991-92 that the league took steps to rein in what in international play is considered unsportsmanlike conduct. N.B.A. rules in that season established a two-tier flagrant foul rule: Flagrant foul 1 awarded two foul shots to the fouled player and possession of the ball to his team; Flagrant foul 2, where there was no evident attempt to play the ball, or the foul was so excessive that it could have resulted in injury to the fouled player, made the same shot and possession award but also would result in the automatic ejection of the fouler and a $250 fine.

These rule changes have not significantly reduced the level of hard, bruising body contact in the N.B.A. Nor have they reduced the level of intra-player violence. Indeed, in recent years that violence has extended to coaches, referees, and fans. In the 1996 playoffs between the New York Knicks and the Miami Heat, a bench-clearing brawl resulted in the ejection of nine players, who were also suspended for several playoff games. Also in 1996, Dennis Rodman head-butted a referee who had ejected him, earning a six-game suspension. Rodman was suspended for eleven games in 1997 for kicking a photographer. In 2004, Charles "Bo" Outlaw of the Orlando Magic was ejected from a game and fined $10,000 for physical contact with a referee (Farnsworth, et al).

In 1997, Latrell Sprewell grabbed Golden State Warriors coach P. J. Carlesimo by the throat and choked him for 10-15 seconds before others players pulled him off. He returned from the locker room twenty minutes later, threw a punch at Carlesimo and threatened to kill him. Sprewell was suspended for one year, the longest for any team sport athlete for a non-drug-related offense (Puma).

Meanwhile, on-court fights continued. Two incidents in January of 2002 are indicative. In a rough- hacking Laker-Bulls game, Brad Miller crashed his forearm down on Shaquille O'Neal's shoulders and Charles Barkley elbowed him in the head. O'Neal threw a punch at the back of Miller's head and knocked him off the court with a hard tackle, earning a suspension. The same month, Tracy McGrady of the Orlando Magic got a forearm from Kenyon Martin of the New Jersey Nets that knocked him to the floor. McGrady came up swinging and Martin countered; both players were ejected ("Bulls Win by TKO"; Johnson).

Fan Frenzy and Player Fights: Violence on Court and in the Stands

Predictably, physical contact has expanded beyond the court and hyper-emotional, often alcohol-fueled fans have become part of the game. In March 2003, at a Knicks home game, a drunken fan, Calvin Klein, left his courtside seat and grabbed Latrell Spreewell by the arm as he was attempting to in-bound the ball. Klein was quickly restrained and returned to his seat by Madison Square Garden security personnel. But the incident resulted in the "Calvin Klein" law, whereby New York City banned fans from entering the court or field during a professional sporting event (Anderson).

The most egregious example of fan-player violence was the brawl during the Pacers-Pistons game on 19 November 2004, popularly called the "Basketbrawl" or, more familiarly, "Malice at the Palace" (the Pistons' home court in Auburn Hills, MI). The fight began among the players with 45.9 seconds remaining in the game when Indiana's Ron Artest fouled Detroit's Ben Wallace very hard from behind. Wallace retaliated by shoving Artest in the face, and players from both teams engaged in the struggle. Artest retreated and lay on the scorer's table, taunting Wallace. At that point, a fan, John Green, threw a cup of beer at Artest and hit him in the chest. Artest charged into the stands and confronted a man he mistakenly believed had thrown the cup. Artest was confronted by two other fans and his teammates Stephen Jackson and Jermaine O'Neal joined the melee. Nine spectators were injured, two seriously enough to require hospital care; no players sustained injuries. Nine players were suspended for a total of 146 games (137 for Pacers and 9 for Pistons) and were fined a total of $10 million—Artest got a 68-game suspension (the longest ever for an N.B.A. fight) and was fined $5 million. Five players and five fans were charged with assault and battery, and the players were sentenced to a year on probation and fined $250, while John Green, who had ignited the brawl from the stands, was sentenced to 30 days in jail and two years' probation and banned for life from Pistons' basketball games (Pacers-Pistons Brawl). In a *Sports Nation* poll conducted by ESPN, 83% of respondents ranked the brawl "the ugliest incident of fan-player violence" they had ever seen. Only 46% believed that fans were to blame for the outbreak ("Pacers-Pistons Brawl").

League response to the brawl was to increase arena security in order to keep fans and players apart, and to ban the sale of alcohol after the third quarter. Though statistical evidence is limited, what is available suggests that flagrant fouls have risen each year since the 1994-95 season. There were ten flagrant 2 fouls in 2001 and 13 in 2002. In 2001 there were 130 flagrant 1 and 2 fouls in the N.B.A.; in 2002 there were 71 by mid-season. In 2006, the league instituted a less tolerant policy, in essence "telling its players that the days of hand-to-hand combat were over." Five players received suspensions during the playoffs that season, which led one commentator to argue that N.B.A. had come to stand for "No Bully Antics" (Isola).

But the league's efforts seem to have been ineffectual in controlling hard physical contact. In the 2009 playoffs, fourteen flagrant fouls were called in 80 games (18% of games), which represented a 75% increase over the 2008 playoffs, when eight flagrant fouls were assessed in 86 games (9% of games), a figure was double that of 2007. The rate in 2006 was twelve flagrant fouls in 89 games (13% of games) (Denton). When the N.B.A. Competition Committee met in May 2009 to review flagrant fouls in the playoffs, it stressed the ambiguous dynamics among players, coaches, referees, and league officials that continue to sustain violent and dirty play. The terms "flagrant," "excessive," and "rescinded," they declared, have dominated an otherwise splendid N.B.A. postseason,

> and now the issue is no longer about whether there is a fine line between "hard" and "dirty" fouls. Those are easy to discern. The hard part is predicting what the referees will call, and whether the league will overrule them the following morning ... leading to the usual protests about playoff officiating and the lack of consistency (D'Alessandro).

And the fans seem to enjoy the vicarious violence, typically escalated during the high stakes of the playoffs. Since players accept hard physical contact as the reality of the game, league officials seem conflicted about controlling it. During the 2009 playoffs, TNT experienced a 14% increase in viewership over the 2008 season. As Scott Reister put it: "[D]eath match atmosphere and high stakes are good for ratings. . . . To win you need some beasts down low to give out (and take) the punishment, good FT shooting, and some strong-willed leaders to rise above the insanity. Do all that, and you may come out alive . . . assuming that you don't end up in a body bag first (Riester).

Since 1984, the N.B.A. has been the preeminent American professional sports association, promoting both extensive international, indeed, global, inter-ethnic contact and bruising physical body contact in an era of "hard ball." Unlike earlier immigrants, international players retain their natal citizenship and many do not establish permanent residency in the United States, but like them they typically come to America in pursuit of economic opportunity. Their experience in the culture of the N.B.A. necessitates their adaptation to a very different culture where the interaction of international cultures and the dominant culture of the N.B.A. has resulted in mutual adaptation and a perceptible internationalization of American professional basketball. Especially since the recension of the ban on zone defenses in 1991, American professional basketball has effectively combined the "old school" African-American street ball, one-on-one and two-on-two game with hard physical contact given and received with alacrity and the sound fundamental five-on-five game relying on pinpoint passing and shooting finesse. In essence reliance on an individual star has been superseded by an increased reliance of team play.

International contact has enriched the sport at the professional and collegiate levels, while physical contact seems to have made the game more exciting and attractive for fans. Less desirable has been the spread of on-court violence—understandable when four to six men, 6'10" or taller, each weighing 250 lbs. or more, are pushing and shoving, and bruising one another in a very confined space around the hoop—to coaches, referees, and fans. The response of league officials has been ineffective in dealing with on-court violent contact, so its spread beyond the players is not to be unexpected.

Globalization has dramatically internationalized and transformed American professional basketball, blending three styles of play—above the rim, in the paint, and beyond the arc, thereby reducing the notion of American exceptionalism in the sport. League-sanctioned diversification has led to significant ethnic and cultural amalgamation in a volatile on-court environment. As a consequence, within a more cosmopolitan cultural, social, and physical space, those elements that make American culture so tolerant of interpersonal violence have continued to prevail in the bruising physical play of the N.B.A. [6]

In the contact space that is the N.B.A. we see the concurrent adaptation to the reality of internationalization of what was formerly seen as the uniquely American sport and the persistence of a popular macho code of physical competition that prides itself on forceful bodily contact and mutual physical punishment. That code insures that any such contact will be taken as a challenge, a mark of disrespect. Honor and on-court status demand retaliation. Only the weak meekly accept being "dissed" by an op-

6 That separateness remains as strong a force as blending was abundantly clear in the 2010-2011 championship series between the Dallas Mavericks and the Miami Heat. The stark contrast between the on-court, off-court, and media relations styles of Dallas' Dirk Nowitzki and Miami's LeBron James was starkly apparent throughout the playoff series.

ponent. Despite its admirable commitment to global service and educational initiatives, in the N.B.A., as in the broader American immigration experience, blending and separateness are combined in the complex rough-and-tumble contact space that is the competitive world of the most turbulent "non-contact" sport—professional basketball.

Works Cited

Abrams, Jonathan. "N.B.A's Undercover Secret: Players Protective Pads." *New York Times. 28 April 2009.* 20 July 2009 <http://www.nytimes.com/2009/04/26/sports/basketball/26pads.html?ref=jonathanabrams>.

"Addidas Nations." *Addidas Nations.com. 2009.* 20 July 2009 <http://basketballrecruitint.rivals.com/content.asp?SID90108=659011>.

A.S. "Limbaugh on the N.B.A.: 'Call it the TBA, the Thu'g Basketball Association . . .They're Going to Watch the Crips and the Bloods." *Media Matters.org.* 10 December 2004. 23 July 2009 <http://www.mediamatters.org/search/20041210008>.

"Basketball U on International Players." *NBA.com.* 9 October 2003. 20 July 2009 <http://www.nba.com/canada/bu_international.html>.

"Basketball Without Borders." *NBA.com* (2009). 26 July 2009. <http://www.nba.com/bwb>.

Beck, Howard. "In N.B.A., 'Flagrant' is a Matter of Interpretation." *New York Times* 3 June 2009. 21 July 2009 <http://www.nytimes.com/2009/06/04/sports/basketball/04fouls.html>.

Boeck, Greg. "Team-First, Back to Basics Foreigners Changing N.B.A." *USA Today* 21 April 2006. 24 July 2009 <http://www.reg.usatoday.com/community/tags/reporter.aspx?id=230&pg>.

Bucher, Rick. "Above the Rim, Beyond the Arc: AThe Dress Code Didn't Just Change Labels in N.B.A. Locker Rooms, It Pushed Players to Rethink Their Lifestyles." Sports *ESPN* 2009. 26 July 2009 <http://www.sports.espn.go.com/espnmag/story?.id=3898919>.

---. "Why N.B.A. Cares is More Than a PR Slogan." *ESPN, the Magazine* 29 November 2006 <http://www.sports.espn.com/nba/columns/ story?>.

Bulls Win a TKO: O'Neal, Miller Cause Melee: Lakers Fail to Hold 17-Point First-Half Advantage." *Chicago Tribune* 12 January 2003. 23 July 2009 <http:www.articles.chicagotribune.com>collections>Kobe Bryant>.

Callimachi, Rukmini. "N.B.A. Camp to Show Africa Future in Basketball." *Boston Globe* 15 August 2010, D7. <http://www.usatoday.com/sports/2010-08-12-1002793699_x.htm>.

D'Alessandro, Dave. "Too Many Flagrant Whistles in N.B.A. Playoffs Have Players, Coaches, Crying Foul on Officials." *Newark Star Ledger* 28 May 2009. 21 July 2009 <http://www.njcom>New Jersey Nets>Around the NBA>.

Denton, John. "Flagrant Fouls Hit Highlight Reel." *Realgm.com.* 26 January 2002. 20 July 2009 <http://www/rea;gm/com/SRC_wiretap_archives/11541/2002/26/flagrant_fouls_hit_the_highlight_reel>.

Farnsworth, Elizabeth, et al. "Out of Bounds." *PBS Newshour*. 5 December 1997. Transcript. <http://www.pbs.org/newshour/bb/sports/July . . ./nba_12-5.html>.

Foucault, Michel."Of Other Spaces, Heterotopias" (1967). 15 Aug. 2009 http://foucault.info/docunents.heterotopia/foucault/heterotpoia.en.ht.

Hammann, Joshua. "In Senegal an Academy Develops the Minds (and Game) of Promising Players." *ESPN.com.* 2009. 24 July 2009 <http://sports.espn.go.com/espn/print?id=3269366+type=story>.

"Inter Basketball Profiles: Glouchkov." *Interbasket.net.* <http://Interbasket.net/players.glouchkov.htm>.

Isola, Frank. "Changes Are Flagrant: N.B.A. Gets Rough on Hard Fouls." *New York daily News* 19 June 2006. 20 July 2009 <http://www. articles.nydailynews.com/183240651_hard_fouls_mavs_jerry_stack house>.

Johnson, K.C. "Kenyon and Nets Fight Off McGrady, Magic." *New York Daily News* 13 January 2002. 27 July 2009 <http://www.dailynews.com/topics/Kerry&Kittles>.<http://blogcritics/culture/article/nba_brawl_renews_interest_in calvin>.

"Key Playoff Trends: Rough Play, Poor Shooting." Articles Base.com. 18 May2009. 17 July 2009 <http://www.articlesbase.com/basketball_articles/key-playoff-trends-rough-play-poorofficiating_922035.html>.

Lacy, D. Aaron. "Is the N.B.A. Dress Policy a Pretext for Racial Discrimination?" *Hiphopla* 14 April 2009. 23 July 2009 <http:// www.hiphoplaw.blogspot.com/ .../is-nba-dress-policy-pretext-fo-racial.html>.

Marlin, Brooks. "The Punch: Kermit Washington vs. Rudy Tomjanovich." *Everything* 21 October 2002. 23 July 2009 <http:// www.everything2.com/title/the+punch%253+Kermit+Washington+Rudy+Tomjanovich>.

McCormick, Brian. "Basketball Development in Africa." *World Press.com*. 2009 24 April 2009 <http://www.darfurdreamteam.org>.

---. "The European Invasion: A Good Thing." *College Hoopsters.com.* 2009. 20 July 2009 <http://www.collegehoops.net.com/coaching/Euros.html>.

"McDonald's Championship." *Hoopedia* (2003). 20 July 2009 <http://www.hoopedia.nba/com/index.php?title=McDonald's>.

Monroe, Mike. "Veni, Vidi, Vici: How David Stern and the N.B.A. Conquered the World." *American Way 1*5 February 2009. 12 July 2009 <http://www.americanwaymag.com/nba.david.stern.China'Yao. ming.parker.jr.>.

Murray, Steve. "The N.B.A.'s Hip-Hop Image Problem." *Midweek.com.* 2009. 23 July 2009 <http://www.midweek.com>Sports/Fitness> Hot Air>.

"N.B.A. Cares." *NBA.com* (2009). 26 July 2009 <http//www.nba.com/nba_cares>.

"N.B.A. Cares and W.N.B.A. Launch Vaccines for Teens Campaign." *NBA.com* 2009. 26 July 2009 <http://www. http://www.nba.com. nba_wnba_caares>.

"N.B.A. Draft 2009." *Hoopedia* 2009. 24 July 2009 <http://www.hoopedia.nba.com/index.php?title=2009_NBA_Draft>.

"N.B.A. Growth Table." *Basketball.com* (2009). 26 July 2009 <http://www.basketball.com/nba/history/shtml>.

"N.B.A. International Historic Timeline, 1946-2000." 26 July 2009 *Hoopedia* (2009). 20 July 2009 <http://hoopedia.nba.com/index.php?

"N.B.A. Rules History, 1980-Present." *NBA.com.* 2009. 15 July 2009 <http://www.hoopedia.nba.com/index.php?title=NBA_Rules_History >.

"National Basketball Association Criticisms and Controversies—Racialized Cultural Issues." *Wikipedia* 2009. 26 July 2009 <http://www.mynba.com/thread.jspa?threadID=5700034138>.

"National Basketball Association and Hip-Hop Culture Month." 26 July 2009 <http://mynba/com/thread.jspa?threadID=5700034138>.

"Official Rules of the National Basketball Association." *NBA.com.* 8 September 2004. 15 July 2009 <http://www.Nba.com/analysis/rules_index.html>.

"Pacers-Pistons Brawl." *Wikipedia.* 2009. 17 July 2009 <http://www.en.wikipedia.org/wiki/Pacers_Pistons_brawl>.

"Paul Pierce Gang Sign." *Mahalo.com.* 2009. 23 July 2009 <http://www.mahalo.com/paul_pierce_gang_sign>.

Pollakoff, Brett. "LeBron Upset His 'Crab Dribble' Was Called a Travel in Final Seconds. Against Wizards." *N.B.A. fanhouse.com.* 28 April 2009. 15 July 2009 <http:www.aolnews.com/ . . .lebron.upset.his-crab-dribble-was-called-a-travel-in-final-sec/>.

Pratt, Mary Louise. "Art of the Contact Zone. *Profession* (NY: MLA) 91 34-35.

Puma, Mike. "The 'Choke' Artist." *ESPN Go.com.* 4 December 2004. 25 July 2009 <http//:www.espn.go.com/classic/s/add-sprewell-latrell.html>.

Riester, Scott. "The anchor's Desk: Brutal Fouls, Confusing Whistles, and High Ratings Just Another N.B.A. Season." *Midwestern Sports Fans.com* 2009. 27 July 2009 <http://www.midwesternsportsfans.com/2009/05/2009_nba_playoffs_ratings_strong_despite_hard_flagrant_fouls>.

Rhoden, William G. "Foreign Players, American Courts: A Special Report—Basketball Talent Search Brings Schoolboys to U.S." *New York Times* 13 August 2009: 36. 20 July 2009 <http://www.nytimes.com/topic/news/williamrhoden/index.html> . <http://www.reg.usatoday.com/community/tags/reporter.aspx?id=230&pg>.

"Shouler, Ken. "Daly Left Mark on Pistons, Dream Team." *Sports ESPN.com.* 11 May 2009. 23 July 2009 <http://www.motorcitybadboys.com/index.php>.

Sports for Education and Economic Development." 2009. 6 August 2009 http://www.seedsproject.org.

Thomas, Vincent. "The N.B.A. and Hip-Hop Pull Off an Amazing Reunion." *NBA.com.* 2009. 26 July 2009 <http://www.nba.com/2009/vince_thomas/D4 . . ./amazing 2090423>./

U.S. Men's National Basketball Team." *Wikipedia*, 2008: Pars. 4-6, 8. 15 July 2009 <http//www.en.wikipedia.org/...United_States_Men's_National_Basketball_team>.

"U.S. Senior National Team (Men's)." *Hoopedia* (2009). 12 July 2009 <http:/www.hoopedia.nba.com/index.php?title=USA_Senior_Team>.

Vollrath, Amanda. "New N.B.A. Dress Code Too Strict at Best, Racist at Worst." *The Dog Street Journal.* 7 November 2005. 20 July 2009 <http://www.dogstreetjournal.com/story>. <http://www.nytimes.com/2009/04/26/sports/basketball/26pads.html?ref=jonathanabrams>.

Washburn, Gary. "Good Report Card: Diversity Not an Issue Here," *Boston Globe*. 19 June 2011: D11.

Windhorst, Brian. "Special to ESPN." *Sports ESPN.com.* 24 April 2008. 23 July 2009.

"Wiz's Haywood Says LeBron Should Stop complaining About Rough Play." *Sports ESPN Go.com.* 29 April 2009. 26 July 2009 <http://www.sports.espn.go.com/nba/playoffs.2008/columns/story?/page>.

Hip-Hop Culture as a Medial Contact Space: Local Encounters and Global Appropriations of "Wild Style"

Sina A. Nitzsche

Sina A. Nitzsche's essay analyzes the myriad contact spaces in the hip-hop movie Wild Style (1983). Taking cues from Pratt's concept of the contact zone, Nitzsche proposes a difference between two levels of contact: on the film's diegetic level, there are various spaces that foster contact between different social groups, most notably the hip-hop street culture on the one hand and the Manhattan established art scene on the other; on the level of the film's dissemination, Wild Style generated a contact space for global audiences which led to the formation of New York Style street cultures in various contexts outside the United States.

Introduction: New York Street Cultures

Streets are democratic public spaces which are generally free of charge and accessible to everyone. Integrated into larger global processes such as immigration, globalization, and popular culture, they allow manifold encounters between different social groups from diverse backgrounds. Immigrant street vendors in New York City, for instance, sell a variety of sweet and savory foods, I (heart) NY souvenirs, illegal copies of popular CDs and DVDs, and even xeroxed street literature.[1] The vendors import their cultural practices and transplant them onto the streets of New York. In addition to their imported practices, they also offer New Yorkers an affordable alternative to the high-priced restaurants, music or

1 This is a recent development where African Americans sell their copied literature on the street. In the following video, Terri Woods, the key figure of this phenomenon, talks about how she sold her novels on 125th Street in Harlem: http://www.youtube.com/watch?v=ddafBrKcZ1k

book stores. They generate a "street economy" within the greater realm of New York City's retail industry, competing with established businesses over the needs of their customers. Street vendors illustrate how global developments are literally grounded on the streets.

Likewise, hip-hop is a cultural practice that originated in New York City and has been inextricably tied to the public space of the street. Commonly understood as a cultural form which consists of the four elements DJing, MCing, graffiti, and breaking, hip-hop "emerged as a source for youth of alternative identity formation and social status" (Rose 34) in the deindustrialized and financially shaken parts of the South Bronx, Harlem, and Brooklyn of the 1970s. Young and mostly male Afro-Caribbean immigrants brought their musical style and party traditions with them and organized so-called block parties, i.e. loud outdoor festivities where people from the neighborhood meet and dance. As it is for street vendors, the street is therefore a crucial public space in the emergence of hip-hop, the local turf where greater global developments reemerge and solidify.

In this vein, hip-hop culture is a form of contact zone as defined by Mary Louise Pratt. This is especially evident in the film "Wild Style" (1983), directed by Charlie Ahearn. "Wild Style" is a key film in the emergence of hip-hop inside and outside of the United States. The low-budget production reveals the "uptown-downtown synergy" (George 13) between DJs, MCs, breakers, and graffiti artists embodied by graffiti writer Raymond Zoro (Lee Quinones) as well as the art journalist Virginia (Patti Astor) who is interested in bringing graffiti to the Manhattan art world. The movie presents a community which is marginalized by authorities but which manages to develop its own cultural style and musical expression.

I argue in this paper that "Wild Style" constitutes a medial contact zone. By medial contact zone I refer, firstly, to the fact that the personal encounter between different groups of people in different positions of power is recorded, filmed, photographed, or written on a medium. "Wild Style" presents the personal encounter of Virginia with the uptown street culture on screen. The second aspect of the medial contact zone involves the film's distribution. The film is accessible to other groups in other local contexts by means of TV broadcasting or film distribution systems. The medial contact zone invites a reassessment of the contact zone, not only on a local level but also on a global scale. As I will show, "Wild Style" has triggered hip-hop movements in several countries and contributed greatly to the current global status of this form of popular culture. Pratt's idea of the contact zone offers a new way of reading hip-hop. Most of the scholarship in hip-hop is concerned with spaces and places (most notably Forman 2002, Rose 1994, Klein and Friedrich 2003, 2010) and there has been no major effort to conceptualize hip-hop as a contact zone. So far, only Pancho McFarland investigated the multiracial contact zone between African Americans and Latinos in Chicano hip-hop (2008). While McFarland examined the specific contacts and conflicts between those two groups, I aim at a closer reading of the encounter between the "colonized" and the "colonizer" figures exemplified in the movie "Wild Style."

MCs, B-Boys, and Fly-Girls: Mediating Hip-Hop

In Mary Louise Pratt's sense, contact zones are "social spaces where cultures meet, crash, and grapple with each other, often in contexts of highly asymmetrical relations of power" (76). Pratt conceptualizes the contact zone in her article "Arts of the Contact Zone" as a space of personal encounter between the colonized Inca population and the Spanish colonizers. Likewise, hip-hop is a cultural form that emerged as a movement of resistance, thus being an *a priori* counter-hegemonic cultural practice. In contrast to Pratt's described colonial encounters which took place after a cumbersome transatlantic ship voyage in the sixteenth century, hip-hop as a twentieth century phenomenon is much more hybrid, open, and flexible. This can be explained in the multiplicity of media in which hip-hop appears, such as records, music videos, films, but also on walls, subway cars, and in fashion. In this sense, hip-hop offers a much greater potential since a contact zone than Pratt's described colonial encounters as those media forms constantly reference and appropriate each other.

Several global tendencies manifested themselves when hip-hop emerged as a personal contact zone on the streets of the South Bronx in the 1970s. First, post-World War II immigrants from Latin America and the Caribbean settled in New York, making the city their new home and bringing in their cultural and spatial practices, such as the positioning of sound systems in the streets. Second, the aftermath of the 1960s Civil Rights Movement brought forth a large African American musical and cultural output, such as funk, soul, or the Blaxploitation film which constituted the audio and visual basis for the development of hip-hop. Those tendencies challenged the American music and film industry's lack of integration for African American and Latino popular cultural forms. All these tendencies are grounded and localized on 1520 Sedgewick Avenue in the mid-1970s, the mythical birth place where hip-hop emerged as an urban street culture. Jamaican-born DJ Kool Herc organized the first so-called outdoor block parties (Chang 77) with his Jamaican sound system. In this context, the street has been the main turf where larger global developments solidify, interrelate, and re-emerge in hip-hop since the final decades of the 20th century. The street is thus an important instance in the personal contact zone. Its four elements and its philosophy of "keeping it real" or remaining "true to the game," as the West Coast MC Ice Cube famously put it, are closely connected to the street from the very beginning.

Hip-hop combines both the personal and the medial contact zone in its four elements. For instance, Graffiti writers from many different backgrounds collaborate in crews where they share their styles and work on their tags (short signatures), outlines, or full pieces. This personal mode is then transformed into a mediated mode where the tags, outlines, and full pieces, in a further step, are sprayed onto walls or subway cars to make them visible to a large urban audience. It takes the crews a mutual effort to apply the small sketches drawn in a scrap book to the walls or subway cars. The collective production process of the pieces is conducted in spaces inevitably avoiding contact with the police or other authorities. While the artists remain outsiders and mystic figures by concealing their identity, the visual representation of tags and nicks (nicknames) tell passengers and pedestrians of the subversive nature of this street culture. The contact to a greater audience is established by way of graffiti on walls and on subway cars. In the 1970s, for example, graffiti writers managed to 'bomb' the New Yorker Metropolitan Transportation Authority (MTA) subway system. 'Bombing' refers to the excessive painting of subway cars when pieces are painted faster than the removal services can clean them. The term further indicates the battle/war/conflict between the graffiti groups and the public transportation authorities. This visibility in the city is also a means of re-claiming the urban territory as African Americans have been excluded from urban spaces for most of American history and raises questions of authority and ownership. Graffiti conflicts with the official institutions, such as the MTA, and the police, who treat graffiti as a criminal act of demolition of public property.

While graffiti constitutes a medial contact zone avoiding personal contact with a greater audience, breakdancing strives on the face-to-face interaction of the artists with their audiences. In the 1970s, crews like the Rock Steady Crew performed on makeshift stages on the sidewalk, in parks, or other public areas. These makeshift stages are personal contact zones where individuals or members of different crews enter into a battle over the best moves, such as six-step (moving the body in a circle on the ground), freeze (pausing the body movement) or head spin (rotating the body upside down on the head). The audience gathering around the stage provides the dancers with instant feedback by indicating their enthusiasm or rejection for certain groups or moves in the competition.

Hip-hop jams or block parties best combine the personal and medial mode of the contact zone. At these parties, participants who represent all four elements of hip-hop and different cultural backgrounds exchange ideas, celebrate together, and inspire each other. DJs play music, MCs perform their rhymes, breakers dance to the beat while graffiti artists paint the walls with pieces (smaller artwork) and murals (larger paintings). Those practices illustrate the unifying aspects of hip-hop culture as a personal contact zone which are based on resistance against a larger white hegemonic culture. However, such jams are not only smooth encounters. One of the key features of hip-hop culture is competition. MCs compete for the perfect rhyme, DJs for the perfect beat and best sample, and breakers for the most impressive moves. Furthermore, many rap crews often belong to opposing street gangs who fight over dominance in the neighborhood.

"Wild Style" as a Medial Contact Zone: From Exploration to Appropriation

Like hip-hop itself, the film "Wild Style" is a medial contact zone in two regards. Firstly, it represents the manifold interactions of different groups of people in New York City in the early 1980s on screen, such as African American, Afro-diasporic, and Hispanic artists, breakers, graffiti writers, DJs, and MCs, but also artists from Manhattan. In displaying the innovative potential and cross-cultural vibrancy of the street culture, the film constructs a democratic community. Secondly, this on-screen contact space is then distributed via TV stations, video rental stores, and cinemas in many parts of the world. Since "Wild Style" conveys a positive, enthusiastic and liberal image of street culture, it inspired the global audience to appropriate this special sense of creativity and community into their respective local contexts. Both aspects or modes of the medial contact zone in "Wild Style" are interrelated with each other.

The most prominent figure in my discussion of the medial contact zone is the protagonist Virginia, who at first glance may signify the hegemonic Anglo American culture. Her name is reminiscent of the state of Virginia which had a pivotal position in the nation-building process in American history. Her white ethnicity signals purity and explains the allusion to the "Marilyn of the eighties" (Hoban 152). Although belonging to the dominant culture in terms of her ethnicity, she transcends the audience's expectations beyond this category. She crosses the cultural boundaries much more easily than white men in her position, probably because her appearance, clothing style, and attitude bears striking similarities to Debbie Harry, legendary singer of the American new wave band Blondie which was also involved in early hip-hop. As an art journalist, Virginia represents the art scene that is critical of American consumer culture. Although part of the dominant culture, Virginia does not function as a colonizer in Pratt's sense. She encounters the various uptown street artists on a democratic basis and undergoes a cross-cultural learning process. She appreciates the street culture she is introduced to and even wants to establish it within the downtown art scene. Coming from a hegemonic background, the film suggests that the platinum blonde heroine moves beyond this binary opposition of the colonizer and the colonized groups. Virginia's first encounter with the locals on the street ironically invokes the perspective of authorities and the media who view the inner city as an uncivilized and dangerous urban territory. She drives uptown to meet The Union Crew, a local graffiti crew, to conduct an interview about their work. When her car breaks down on the final part of the trip, children from the neighborhood spontaneously approach her and surround the car. Virginia, who is sitting in the safe interior space of her car, is scared of them. She exerts her hegemonic outside attitude by hysterically shouting: "You can't touch the car! I am calling the police!", as the over the shoulder shot in the image[2] demonstrates:

2 All screenshots are printed with permission of Charlie Ahearn.

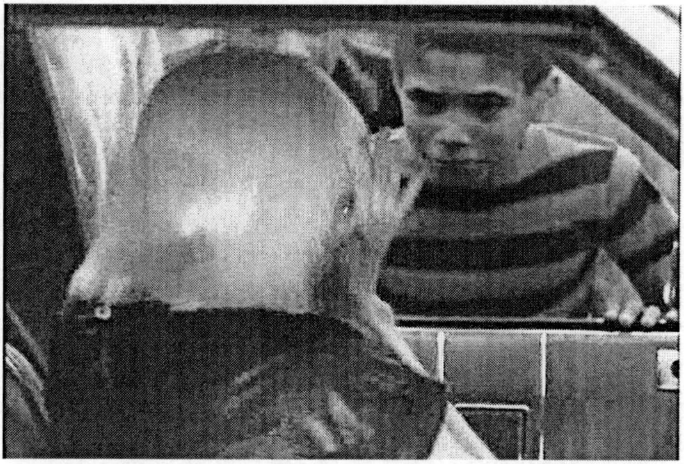

Virginia's reaction resembles a fear of the allegedly criminal area of the inner city. In so doing she exaggerates the prevalent assumption about African Americans as unlawful individuals or criminal gang members which is based on their stereotypical representation in the news media (Macek xviii). For a moment Virginia takes on this hegemonic attitude, but she becomes immediately aware of her own limited and prejudiced view. Smilingly, she asks the children: "Where is the telephone?" Her self-reflexive behavior distinguishes her from other colonizer figures who are less likely to change their perspective. As a result of this changing attitude, the kids even help Virginia and move her car to her sought-for destination, The Union Crew.

This incident characterizes the street as a cultural zone which enables a first contact between Virginia and the African American children and teenagers. The film constructs the street as a free and open space, facilitating spontaneous encounters which lead to an exertion of cultural stereotypes, but also to their revision.

Virginia functions as an agent who discovers the potential of this street culture. Her interview is shot in a shot-reverse-shot pattern which alternates between the interviewer and the interviewed who are standing in front of a mural at the Dixie Club:

During the interview she learns about the artists' reasons for doing graffiti, which writer Johnny 'Crash' Matos compares to a "virus," a metaphor which suggests that this urban practice is highly contagious. Virginia finds out that painting is a communal activity which enhances the crew's sense of community. Female writer 'Lady Bug' Rose (Sandra 'Pink' Fabara) also explains that in addition to being a means for community improvement, painting murals for commercial purposes constitutes a way of earning a living. The interviewees' responses challenge the prevalent assumption of economic stagnation in a marginalized urban area and graffiti as a solely criminal act. Hence, the interview offers the graffiti artists a means of articulating their difficult circumstances and the meaning of graffiti as a means to escape them. Along with Virginia the audience learns about the meaning of the street culture for the local youth.

Yet, the encounter with hip-hop culture does not always run smoothly. When Virginia enters the club with writer Raymond and promoter Phade, she feels uneasy among the African American party crowd who look her over critically. She is seen as an outsider to the rest of the guests because of her appearance which is also underlined in the *mise-en-scène.* The screenshot shows Virginia positioned in the middle of the frame. Two guests look at her from behind at each side of her shoulder.

At first glance, the *mise-en-scène* suggests that she does not fit in with the rest of the party crowd. Virginia wears an elegant tight long grey-green cashmere dress and a pearl necklace which signifies a quite affluent background. Her rather classy and feminine outfit does not match with the casual street fashion worn by many guests, such as Kangol hats, Adidas sneakers, glossy wind breakers, or crew sweatshirts. This initial party scene can be read as a sign of what Pratt identifies as the asymmetrical nature of the contact zone. Clearly, the party is the place where two worlds come in contact with each other in terms of class and ethnicity: The downtown art journalist encounters the uptown African American street culture. The jam creates a contact zone between the Anglo Saxon American and African American culture where an asymmetrical relationship is temporarily acted out.

Eventually, Virginia manages to transcend boundaries, which is at first not easy due to her appearance and class. She starts to feel comfortable and becomes part of the crowd. The music at the club facilitates the contact between Virginia, the other guests and the DJ, Grandmaster Flash, the performers Cold Crush Brothers, and the Rock Steady Crew. Bystanders direct her to the cipher, the circle of dancers and she starts performing rudimentary dance moves under the friendly laughter of the audience in the background of the frame.

Virginia lacks the knowledge of the breakdancers but performs her moves in a clumsy and ironic way while simultaneously being aware of her outsider status. She does not aim at imitating the dance styles of the breakers but finds her own approach. In this sense, she has incorporated the hip-hop philosophy of 'keeping it real,' that is, staying true to oneself.

Her self-reflexive attitude is rewarded with approving joy by the audience, and she becomes part of the community. In contrast to Pratt's idea of the contact zone as an encounter of asymmetrical power relationship, the party creates an intercultural contact zone where class, ethnic, or ideological conflicts are temporarily dismissed in favor of style, flow, and the philosophy of 'keeping it real.' This contact is facilitated through the music and the special jam atmosphere which reinforces a democratic encounter as well as a mutual feeling of togetherness and community.

"Wild Style" suggests that this contact zone between street culture and art world is bound to this specific local place and cannot be transferred to another, less open-minded context. The film features a second party sequence which takes place at Manhattan's wealthy East Side. Virginia aims at promoting graffiti in the downtown art scene and takes the graffiti writer Zoro (Lee George Quinones) and promoter Phade (Frederick Braithwaite) to an art reception. Here, the party crowd is inverted in relation to the party at the Dixie Club: by comparison, the majority of the guests consist of art and media experts while there are only a few members of the street culture. The gathering reveals the ideological conflict between avant-garde and hip-hop culture, a conflict which manifests itself in the framing and attitude towards graffiti and rapping. The screenshot shows that Phade is visually separated from the other party guests, modern art patron Niva (Niva Kieslac) and the museum curator (Glenn O'Brien):

Phade stands in front of a black background whereas the art patrons are standing in front of a grey background. This visual division signifies an ideological difference between the party guests and it is reinforced by Niva's upper body which is moved away from Phade that she can examine him.

Conversations further reveal the ideological conflict between street culture and established art world. The art expert, the museum curator, and the TV producer all display different prejudices towards graffiti. Art dealer Niva, for instance, is attracted by the mysterious writer Zoro and sees an exotic sexual adventure in the Puerto Rican male from the Bronx. The museum curator explains his disapproval of graffiti as an act of vandalism to Phade: "I've probably seen [Zoro's pieces]. We've spent $50,000 last year removing graffiti from the façade of our building." Similarly, Zoro is exposed to prejudice and arrogance from the TV producer (Bill Rice). The tired-eyed producer reminds him of the fact that graffiti is a criminal act while standing in front of a postmodern Frank Stella painting: "Raymond, you cannot paint in the subway stations." He even ridicules rapping when Zoro tries to explain MCing and downright rejects street culture as a form of culture altogether.

"Wild Style" constructs the art party as a failed contact zone between the established art industry and street culture. As do the local authorities and officials, the party guests exoticize, ridicule, or arrogantly neglect street culture and its philosophy, practices, and innovative potential. Neither of them appreciates the innovative character of the urban art form which "is black urban renewal" (Rose 61). Only Virginia exposed herself to the uptown culture and engaged in an intercultural dialogue. Her transcending of class, ethnic, and cultural boundaries further contributes to her characterization as the film's heroine. In this sense, "Wild Style" proposes that the success of the contact zone depends on the curiosity of an open-minded recipient and on an egalitarian context. The street is such a space that provides an inclusive and democratic framework for the intercultural exchange between the different groups. While the street is envisioned as a space that does not have formal boundaries or special entrance rituals which could prevent Virginia from entering, the art party, by contrast, is not easily and openly accessible as the street. The failure of successfully introducing the contact zone downtown is confirmed at the end of the movie when Virginia is back in the Bronx with Phade at the final amphitheater jam.

As a result, the film's global success depends on this particular idea of the contact space. In presenting a tightly-knit network of various local artists and activists of the early hip-hop culture, "Wild Style" constructs a community united against politics, authorities, and the established art world. It provided many teenagers around the world with a detailed audio-visual hip-hop manual and inspired them to start their own hip-hop culture. Long sequences of performances at jams demonstrate how the four elements interact with each other and convey the atmosphere at such gatherings. Close-up shots of Grandmaster Flash DJing in his kitchen, for instance, display the techniques of mixing and scratching. Zoro's nightly train writing session shows spraying techniques while panoramic shots of trains reveal the composition of the overall artwork. Sven Franziko, German producer and former member of the hip-hop formation Fischmob from Hamburg, notes that the film added an important visual dimension to the music that he had already known by showing the interaction between the four elements. He explains that he paused the home video in order to photograph (qtd. in Loh and Verlan 167) or copy the graffiti pieces from the TV screen with paper and pencil. In showing the techniques of DJing, MCing, breaking, and graffiti, "Wild Style" embodies the hip-hop philosophy of 'Each One Teach One.' This idea is based on the assumption that everybody can pass their knowledge on to their peers without the influence of an educational authority. Hence, the on-screen encounters, practices and techniques facilitate an intercultural and intermedial learning process which served and continue to serve as a blue print for the creation of many local hip-hop cultures around the world.

The medial contact zone exemplified in "Wild Style" is separated from its own local historical background and cultural tradition through a global media distribution. "Wild Style" had at first a difficult start in the United States, because the topic was not considered of national importance by the public TV channel PBS (Klage). *The New York Times* reviewed the film with little enthusiasm because it did not meet the established cinematic conventions (Canby). However, it almost immediately jump-started graffiti and breaking in Australia, Japan, and Germany. Australian Cultural Studies scholar Tony Mitchell points out that the release of "Wild Style" triggered a graffiti boom in Australia in the 1980s (39). American media scholar Ian Condry explains that "Wild Style" (along with the later Hollywood production *Beat Street)* generated the breakdance movement in Japan when the film appeared in Tokyo in 1983 (228). The movie was particularly successful in (Western) Germany.

Partly financed by the German public TV channel ZDF (and British Channel 4), it appeared on German TV in April and in movie theaters in November 1983. German music scholar Dietmar Elflein emphasizes that "Wild Style" was the first important impetus for the breakdance and graffiti movements in Germany, because it conveyed the idea that "hip-hop was more than rap music" (256). American scholar Inez Templeton confirms this idea by arguing that *Wild Style* enabled German teenagers to discover the New York street culture connected to the music (194). The film was successful outside the United States because it was detached from the American debates around the inner city as a zone of danger and the street culture as something that would not attract much interest among American viewers.

"Wild Style" as a medial contact zone speaks to different marginalized audiences worldwide. In Germany, for instance, DJ Friction, German producer and former member of the Stuttgart hip-hop collective Freundeskreis, remembers watching the movie on ZDF and being impressed by the tightly knit community it conveys ("DJ Friction"). *Wild Style* inspires teenagers from a middle class background who do not identify with the traditional German value system. At the same time, the independent production speaks to ethnic Germans. The Frankfurt-based MC D-Flame observed that the German Turkish youth identifies with Puerto Ricans whereas Afro Germans identified with African Americans in the film (qtd. in Loh). Through the global distribution system of "Wild Style," teenagers identify with the marginalized and appropriate the asymmetrical power relationship of the filmic contact zone to their own local contexts. The asymmetrical nature of the contact zone is thus reproduced in other contexts with other individuals. In this sense, the medial distribution extends Pratt's notion of the contact zone as a predominantly localized personal encounter. Thus, the medial contact zone, discussed here in the example of "Wild Style," has a much greater impact on its audiences than the personal contact zone described by Pratt. Since its first release in the early 1980s this filmic contact zone triggered a global cultural form.

Conclusion

My analysis of "Wild Style" has shown the manifold encounters and interactions of early hip-hop artists through the character of Virginia who, along with the movie's audience, discovers the street culture. The international reception of "Wild Style" also demonstrates the ways in which global media distribution creates an additional filmic contact zone which inspired global audiences to start their own hip-hop culture in their own local contexts.

As a result, the medial contact zone exemplified in "Wild Style" accelerates the global commodification of hip-hop. Ironically, the film already foreshadows this development. In exposing graffiti to the downtown art scene, Virginia triggers the process of commercialization and commodification of graffiti in a larger context. Since the early 1980s hip-hop has grown into one of the most widely-spread popular forms and evolved into a global multimillion dollar business including music, street wear, and literature. Another result consists of the myth that this on-screen contact space has produced. "Wild Style" presents a romanticized version of a grassroots street culture as a peaceful, non-commercial, and creative urban endeavor. With the enormous commercial success of hip-hop, there is also an increasing global interest in its local origins. People who are familiar with the film visit the birthplaces of hip-hop in New York City, thus, completing the circle of the medial contact zone. Attending "The Birthplace of the Hip-Hop Tours," tourists visit the setting they know from "Wild Style", thus touching ground with a space that shaped their perception of hip-hop. The contact zone which originated in a specific local context, which was filmed and distributed to a global audience, then travels back to its origins in New York City. The medial contact zone is therefore a transnational phenomenon.

Works Cited

"DJ Friction." *Musikbase.de.* 20 September 2010 <http://www.musikbase.de/Bands/D/DJ-Friction/Biographie/>.

Canby, Vincent. "Wild Style, Rapping and Painting Graffiti." *New York Times*. 18 March 1983. 27 August 2010 <http://movies.nytimes.com /movie/ review?res=9C0DE0DA103BF93BA25750C0A965948260>.

Chang, Jeff. *Can't Stop, Won't Stop: A History of the Hip-Hop Generation*. New York: St. Martin's P, 2005.

Condry, Ian. "A History of Japanese Hip-Hop: Street Dance, Club Scene, Pop Market." *Global Noise: Rap and Hip-Hop Outside the USA*. Ed. Tony Mitchell. Middletown, CT: Wesleyan UP, 2001. 222-47.

Elflein, Dietmar. "From Krauts with Attitudes to Turks with Attitudes: Some Aspects of Hip-Hop History in Germany." *Popular Music* 17.3 (October 1998): 255-65.

Forman, Murray. *The 'Hood Comes First: Race, Space and Place in Rap and Hip-Hop.* Middletown, CT: Wesleyan UP, 2002.

Friedrich, Malte. *Urbane Klänge: Popmusik und Imagination der Stadt.* Bielefeld: Transcript, 2010.

George, Nelson. *Hip-Hop America.* New York: Penguin, 2005.

Hoban, Phoebe. *Basquiat: A Quick Killing in Art.* New York: Viking Press, 1998.

Klage, Jan. "Wild Style Regisseur Charles Ahearn." *De:Bug Magazin.* Issue 121 11 May 2008. 20 September 2010 <http://de-bug.de/mag/5564.html>.

Klein, Gabriele and Malte Friedrich. *Is this real? Die Kultur des HipHop.* Frankfurt: Suhrkamp, 2003.

Loh, Hannes. "20 Jahre 'Afrodeutsch' Ein Exkurs über Sprache, HipHop und Verantwortung." *Rock Links.* 20 September 2010 <http://www.rock-links.de/texte/loh/ 20afrodeutsch.html>.

---. and Sascha Verlan. *25 Jahre HipHop in Deutschland.* Höfen: Hannibal, 2006.

Macek, Steve. *Urban Nightmares: The Media, the Right, and the Moral Panic over the City.* Minneapolis and London: U of Minnesota P, 2006.

McFarland, Pancho. "Chicano Hip-Hop as Interethnic Contact Zone." *Aztlan: A Journal of Chicano Studies.* 33.1 (Spring 2008): 173-83.

Mitchell, Tony. "HipHop und die Aborigines: Die moderne Corroboree." *HipHop Meets Academia: Globale Spuren eines lokalen Kulturphänomens.* Eds. Karin Bock, Stefan Meier, Gunter Süß. Bielefeld: Transcript, 2007. 39-56.

Pratt, Mary Louise. "Arts of the Contact Zone." *Conversations in Context. Identity, Knowledge and College Writing.* Eds. Kathryn R. Fitzgerald et al. San Diego: Harcourt Brace, 1998. 74-87.

Rose, Tricia. *Black Noise: Rap Music and Black Culture in Contemporary America.* Middletown, CT: Wesleyan UP, 1994.

Templeton, Inez. "Was ist so Deutsch daran? Kulturelle Identität und die Berliner HipHop-Szene." *HipHop Meets Academia: Globale Spuren eines lokalen Kulturphänomens.* Eds. Karin Bock, Stefan Meier, Gunter Süß. Bielefeld: Transcript, 2007. 185-95.

"Wild Style." Dir. Charlie Ahearn. Rhino Home, [1983] 2002.

Challenges to the Spatial Order: Smashed Windows in "Do the Right Thing" and the Battle of Seattle

Georg Drennig

Georg Drennig compares the smashing of a shop window in Spike Lee's film "Do the Right Thing" (1989) to a photograph of a protester at WTO riots of 1999 entering a Starbuck's through a smashed window. Drennig argues that the ghetto riot is often perceived as localized. The Seattle protest, in turn, often confounded commentators because it took place in a revitalized and commercialized downtown area and because of the predominantly white protesters. In both cases, the glass wall separating private from public and commercial from non-commercial spaces is broken down and establishes a violent contact zone.

When Mookie, the protagonist of Spike Lee's "Do the Right Thing" (1989), throws a garbage can through the window of the pizzeria he works at, a reading of this act suggests itself to be understood as an act of violence against the ghetto's spatial order.[1] The film's economically disenfranchised ghetto characters unleash their anger at Sal's Famous, the white-owned pizzeria that reminds them of their position at the bottom of the spatial and economic order. If Lee's representation of the logic of the ghetto riot proposed an explanatory model of violence against property, then this model faced a major challenge at what came to be called the Battle of Seattle. At the World Trade Organization (WTO) riots of 1999, the battlefield was not the ghetto street but the globalized downtown, and the rioters were not racially marked, but protesters in a seemingly unclear relationship with the windows they smashed.

What is the relationship between the spatial order of North American cities and rioting? This essay will suggest that in the cases of Spike Lee's fictionalized Bedford Stuyvesant and Seattle's downtown, the commercial space becomes a target of violence because it represents larger-scale economic forces that have come to shape the protesters' lives and curtail their

---

1 This is indeed one of the most common readings of the film, as in the essays by Lyne, McKelly, W.J.T. Mitchell, and Hanson.

opportunities for representation. The broken window of the invaded commercial space is thus a manifestation of rioters' attempts to change the extreme asymmetry of power and ability to inscribe their meanings into their everyday spaces. In other words, smashing shop windows can be read as a violent exercise in changing the context of the grappling over meaning that is the contact zone. This logic then applies to both, the fictional representation that is Lee's work, and the media images that abounded after the Battle of Seattle. My essay is interested in the collusion of material and imaginary space that this paper is interested in.[2]

In this context of 'fighting the power,' Spike Lee's "Do the Right Thing" is a Marxist reading of the urban riots of the 1960s, 70s, and 80s, and a prefiguration of the L.A. riots of 1992[3]. As the film follows the young black protagonist Mookie through his day working as a pizza deliveryman for the Italian-American Sal, the issue of spatial representation of African Americans in Brooklyn's Bedford Stuyvesant district plays out in increasingly tense conflicts. In Sal's Famous, Mookie is reminded of his precarious position in the family-run business by Sal's son Pino, whose racist attitudes and testy exchanges with Mookie lose their initial comedic tone as the day wears on. Tensions also build on the streets, shown in several hostile encounters between the film's characters, and the menacing appearance of a police patrol car. After a scene in which several characters hurl racist epithets directly at the camera, the character of DJ Mister Señor Love Daddy, the neighborhood radio's voice and film's occasional Greek chorus, effects a preliminary truce of sorts which will fall apart in the climactic riot.

What is at stake here, however, is not just the human drama of racist prejudice. The oppressing forces that create the potential for violence in "Do the Right Thing" are depicted as structural and inscribed into the

2 After this essay was written, two events took place in which some of the mechanics mentioned in this essay could be analyzed. The riots in English cities in August 2011 provided something of a discursive Rohrschach test, with interpretations spanning the full range of political and social models of explanation for ghetto riots. The Stanley Cup riot on June 15th in Vancouver, in contrast, baffled observers for the exact same reason that the Battle of Seattle elicited such a strong response: It was not on the geographical and social margins of the city, but in its commercial disctrict/downtown that the violence took place. The fact that some of the rioters who were identified came from the upper (white) strata of Vancouver society only served to increase the bafflement.

3 See Davis for an extended discussion of urbanophobic discourses that guided perceptions of ethnicity and violence in urban settings in the nineteen-nineties.

everyday space. Though it is mainly blacks and Puerto Ricans that populate the public sphere of Bed-Stuy, they are excluded from ownership of it, and thus denied the ability to permanently assert meaning within the order they inhabit (Hanson 59). Instead, the structure of the neighborhood is a "stew of economic imperialism" (Lyne 50), in which the inhabitants take the role of colonized subjects (Hanson 47). Thus it is outsiders—but, critically, property owners—like Sal, who can determine the rules of permanent representation, while the inhabitants have to struggle to even fleetingly articulate other meanings such as pride in black achievement, and insert them into the public sphere.

Three characters in particular, Smiley, Radio Raheem, and Buggin' Out, represent this struggle over representation. Smiley, suffering from a stutter and cerebral palsy, strives for visual representation of African Americans by selling photo prints of Martin Luther King and Malcolm X. He has, however, no means to give those images a permanent place, and his speech impediment further denies him the critical "capacity for self-representation" of speaking (Olaniyan 100-101). It is only at the end of the film that Smiley is able to affix one of his pictures in a privileged spot, and therefore insert his meanings into public space in a manner that seems satisfactory to him, if only temporarily.

In contrast to this visual tactic, Radio Raheem's mode of challenging the spatial order is acoustic: carrying a ghetto blaster and continuously playing Public Enemy's *Fight the Power*, he claims the streetscapes as his own by means of "sonorial graffiti" (Forman 65). This tactic seems successful for most of the time, yet its effects are fleeting and still subject to the constraints imposed upon him by his position; he is dependent on buying batteries for his ghetto blaster from Korean store owners, and the ensuing exchange shows that despite his display of self-confidence and aggression, Radio Raheem is unable to set the terms of such encounters. When he enters Sal's Famous, defiantly turning the volume up on his way in, he has to accept his powerlessness in the commercial space. Sal states his terms clearly: If Radio Raheem wants to have pizza, he has to turn the music off, which he eventually does.

Buggin' Out explicitly rejects these spatially and economically determined rules imposed upon him as an African American. After an already testy exchange with Sal, he notices that the pizzeria's 'Wall of Fame' features no images of African Americans. Demanding that Sal add "brothers" to the framed photographs of famous Italian Americans, Buggin' Out refuses to follow the logic of the "liberal bourgeois notion of property rights" (Lyne 49) that Sal articulates—arguably understandably, given his emotional investment in his family business—by saying: "Get your own place, you can do what you want to do." Since Buggin' Out is denied this option, he chooses to reject the discourse of representation through ownership and his "subject status as a consumer" (McKelly 222), and launches a comically unsuccessful boycott of Sal's Famous.

As they refuse to take Buggin' Out's calls not to eat at Sal's seriously, the other customers clearly privilege the personal connection they have forged with Sal and his place over a reading of the structures it represents and the political implications of a boycott. It is, however, also clear that this is an uneasy equilibrium, as the constant tension between Mookie and Pino serves to highlight. Thus, while the primary personal choice of most characters is co-existence as individuals, and not acting out larger political struggles, the narrative sets the stage for a shift into a mode of interaction in which the oppressive structural forces take center stage. When they are finally foregrounded, their destructive potential is unleashed.

This simmering conflict escalates at the end of the day when Radio Raheem, who has joined Buggin' Out in his boycott of the pizzeria, enters Sal's Famous and this time refuses to stop playing Public Enemy's *Fight the Power* at full volume. After an exchange of insults, Sal smashes Radio Raheem's ghetto blaster with a baseball bat, depriving him both of property (Hanson 59) and the key means of representation that he had access to. This sets off a melee between Radio Raheem, Smiley, Buggin' Out, and several patrons on one side, and Sal and his sons on the other. As the fight spills onto the street, the scene turns tragic through the intervention of outside forces. The police, already depicted as a menacing presence earlier, arrive and in trying to subdue Radio Raheem, strangle him to death in a shot that is framed in such a way as to draw explicit parallels to a lynching. In a close up, Radio Raheem's feet are seen lifted above the ground, twitching, before not moving anymore. Shocked silence follows the police's departure with the arrested Buggin' Out and the dead body of Radio Raheem, and Sal and his sons face the neighborhood's inhabitants. In a scene that "would result in the spillage of gallons of critical ink across hundreds of newspapers, magazines, and academic journals" (Lyne 48), Mookie then picks up a garbage can and throws it through the window of Sal's Famous, initiating the looting and burning-down of his place of work.

In the context of my essay, the significance of this act lies in reading the broken window of the pizzeria as a space in which Mookie renegotiates the terms of encounter and meaning-making in the contact zone. This is not to deny the rage over the killing of Radio Raheem as Mookie's and everybody else's immediate motivation, succinctly phrased by Mookie when he talks to Sal the following day: "Motherfuckin' window. Radio Raheem is dead!" Still, Mookie's attack was not against a random target or the police but "a public symbol ... the plate-glass window that marks the boundary between public and private property, the street and the commercial interest" (W.J.T. Mitchell 896). The breaking of this boundary opens up a contact zone; whereas the intact window sets a clear marker of ownership and privileged meaning making, breaking that window provides a rejection of such privilege, albeit one that offers little in the way of a fixed meaning by itself.

The nevertheless radically changed potential for meaning-making is soon used by Smiley, who enters the looted and burned-out pizzeria to the—for the first time non-diegetic—sounds of *Fight the Power* and puts a photograph of Martin Luther King and Malcolm X on the scorched Wall of Fame. Though his success is still bound to be temporary, Smiley has achieved in the violently and tragically reshaped commercial sphere what he had strived for on the street. With the window and protective borders of Sal's Famous broken, the asymmetrical terms of grappling over representation have been altered in favor of Bed Stuy's inhabitants, who briefly succeeded in challenging the spatial order that has excluded them from permanent means of inscribing their meanings in the public sphere (W.J.T. Mitchell 894).

In a reading that focuses on the underlying structural causes of the riot, it is striking to see how familiar—in all senses of the word—the attacked business is to those who then loot it. The rioters, many of whom repeatedly voice their appreciation of Sal's pizza prior to the violence, are Sal's customers. Though the pizzeria represents the economic order that shuts them out as active and equal participants, the film's characters had accepted their status as consumers on whose support the order relies, or at least privileged the human relationship and its immediacy over the large-scale forces at work. They then reject this positioning by destroying Sal's Famous as a representation of oppressive and exclusive macro-scale settings, since no other such representative space or agent is at hand. Lee even shows the logical extension of this logic of destruction by having the protesters proceed to the Korean corner store across the street, but then uses artistic license to spare that business the fate of Sal's Famous by making the rioters accept the storeowner's problematic claim that he, too, is basically black (Hanson 60-61).

Both businesses, the one destroyed and the one left intact, are the immediate representation of a larger order that has a direct bearing on the space in which the inhabitants of Bedford Stuyvesant live their daily lives and struggle for representation. Their violent reaction and fight for the possibility of inscribing new and different meanings then takes place in this same environment, never leaving the colonized space; within the New York City of "Do the Right Thing," fighting the power is a local affair that can be written off as "just another ghetto riot." This was not the case, however, in the media and academic landscape that reacted to the film by spilling "gallons of critical ink," as Lyne has noted (48). When Spike Lee as Mookie throws the garbage can, Lee the director has furnished him with a background and a motivation. As the hegemonic interpretive template of ghetto violence relied on (black) anonymity and senselessness in its description of events, any other treatment was bound to be received either as a challenge or as opening up new meanings.

At a first glance, the anti-WTO protests of 1999, which would become known as the Battle of Seattle, could hardly be a more different case of rioting. They defied the explanatory model of ghetto violence and did not offer images of easily-categorized and neatly-defined ethnic or social groups taking their protest to the streets; even the question of what exactly had happened was, and still is, a matter of debate. If we take 1990s Downtown Seattle as an example of a global economic and spatial order that curtails the possibilities of representation in the public sphere, parallels to Lee's film emerge. The often-printed image of a protester smashing and entering through a window of a Starbucks franchise thus offers a reading along similar lines: the shattered glass as a contact zone in which the asymmetry in the relationship of power between meaning makers is challenged and temporarily shifted. This is not meant to justify through theorization the violence that took place, or to deny the upsides of the economic revitalization that changed many U.S. downtowns in the 1990s, but to offer a framework for analyzing the collusion of imaginary, abstract, and material spaces that can be found in the broken window.

Since the logic of the ghetto riot, and thus the entire notion of urban unrest in North America, relied on ethnicity as a factor, it was the pronounced absence of non-whites at the Battle of Seattle—around five percent of protesters (Martinez 143)—that confused commentators. So did the social background of the protesters, from union members to white-collar workers. Journalist Rick Moody's personal experience provides some glimpse of the socioeconomic diversity of those who protested or through their mere presence swelled the numbers of people on the streets, as he related how his "daughter Caitlin's high school AP Government class had been preparing for weeks for the convention and demonstrations as a kind of live-history-as-it-happens class project" (2). Equally instructive is an article from *Time* magazine in the way that it struggles to make sense of events and provide labels for participants in the protests and riots:

> Things got serious when scattered groups of self-described Black Block anarchists, wearing all-black outfits with handkerchiefs or hoods covering their faces, started to smash windows ... Peaceful protesters, horror-struck, shouted, "Shame! Shame!" at the rioters. Once word got out that the streets were haywire, however, a wave of garden-variety thugs headed downtown ... (Lacayo 2)

Making the distinction between "peaceful protesters" and "vandals—wearing black and calling themselves anarchists" (Hunter), may have helped media commentators, and has set the interpretative scheme for future WTO protests ever since; I would argue, however, that the difference in means of protest is, for the specific purpose of this analysis, secondary to the spatial dimension of events.

As images of rioters smashing windows and looting stores had been inextricably linked to ethnic violence, such scenes had been considered unlikely in the quality-of-life capital of 1990s America. Thus the visuals of the WTO riots were especially jarring, as Moody's account makes clear: "[S]eeing in the mist the ghostly silhouettes of protestors and gas-masked police, I thought I was looking at a weird experimental overlay: a 1960s Detroit riot against a 1990s Seattle background" (Moody 2). Clearly, older iconic representations of such events had set a template for interpreting them that was bound to fail when rioting occurred in the "Emerald City." The confusion over what exactly happened was thus exacerbated by an inability to reconcile events with their physical setting, so that marching unions and anarchist activists were caught just as unprepared as Seattle's mayor Schell, leading to attempts at containment from all sides:

> Anarchist websites subsequently complained that their boys in black were blamed for the apolitical looting by the later group that ruined their well-planned attack ... [The mayor] slapped a dusk-to-dawn curfew on the city's downtown and imposed a 50-square-block no-protest order on downtown, which left demonstrators furious. (Lacayo 1-2)

At the end of that first day of unrest, a downtown that had symbolized the rise of the post-Fordist metropolis[4], had been scene to events that bore several key features of the logic of ghetto riots, including "excessive use of force" by the police (Hunter), and the type of smashed window this paper is interested in: "I walked past a looted Starbucks, its windows shattered, the machinery and crockery and display cases on its counters destroyed, and much of the store's merchandise, furniture, and equipment tossed out in the street" (Moody 3).

4 See Lyons for a comprehensive cultural analysis and Moody for a more personal chronicling, of the changing (self) representation of Seattle in the course of the nineteen-eighties and nineties.

One of the arguably most iconic images to emerge from the Battle of Seattle is an Associated Press photograph showing a scene alluded to previously: a rioter stepping through the smashed window frame of a Starbucks franchise. This is a case of the "experimental overlay" at work: A scene uncannily familiar from depictions of ethnic rioting, yet in a setting that does not correspond to the expectations set up by the interpretive template that North American culture had provided. Mookie in "Do the Right Thing" ultimately stays within a cultural logic that, though very critically examined by Spike Lee, is in itself coherent. The rioter in Seattle, who even used the exact same way of breaking the window—the garbage can is still visible in the background—caused confusion exactly because of the jarring contrast between the familiar and the unexpected. Broken storefront windows are a part of the iconography of urban rioting. Yet it seems as if nothing had prepared observers for the fact that it was a Starbucks café in a revitalized downtown that was targeted, with the rioter not being clearly identifiable as black.

Though the stores of "companies such as the Gap and Nike that have been accused of using low-wage or child labor to produce some of their merchandise" (Lacayo 2) had been equally target of violence against property, the looting of the Starbucks franchise received privileged media coverage, a "choice … over and above a number of other damaged downtown retail outlets in Seattle [that] suggested something more" (Lyons 162). The identity and geographical background of the individual who picked up a garbage can and threw it through the window may be unclear; the man's dress—beige slacks, down jacket, and nondescript shoulder bag—seems rather innocuous, though clearly not part of ethnically-marked fashion, or, if anything, white middle class. Additionally, the setting that is depicted in the photograph—the ultimate non-ghetto urban location—the downtown Starbucks looted in the picture, had been seen to be immune from exactly this kind of violence. Originally a business that emerged in Seattle, the chain's coffee shops were deeply familiar sites for Seattleites, providing a space for urban society to watch its own performance of a leisure lifestyle in a revitalized urban setting (Lyons 149). As in "Do the Right Thing," the attacked businesses were clearly part of the protesters' everyday space.

The transformation that Seattle underwent over the 1980s and 1990s has been much commented on. With economic and demographic change, however, came a restructuring of commercial space that was not unanimously seen as positive:

> Downtown Seattle had spent the 1990s undergoing a depressing renaissance. By 1999, it sported arguably the spiffiest, newest, most fashion-forward and prosperous major urban retail core in the country. National chains moved here in droves, the past few years having seen Barney's New York, FAO Schwarz, Banana Republic, Nike, Sega Gameworks, Planet Hollywood, Restoration Hardware, Tiffany's, and other upscale merchants set up shop, muscling out locally owned businesses. (Moody 9)

Not only did this restructuring visibly establish a stronger presence of the national and global economic order over the local, but it also privileged consumption over other ways of being in the public sphere that could then be negatively framed as loitering (Lyons 91, 147). Representing an order set apart from the local, and reducing those present in it to the role of consumers, downtown Seattle had turned into an Augéan non-place that confronted its inhabitants with their inability to participate in permanent meaning making in it.

The choice of Seattle's globally-inscribed downtown as the site for the WTO talks then served to highlight how globalization reorders everyday space. Yet it also allowed protesters to use the city streets to draw attention to their cause and to give a spatial dimension to their opposition against the modus operandi of global trade. By attacking the physical manifestation of abstract concepts—both the national economic order represented by chain stores and the infrastructure used by the WTO itself—rioters engaged in a process that was a mirror image of what had happened to Seattle's downtown in the 1990s. If, during the conference, the city's streets would be read as "the thoroughfares along which illegitimate global traffic would be enabled" (Herbert 607), then blocking these avenues was an example of the local space impacting the larger spatial order. Global processes thus triggered the reassertion of local public space (Kellner 296).

In the reemergence of a public space that became stage for the expression of a multitude of meanings instead of a non-space dedicated to consumption, the challenge the WTO and Seattle authorities were faced with went far beyond inconvenienced or accidentally tear-gassed conference delegates and destroyed businesses. Controlling their public spaces and the meanings inscribed in them is part of governments' "territorial imperative, or imaginative scripting of space" (Katharyne Mitchell 289), an imperative that was threatened by the disorder and potential for representation that the protests returned to the streets. As the city reacted by denying access to large parts of downtown to anybody "not necessary to the normal functioning of the area" (Herbert 602), it rejected all notions of public space as fundamentally democratic and necessarily unpredictable (Don Mitchell 130). Instead, the spatial order of consumption was by implication declared to be the norm, a norm rejected by rioters who smashed the commodified spaces of leisure that the large windows of Starbucks had provided (Lyons 159).

Global trade and its injustices brought the anti-WTO protesters onto the streets, yet once there, the rioters targeted the material everyday spaces into which this economic order was inscribed. James Lyons' analysis of the rise of Starbucks and the iconic images of, and media response to, its looting in 1999, poignantly expresses the relationship between the transformation of public space as a non-place dedicated to consumption, and the violent reaction against everything this change represented: "If Starbucks profited from inviting customers to 'eat the street,' then events in Seattle witnessed the streets bite back" (163). Ultimately, the violence on the streets of Seattle succeeded in inscribing new meanings in the post-Fordist urban landscape. Though reactions to the events differed, working as what Washington Post writer Anne Swardson titled "A Rohrschach Test on Trade," the Battle of Seattle resulted in a reassertion of the public space as the site of oppositional representations, and as a contact zone in which the grappling over meaning could not be ignored by the powers that be (Lacayo 4).

Implicit features of the ghetto riot—the fight against exclusion from permanent representation in the public space, and the order that brings about this exclusion, are often overshadowed by simple explanatory models of race and poverty in public discourse. In a way, the logic of destruction at the WTO riots of 1999 made the underlying spatial dynamic of the ghetto riot explicit by forcing the struggle over representation into public debate, yet not giving recourse to explanations through ethnicity. It also provided visuals that challenged observers, thus inserting ambiguity into the debate, and forcing a reexamination of the logic of urban riots as represented through culture. The riot, read spatially, voices a challenge to the economic order by attacking its material manifestation and violently altering the semi-permeable border between commercial and public sphere. Though the trigger of the rioting is a specific act of violence in Lee's "Do the Right Thing" while the Battle of Seattle brought together a multitude of motivations and modes of protest, both cases show a rejection of the status protesters find themselves reduced to. Lacking the means to inscribe lasting meaning in a space that is less and less public and increasingly encroached upon by structures above the local, rioters not only reassert the disorderliness of, and multiplicity of meanings in, truly public space, but also challenge its borders.

Yet the smashed window is more than a forced entry into a representative space. Sal's Famous and the Starbucks franchise in Seattle are deeply familiar sites for the rioters and looters. As much as these businesses are inscribed by a larger national or global order, they are also part of the local everyday space; the traces and repercussions of any attack on them thus will be present in the same public space rioters tried to claim as theirs for representation. In the temporarily empty window frame, the collusion of local, national, and global spaces is therefore visible as an order that can hardly be broken. Only the many shards of glass that lie on the ground may reflect the multitude of meanings that had been made possible and widely visible, albeit only for a limited time. "Do the Right Thing" ends on a note that allows for conciliation; the Battle of Seattle has changed the dynamics of WTO talks that followed it. At the end of this essay, perhaps an optimistic outlook is thus possible: physical damage can be repaired, and though the presence of the global economic order in everyday spaces cannot be erased, the temporary change of power symmetry in the contact zone of the broken window may allow for the lasting emergence of previously underrepresented meanings. Or, in the words of "Do the Right Thing's" voice of reason DJ Mister Señor Love Daddy: "Are we gonna live together? Together are we gonna live." Spaces that facilitate a multiplicity of representations might just work towards that goal.

Works Cited

Davis, Mike. *Dead Cities*. New York: The New Press, 2002.

Forman, Murray. "'Represent': Race, Space, and Place in Rap Music." *Popular Music* 19.1 (2000): 65-90.

Hanson, Philip. "The Politics of Inner City Identity in *Do the Right Thing*." *South Central Review* 20.2/4 (2003): 47-66.

Herbert, Steve. "The 'Battle of Seattle' Revisited: or, Seven Views of a Protest-Zoning State." *Political Geography* 26 (2007): 601-19.

Hunter, Jennifer. "WTO Seattle Riots." *MacLean's*, 13 Dec. 1999. N.pag. Quoted in *The Canadian Encyclopedia*. 2010. Historica Dominion. 17 Dec. 2010. <http://www.thecanadianencyclopedia.com/index.cfm?PgNm=TCE&Params=M1ARTM0012058>.

Kellner, Douglas. "Theorizing Globalization." *Sociological Theory* 20.3 (2002): 285-305.

Lacayo, Richard, et al. "Rage Against the Machine." *TIME.com*. Dec. 13, 1999.Time Inc. Jan. 7, 2011. <http://www.time.com/time/magazine/article/0,9171,992808,00.html>.

Lyne, William. "No Accident: From Black Power to Black Box Office." *African American Review* 34.1 (2000): 39-60.

Lyons, James. *Selling Seattle: Representing Contemporary Urban America*. London: Wallflower, 2004.

Martinez, Elizabeth. "Where Was the Color in Seattle? Looking for Reasons Why the Great Battle Was so White." *Monthly Review* 52.3 (2000): 141-48.

McKelly, James C. "The Double Truth, Ruth: *Do the Right Thing* and the Culture of Ambiguity." *African American Review* 32.3 (1998): 215-27.

Mitchell, Don. *The Right to the City: Social Justice ad the Fight for Public Space.* New York: Guilford, 2007.

Mitchell, Katharyne. "Ungoverned Space: Global Security and the Geopolitics of Broken Windows." *Political Geography* 29 (2010):289-97.

Mitchell, W.J.T. "The Violence of Public Art: *Do the Right Thing*." *Critical Inquiry* 16.4 (1990): 880-99.

Moody, Fred. *Seattle and the Demons of Ambition: A Love Story*. New York: St. Martin's P, 2003.

Olaniyan, Tejumola. "'Uplift the Race!': 'Coming to America,' 'Do the Right Thing,' and the Poetics and Politics of 'Othering.'" *Cultural Critique* 34 (1996): 91-113.

Swardson, Anne. "A Rohrschach Test on Trade; Nation's Diverse Goals Color Reactions to Protests." *Washington Post*3 Dec. 1999. A32+.

Makeshift Heterotopia(s): Tent Cities in North America

Kathy-Ann Tan

> The question of homelessness is [...] necessarily always also a question about public space—of who the public is, of who may inhabit public space, and of how such space will be constituted and controlled. - Samira Kawash, "The Homeless Body"

In the light of the "spatial turn" that has infiltrated and influenced the realms of American literary and cultural studies[1], this essay proposes a revisiting of Foucault's concept of heterotopia with regard to sites of social heteronomy in North America. Specifically, it will examine the phenomenon of modern-day heterotopias in the form of tent cities, ranging from organized communities to provisional encampments for the homeless. As makeshift heterotopias that find their global counterparts in the slums of India, the *favelas* of Brazil, and the rooftop housing of Hong Kong, tent cities across the United States and Canada represent a (wake-up) call to scrutinize the ways in which the globalizing processes of late capitalism have impacted on local spaces of American culture.

My point of departure for a reading of tent cities as contemporary sites of heterotopia lies in Foucault's examination of the relationships between structures of power, knowledge, and space. The introduction to this present collection of essays already charts out some of the widely-used concepts that have acquired currency in contemporary debates on contact spaces, but I wish to briefly recall the oft-cited passage from Foucault's "Of Other Spaces," which sets out the definition of "heterotopia" explored within the scope of this essay:

---

1 For a good overview of this paradigm shift, see, for example, Spatial Turn. Das Raumparadigma in den Kultur- und Sozialwissenschaften (2008), eds. Döring and Thielmann, Raumtheorie. Grundlagentexte aus Philosophie und Kulturwissenschaften (2006), eds. Dünne and Günzel and The Spatial Turn: Interdisciplinary Perspectives (2008), eds. Arias and Warf.

> There are also, probably in every culture, in every civilization, real places—places that do exist and that are formed in the very founding of society—which are something like *counter-sites*, a kind of effectively enacted utopia *in which the real sites, all the other real sites that can be found within the culture, are simultaneously represented, contested, and inverted. Places of this kind are outside of all places, even though it may be possible to indicate their location in reality.* Because these places are absolutely different from all the sites that they reflect and speak about, I shall call them, *by way of contrast to utopias, heterotopias*. (24, my italics)

While tent cities are clearly not "effectively enacted utopia[s]", they might still be regarded as sites of heterotopia in the light of the above definition: They are located, more often than not, in the penumbra of large cities, in liminal spaces (unused plots of public land with low visibility to the public and away from residential developments) on the fringes of society, and they are "other spaces", counter-sites that are an "inver[sion]" of the "real" sites of permanent housing. More specifically, it can be argued that tent cities conflate two of the several types of heterotopia that Foucault distinguishes: "heterotopias of crisis" ("places reserved for individuals who are, in relation to society and to the human environment in which they live, in a state of crisis") and "heterotopias of deviation" ("those in which individuals whose behavior is deviant in relation to the required mean or norm are placed") (Foucault 25). The subjection of tent cities to municipal legislation that effectively criminalizes homelessness on public property, hence making eviction at short notice a real threat, also renders them as transient and makeshift heterotopias.

If, however, tent cities are makeshift heterotopias, how does their ever-increasing presence in the U.S.A. and Canada impact on prevailing discourses by which dominant spaces operate? Do they really "represent, contest and invert" the (written and unwritten) social codes of public spaces, or are they rather unfortunate manifestations of socio-economic exclusion and the failure of housing and welfare policies? This essay seeks to address these questions, and, in so doing, is divided into three sections. The first examines the upsurge of media attention to tent cities in the last few years and argues that this has come at a timely juncture to potentially undo the public's dominant perceptions and stereotypes of tent cities and their residents as dangerous and criminal usurpers of public space, and thereby challenge the "official" logic by which public spaces operate.[2] Ultimately, however, I argue that media coverage tends to fall back on two underlying modes of reportage that do not proffer a "neutral" or unbiased way of engaging with the issues of homelessness and urban poverty. The second section of this essay turns to look at several projects and creative interventions by socially-conscious artists who have similarly sought to challenge public attitudes toward the homeless and the destitute. Like tent cities and portable shelters, these artworks disrupt the hegemonic norms by which dominant social spaces operate when they are performed as site-specific, street-level interventions; they, too, become contestation[s] of the spaces in which we live. As highly conceptual pieces of art and powerful social statements, they challenge the prevalent exclusionary attitudes of the public with regard to homelessness. Finally, the third section of this essay examines some of the statistical reports published on tent cities in the Pacific Rim. Using case studies of four tent cities—Dignity Village in Portland, as well as Seattle's Nickelsville, Tent City 3, and Tent City 4 –, this section explores the disparate attitudes of the tent city residents themselves, as well as their different living conditions.

Following theories in the fields of sociology and political geography that posit space as a socially-constructed entity,[3] this essay concludes with the contention that, as modern-day sites of heterotopia, tent cities across North America are counter-sites that throw a spanner in the works of, and thereby challenge, the neo-liberal discourses of economic progress by which dominant spaces operate. However, at the same time, their dependency on the sanction of the governing political system keeps them tied to a socially imbalanced relationship. It is this disproportion that cre-

2 In her essay "The Homeless Body," Samira Kawash's claims that "[c]ontrary to expectations raised by recently developed understandings of the power of representation, positive representations of the homeless and increasing public visibility have had little impact on the widespread tendency to see the homeless as dangerous usurpers of public space" (335).

3 I am referring here to Henri Lefebvre's influential book *The Production of Space* (1974; 1991), as well as Edward Soja's seminal study, *Postmodern Geographies: The Reassertion of Space in Critical Social Theory* (1989), which initiated his long-standing championing of a reinsertion of spatial interpretations into critical social theory, as well as *Thirdspace: Journeys to Los Angeles and Other Real and Imagined Spaces* (1996). Soja's most recent book, *Seeking Spatial Justice* (2010), turns his inquiry to the idea that "justice [...] has a *consequential geography*" (1), and aims to "stimulate new ways of thinking about and acting to change the unjust geographies in which we live" (5).

ates the "contact zones" between tent cities and their immediate surroundings, making them "social spaces where cultures meet, clash, and grapple with each other, often in contexts of highly asymmetrical relations of power" (Pratt 33).

Media Coverage of Tent Cities

The recent wave of media attention showered upon tent cities in the United States was largely initiated by Lisa Ling's special report for the Oprah Winfrey Show in March 2009, where she visited the tent city in Sacramento now known as Safe Ground (formerly American River Tent City).[4] This report was swiftly followed by the publication of journalist Justin Sullivan's photo essay which juxtaposed images of the same tent city in Sacramento with those of "Hoovervilles" during the Great Depression that occupied almost the very identical location on the banks of the American River.[5]

These and the many other reports that followed in their wake came perhaps as a timely response to a polarization of attitudes in the American public imagination about tent cities and homelessness, although it is of course questionable to what extent the media played a role in disseminating these prevailing opinions in the first place. On the one hand, there is the tendency to romanticize life in tent cities as a chosen lifestyle, a Tho-

4 According to *The Golden Door* website, Dignity Village's internet presence, the Safe Ground tent city in Sacramento was disbanded in the fall of 2009, after an agreement to move its residents to motels. On November 6, 2009, the mayor of Sacramento, Kevin Johnson, launched the "Sacramento Steps Forward" initiative, with a three-year plan to establish and fully fund 2,400 housing units for homeless people.

5 The political reverberations that tent cities across the UNITED STATES have caused has invited their comparison, as Sullivan's photo essay illustrates, with the "Hoovervilles" (named after Herbert Hoover, President of the United States at the time, who was blamed for the problems that led to the depression) or shantytowns erected during the Great Depression in the 1930s. It must be said, however, that the "Hoovervilles" did not disappear overnight; indeed, tent cities continued to remain on America's landscape long after the end of the Great Depression and America's official entry into World War II. The surge in recent media coverage of homelessness in the current economic crisis has, therefore, simply given tent cities renewed attention.

reauvian returning to nature in order to find one's roots.[6] On the other, there is the widespread depiction of tent cities as dystopian slums and shantytowns rife with alcohol and drug addictions, prostitution, violence and mental illness—they have been called the "ground zeroes" for robbery, prostitution and intravenous drug abuse.[7] The former dominant perception of tent cities, which foregrounds the sense of community, Christian charity and goodwill, has been attacked by those who are critical of the way tent cities have become seats for the spread of religion under the guise of benevolence and generosity. Tom Armstrong, or "Homeless Tom," a former inhabitant of the Safe Ground tent city featured in the Oprah Winfrey Show, comments on his blog that

> [t]he reason Sacramento was in the news for so long for such a small thing as its tent city is because too many had a stake in maintaining the illusion. The greatest share of the blame and shame belongs to the organization Loaves & Fishes [a Sacramento-based religious charitable organization]. (Sacramento Homeless Blog)

Armstrong's skepticism regarding the philanthropic activities of Loaves & Fishes reflects his more deep-seated cynicism about the way in which local governments have not been doing enough to solve the problem of urban poverty; he suggests that "[t]hey use homeless people as puppets for their own [...] dangerous political games" (ibid.). Addressing what he perceives to be the real problem—that of chronic unemployment—he

6 These depictions, admittedly, have themselves been fuelled by first-hand accounts of some tent city residents, who see living in an encampment as a self-chosen, alternative form of community lifestyle. Sheila Shortell, for example, writes in an article titled "Friday Night in Dignity Village" on April 10, 2001, "Why not allow some people the freedom to live as they choose, as long as they are not disrupting the lives of people who believe in the conventions of owning private land and living as nuclear families? Dignity Village is a kind of tribe."

7 See "The Road to Tent City," an article posted on the "Save Feral Human Habitat" website by John Green, a social(ist) worker, on May 6, 2009. Defending such slanderous accusations of tent cities, "Dignity Village," the model alternative community and former tent city in Portland, Oregon, states the following in its "Tent City Toolkit" resource on the Internet: Most homeless people do not become criminals or drug or alcohol users. On the streets, integrity, dignity, privacy, and respect for one another are highly valued. People without this strength of character don't hit the streets--they commit suicide. Period. The fact of the matter is homeless people are the constant and unprotected victims of crime. Drug dealers, sexual predators, thieves, and violent people prey on homeless people day in and day out.

writes, "[b]eing unemployed is daunting and damning, and is ever more-so disheartening the longer you are daunted and damned! The spiraling downward road to homelessness grows wider and slippier [sic.], and homelessness, itself, more achingly difficult to escape" (ibid.). Armstrong's "Sacramento's Homeless Blog" is, notably, an important resource for Sacramento's homeless population—at least, for those who have access to the Internet. Posts with cold weather alerts, information on warming centers, as well as the dates and times of community breakfasts and dinners are updated on his site on an almost daily basis.

In a similar vein, Shaughnessy Bishop-Stall, a Canadian journalist, writes in the introductory chapter of *Down to This: Squalor and Splendour in a Big-City Shantytown*, his account of voluntarily spending a year in a tent city on the outskirts of Toronto:

> Tent City is not a city and we don't live in tents. We live in shacks and shanties on the edge of Canada's largest metropolis where the river meets the lake. There's a fence dividing these 27 acres from the rest of Toronto, and on this side we've built what dwellings we can with the rubble of a scrapyard, a no-man's landfill caught in confusion between the city and private business. Sometimes it seems like a community and sometimes like chaos. Junk Town would be a better name. ... The singularity of this place has drawn media attention from all over the world, as well as a flood of well-meaning, but mostly redundant, donations—if only salvation could be bought with wool hats and toothbrushes. This remains, as much as such as thing is possible, a society of anarchy. (1-2)

Bishop-Stall's portrayal clearly seeks to demystify "romanticized" depictions of living in a tent city and to reveal the idiosyncrasies, contradictions, and disorder at the heart of its establishment. It also reflects his dissatisfaction with the way in which the surge in media attention has done little to actually alleviate the problems of homelessness. Interestingly, however, in its use of the phrases "shacks and shanties," "Junk Town" and "a society of anarchy," Bishop-Stall's narrative also veers toward the other widespread depiction of tent cities as slums rife with alcoholism, drug abuse, and violence.

Such polarized viewpoints of tent cities perhaps unintentionally reflect and reinscribe the prevalent moods of fatalism and fear in the first decade of the 21st century. Interestingly, in its attempts to dispel stereotypical notions of life in tent city encampments, media coverage itself has been underwritten by two prevailing "aesthetic" modes of commentary: one that privileges first-hand accounts, letting the residents "speak for themselves," emphasizing the humanistic aspects of life in a tent city, and the other, that glosses over these subjective narratives in favor of more "objective" cultural anthropological and sociological modes of analyses which critique the failure of neo-liberal economic policies, as well as the problems of ecologically unsustainable urbanization in the West. This raises the question of whether tent cities can actually be represented or discussed in a "neutral" discourse that neither patronizes its residents, nor glosses over their plight in more far-reaching attempts to pursue agendas of economic and socio-political reform on a macro level.

Justin Sullivan's previously-mentioned photo essay and the accompanying long entry recounting his visit to Safe Ground on his blog, *At Home and On the Road: Stories and Observations from a Working Photojournalist*, exemplify the former mode of media commentary that relies on the first-hand, "authentic" descriptions and stories of tent city residents. The narrative of Sullivan's photo essay and his blog post reveal the humanistic nature of the community, their sense of unfailing humor in the face of hardship (for example, they unofficially name the tent city "the wasteland"). As Sullivan writes, "[t]he community was very tight knit. People really looked out for each other, especially the elderly. Almost every person I met said the same thing, 'we're just trying to survive.'"

The series of photographs that Sullivan took at Safe Ground[8] construct a narrative that champions humanity in the face of adversity. Optimism prevails over despair, and even though the residents are disillusioned by governmental policies that keep affordable housing and sustainable employment out of their reach, the atmosphere of enduring patriotism is noticeable—American flags are displayed prominently on makeshift poles outside the tents, and one iconic picture even captures a man sitting on a rock in front of his tent wearing an American flag jacket. Snapshots of happiness and moments of compassion prevail—a resident plays frisbee with his dog, while another puppy is captured trying to lick the last few drops of water out of a water dispenser. There is a photograph of Safe Ground advocate Tracie Bailey, decked in hippy gear and braids, praying for the well-being of the Safe Ground inhabitants. The emotional valence of these moments as captured by Sullivan's photographs is not lost on the

8 The location of this particular tent city is particularly ironic, as Sacramento was the centre of the Californian gold rush (1848–1859), and hopeful prospectors had pitched their own tents along the same banks of the American River.

viewer, yet the question remains if their depiction of hope, dignity and a sense of community and goodwill that will prevail over despondency and hardship reflects the "reality" of living in tent cities across North America, or if it glosses over the poor living conditions of tent city inhabitants who continue to experience economic disenfranchisement.

Refuge, Shelter, and Community: Artistic Interventions

Sullivan's photo-essay, which exemplifies the nature of recent media coverage of tent cities, reflects popular culture's as well as art's increasing preoccupation with what Lilian Tone has termed "the poetics of mobility and the aesthetics of the transient." In her article "Placeless Place," Tone makes reference to recent artworks such as Los Carpinteros' *Ciudad Transportable* (Transportable City) and Do-Ho Suh's replicas of his home in diaphanous fabric that have "addressed the transitory nature of what we understand as home by literally recreating and re-contextualizing such domestic spaces in different public spheres" (4-5).

A good example of visual art fuelled by social activism, Lucy Orta's works are a direct engagement with the role of the media in processes of subject- and identity formation and the relationships between individuals and their material environments. As she explains,

> [t]o be homeless in a media culture such as ours is therefore to be rendered invisible, to melt literally into the margins and framework of the city. [...] I began staging Refuge Wear [...] 'interventions' from 1993 onwards, in order to challenge this act of social disappearance, to render the invisible visible once more. (Orta qtd. in Budney and Blackwell, 55)

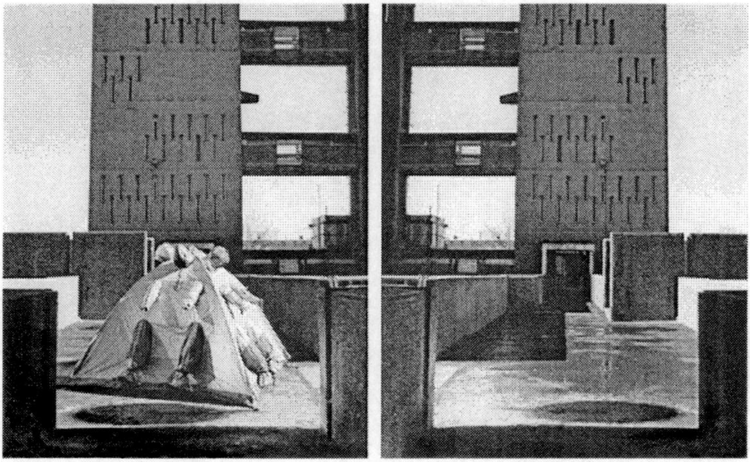

© 2011 by Lucy+Jorge Orta. Refuge Wear Intervention London East End 1998. Original Lambda color photograph, laminated (ed 7). Diptych 150x240cm. Photograph credit: John Akehurst. Courtesy of Collection of the Artists.

As a response to media coverage of "squats, railway stations, housing projects and subways" (ibid.) in the 1990s, as well as to the appeal of Kurdish refugees for protective clothing and shelter toward the end of the Gulf War, Orta designed her series *Refuge Wear* and *Body Architecture* (1993–1996) which feature portable architecture in the form of temporary shelters, canvas tents, mobile "survival sacs" (collapsible bodysuits made of microporous polyester) and cocoons that can be folded up and used as backpacks. These are the results of her attempts to explore the basic notions of shelter, refuge, and community in a material fashion that involves an interaction between the body and the protective fabrics that clothe it. The bodysuits in her *Refuge Wear* and *Modular Architecture* series feature a meticulous attention to detail—micro-porous ripstops coated with a polymide, aluminum coated surfaces to reflect the sun's heat, detachable baby carriers—as well as experimentation with different forms of shelter including the tent, cabin, dome, igloo and teepee.

© 2011 by Lucy+Jorge Orta. Refuge Wear Intervention London East End 1998. Original Lambda color photograph, laminated (ed 7). 150x 120cm. Photograph credit: John Akehurst. Courtesy of Collection of the Artists.

The "survival sacs" and "mobile cocoons" in the *Refuge Wear* series were thus specifically designed with the homeless person in mind, who is forced to carry her/his personal belongings with her/him because s/he has no permanent housing—extra features include visible and hidden pockets might hold food, water and papers. One of the pieces in the series, a bright blue sleeping bag, contains the following inscription:

> Living without shelter for prolonged periods rapidly deteriorates physical and moral health. The lack of adequate sleep increases stress, weakens the immune system and accelerates the loss of identity and desocialisation. (www.studio-orta.com)

In their adaptation of what Brazilian artists in the 1960s termed an "aesthetics of precariousness,"[9] Lucy Orta's *Refuge Wear* series serves as a point of departure for thinking about the ways in which art can critically engage with, and intervene in, processes of social exclusion. Her artworks call to mind other examples of site-specific installations that attempt to challenge the public's perception of homelessness. These include U.K.-based artist Rebecca Kevill's resin casts of coins that feature a homeless person's face instead of the Queen's head, and New York-based Drew Martin's self-portrait sculpture of a sleeping homeless man dressed in an old suit and worn black leather shoes, covered by a white blanket with only his legs and feet sticking out, that resulted in calls to the police when it was exhibited on the pavement in front of his house.[10] Notwithstanding the fact that these works are highly conceptual pieces of art, as site-specific interventions that contest the public's perceptions of homelessness, they act as powerful critiques of the political and economic power structures that have led to the problems of urban poverty, overcrowding, and homelessness in North America.

A Grim Dignity? Case Studies of Tent Cities Along the Pacific Coast

The extent to which global late capitalism has impacted on local spaces of American culture becomes evident from studies and reports that contain statistical data on homeless encampments in the United States. These recent studies are indicative of a partial reversion to a facts and figures-based methodology that reflects a certain weariness with the analytical approach of a wave of seminal articles in the 1980s that sought to examine the dominant social constructions and representations of home-

9 Regina Vater defines the "aesthetics of precariousness" as "a procedure of art invention [in the 1960s] using nonconventional materials that drew inspiration from popular Brazilian creative expression, with an attempt to achieve significance and a feeling of wealth using materials affordable to their precarious economy." (Farris 1999, 229). The "aesthetics of precariousness" has not gone un-critiqued. Taisa Helena P. Palhares, for example, describes it as a "'creative' mimicry of the highly uninspiring situation of generalized poverty that surrounds us." (ibid.)

10 Martin explains in an interview, "[t]he old clothes on my homeless man were basically trash. The homeless in New York are treated like trash. The homeless sculpture was about personifying trash and making it personal to me."

lessness—most notably, Mark J. Stern's "The Emergence of Homelessness as a Public Problem" (1984)[11] and Peter Marin's counterargument, "Helping and Hating the Homeless" (1987)[12]—though, in my opinion, these were important studies that reflected the socio-political climate of that decade, and paved the way for further sociological studies on urban poverty and approaches to its alleviation.

Tent Cities in America: A Pacific Coast Report, released by The National Coalition for the Homeless in March 2010, was the first in a series of publications designed to document the emergence and daily operational processes of eleven tent cities on the upper West Coast of the United States. The report documents its three-fold aim of "understanding the diversity and conditions under which tent cities are created, comparing various levels of community acceptance, regulation, and governance, and advocating safe, legal, and effective methods and practices of encampment" (9). It includes a disclaimer that future publications in the series will include "a section on policy recommendations for local, regional and national policy and decision makers" (ibid.). Of the eleven encampments documented, only six are approved by their respective cities and subject to their ordinances, three are not sanctioned, and two are zoned for camping. The largest communes are Safe Ground in Sacramento and New Jack City & Little Tijuana in Fresno, with 150-200 inhabitants each, and the smallest is the River Haven Community in Ventura with 21 occupants at the time of publication. The names of four of the eleven encampments—

11 As Mark Stern postulates, "[r]ather than getting to the 'facts' about the homeless, I want to ask how the 'homeless' have been conceptualized in the public's mind and what this tells us, not about the homeless, but about ourselves, our officials and our society. Thus, rather than holding the homeless under the microscope of public and professional enquiry, I want to use the homeless as a means of looking at ourselves" (291).

12 Kim Hopper and Jim Baumohl's article "Held in Abeyance: Rethinking Homelessness and Advocacy" offers a reading of both Stern's and Marin's essays, and suggests a reframing of the homelessness debate within the larger Marxist theory of "*surplus populations*" and the institutions and public policies that are pressed to accommodate them. Hopper and Baumohl also argue that homeless shelters often unintentionally illustrate what Mizruchi termed the "abeyance process", the "practice of shunting off unneeded but potentially troublesome people into various forms of substitute livelihood, thereby neutralizing the threat they might otherwise pose" (524). Moreover, they point out, shelters not only contain and accommodate the homeless, but—like the armories in NYC in 1919 and the 1930s that housed the homeless—they also intimidate them, and "in this capacity they recapitulate a long-standing social function of containment" (542).

Dignity Village in Portland, Safe Ground in Sacramento, The Village of Hope and the Community of Hope in Fresno, and River Haven Community in Ventura—illustrate the importance of the preservation of dignity and integrity and community spirit in the face of hard times. It is also significant that three of these four above-mentioned communes have permanent wooden structures, while the other communities use tents as their primary means of shelter.

The mission statements of the eleven tent cities in the *Pacific Coast Report* were similar in the sense that they all placed importance on giving a homeless person the privacy and dignity of their own residence (a tent) and stressed that they were accountable for their own community. The *Report* ends, however, with the following statement:

> The National Coalition for the Homeless believes that now is the time that we, as a country, must embark on a final campaign to Bring America Home and end homelessness once and for all; through a coordinated and comprehensive national response that addresses the housing, income, healthcare, civil rights, and causal factors and consequences of extreme poverty. (67)

The emphasis here is that the root cause of homelessness and vagrancy—the "causal factors of extreme poverty"—can only be solved if there is a "coordinated and comprehensive" nationwide effort to address, acknowledge, and act on the issue. Effectively, this approach entails shifting responsibility from the level of the individual to that of the collective ("we, as a country"), which should ensure a minimum standard of living and affordable housing across the nation. This viewpoint—that homelessness is a nationwide and not an isolated or state-specific problem—is held by bodies such as the NAEH (National Alliance to End Homelessness) and NCH (National Coalition for the Homeless), and reflects a structuralist approach to homelessness whereby policies that create more permanent, long-term affordable housing are viewed as the only effective measure against the problem. This structuralist method, which recognizes that social and economic factors are the underlying causes of homelessness, stands in contrast to the individualist approach in public policy that perceives of homelessness as caused by individual, though involuntary, problems such as social exclusion, mental illness, poor physical health, alcohol and drug abuse (Christensen and Levinson, 598-599). Most homeless assistance organizations now adopt the position that both individual and structuralist factors need to be taken into consideration in order to end long-term homelessness.

Media coverage of the eleven tent cities covered in the *Pacific Coast Report* has, indeed, been intensive, especially via electronic forms of publication. The appendix of the *Report* includes a long list of these various websites, articles, and online blogs. Media attention has especially been showered upon Dignity Village, a tent city established in 2000 and officially recognized in 2001 in Portland, Oregon, has also received its fair share of coverage. According to the mission statement taken off its website, the aim of Dignity Village is to "create a safe, sanitary, self-governed place to live as an alternative ... to the over-burdened shelter system where there are about 600 beds for about 3,500 homeless people, sleeping alone in doorways and under bridges, or in the jails where the homeless are housed for urinating in public, jaywalking, [and] camping" (www.dignityvillage.org/ helping.html). To this purpose, Dignity Village declares itself a "formerly mobile tent city in Portland, Oregon, well on its way to becoming a green, sustainable, urban village" (the 10' x 10' housing structures are even made of recycled materials). With the aim of providing a safe haven for homeless people, Dignity Village also operates under a strict set of five main behavioral rules that include: no violence toward oneself or others; no theft; no illegal substances or alcohol or paraphernalia on the premises or within a one-block radius; no disruptive behavior that disturbs the general peace and welfare of the village; and ten hours of community service per week. Interestingly, in its assessment of Dignity Village, the *Pacific Coast Report* concludes that

> [u]nlike other homeless encampments that are sponsored by local governments or outside non-profits, Dignity Village's model of complete self-governance and funding gives the homeless a unique sense of autonomy and ownership of their community. Having a permanent site ... furthers this sense of ownership and allows the homeless to make both tangible physical and social improvements to their community in a way that is not possible in a mobile community.

The emphasis in the passage above is the idea of permanence instead of temporality or a makeshift quality. As a permanence housing site as opposed to a mobile community, Dignity Village engenders a sense of autonomous ownership in its residents that, in turn, causes them to take pride in their efforts to ensure the community's well-being. The widespread attitude among residents of Dignity Village is that their model offers a viable alternative to the overburdened shelter system in Portland, as well as an ethically responsible and even aesthetically fulfilling lifestyle—their website, for example, also features writings, poems, drawings and songs by the residents and their friends.

Dignity Village also runs a sister website called *The Golden Door* (an obvious reference to last two lines of the sonnet "The New Colossus" by Emma Lazarus, "Send these, the homeless, tempest-tost to me,/ I lift my lamp beside the golden door.")[13] Defining itself as "a grassroots effort to rally Americans to pursue dignity and freedom in U.S. policies to end homelessness," *The Golden Door* takes up the trope of the entranceway to liberty and freedom from oppression in America, stating, "If the US is truly to be a 'golden door' of opportunity, we must guarantee all our citizens basic rights to sleep, dignity, health, and a chance to work hard and provide for their families." *The Golden Door* website also states: "Dignity Village is an extraordinary example of what a group of citizens can accomplish together when they have democracy and freedom to pursue their dreams." The use of the terms "citizen," "democracy," and "freedom" in this statement reflects an emphasis on the constitutional rights and civil liberties that are the birthright of every American national. It also reflects recognition of the importance of self-esteem, dignity, and personhood in relation to the longer-term goal of putting an end to the criminalizing of poverty.

The Golden Door website also features the release of an interactive DVD titled "The Tent Cities Toolkit: a Multimedia Grassroots Primer," a collaborative partnership between Dignity Village and Kwamba Productions that uses Dignity Village as a case study. The Toolkit "aims to raise awareness of the nationwide lack of housing and criminalization of the poor, and to provide a practical set of resources for creating a tent city or alternative housing in communities nationwide."[14] While it does not make any claims toward an eradication of the problem of homelessness, it focuses on the role of grassroots tent city advocacy efforts and is a mobilization call to engender "a cohesive political force for effective social change" (ibid.). Offering "practical hands-on information on the creation

13 These lines are also engraved onto a bronze plague and on display in the Statue of Liberty museum exhibit.

14 Synopsis taken off Film Baby, an independent film website: http://www.filmbaby.com/films/1959, where the DVD is also available for purchase.

of tent city communities," the Tent Cities Toolkit DVD represents an original effort by the inhabitants of Dignity Village to reclaim a sense of agency and to initiate change.

The Tent Cities Toolkit DVD also includes a 41-paged document "'Dignity Village 2001 & Beyond: Outlining Strategies for a Sustainable Future," wherein the residents and supporters of Dignity Village tackle codes of residence and zoning issues, propose a system of self-governance, address the importance of resource management and outline the tent city's development budget. Other resources include a summary of the tent city's bylaws, put together by the Village Council (a.k.a. Board of Directors); a document delineating the judicial process and disciplinary action taken against residents who do not follow the Village's bylaws; an admittance agreement that has to be signed by each new resident of the tent city; as well as carefully-documented protocols with the Portland Police Bureau regarding communications and public safety issues.

The video clips on the Dignity Village DVD feature short interview clips with various residents of the tent city. Significantly, all their responses unanimously convey the idea that they subscribe to a sense of community, belonging, and home. The question "What is Dignity Village to you?" was met almost unanimously with the replies "hope," "love," and "respect". Only one resident replied, "a battle—there is always room for change." Perhaps it comes as no surprise then, that Dignity Village is no longer classified as a tent city today. As a "success story," it has become a role model for government officials and advocates with tent city settlements in their own municipalities. The Village even has its own official website, a MySpace site, Youtube presence, and a Facebook page. It is important to point out, however, that Dignity Village is an exceptional case-in-point. As the *Pacific Coast Report* points out, the success of Dignity Village stands in contrast to many settlements across the nation (17).

Dignity Village's main thoroughfare. Photo courtesy of Joshua Seaman.

An American flag in the window, Dignity Village. Photo courtesy of Joshua Seaman.

Indeed, the situation is very different in tent cities in the Seattle area. Despite being the headquarters of seven companies (Microsoft, Starbucks, Amazon.com, etc.) on the 2010 *Fortune 500* list of the United States' largest companies based on total revenue, Seattle has a large homeless population who reside in shelters and three tent cities—Nickelsville,[15] Tent City 3 (TC3), and Tent City 4 (TC4). Positioning themselves at a tangent to the humanist attitudes and the sense of community spirit, hope, love and respect that, for example, the Dignity Village residents convey, the inhabitants of Nickelsville demand acknowledgement by the public that life in a tent city is a fraught experience. Challenging the use of euphemisms in the wave of recent media coverage, wherein tent cities are commonly referred to as "temporary housing programs," "transitional shelters," and "city-recognized encampments," and whereby the homeless are referred to as "residentially challenged," the Nickelsville residents convey the harsh realities of living in a tent city in the publication of an open-letter titled "Declaration of a State of Emergency in 2010 by and for Homeless People in Seattle & King County" on their website:

> We are unwelcome in your public spaces, and are harassed by your police and private security when we stop to rest. …
>
> We are the working poor who have been set up to fail. …
>
> We are the expendable, the dehumanized, the written off, and the devalued. We are the sick, the disabled, the mentally ill, and the addicted. We are the too poor, too uneducated, too old, and too unemployable to matter. We are the human wreckage of a broken system that denies its responsibility and blames us for our existence.
>
> IT SHOULDN'T BE LIKE THIS. …
>
> OUR STATE OF EMERGENCY MUST BE RECOGNIZED. The Ten Year Plan to End Homelessness is a fraud. The true causes of homelessness—rent increases, gentrification, evictions, and the failure of the market to provide affordable housing—aren't dealt with, measured, or touched. For every unit of affordable housing produced under the plan, three to four have been lost to market forces. (www.nickelsvilleseattle.org/)

15 Residents dubbed the tent city "Nickelsville," in an allusion to the "Hoovervilles" of the 1930s, as a response to Seattle Mayor Greg Nickels sustained efforts to clamp down on homelessness on public property and clear out homeless encampments.

The anaphoric form of these lines, along with their vitriolic tone and subject matter recalls the opening lines of Allen Ginsberg's "Howl"—"I saw the best minds of my generation destroyed by madness, starving hysterical naked" (126). The inhabitants of Nickelsville, however, are not Ginsberg's Beatniks or "angelheaded hipsters", but "the expendable, the dehumanized, the written off, and the devalued", "the sick, the disabled, the mentally ill, and the addicted", "the too poor, too uneducated, too old, and too unemployable to matter". Shattering what they perceive as the veneer of humanist goodwill and humanitarian efforts, the residents of Nickelsville unapologetically decry the local government's "tokenization" of the participation of the homeless, telling them they should "stop pretending" that their plans are effectively resulting in adequate shelter and safety. The message is clear: "Stop the criminalization [of homelessness]. We need housing. Now."[16]

Nickelsville in Seattle, with American flag. Photo courtesy of Indy Fuller.

16 On December 21, 2010, the residents of Nickelsville held a joint press conference with SHARE/ WHEEL as well as with Real Change, the Homeless Empowerment Project based in Seattle that takes the form of "a newspaper, an advocacy group, a Homeless Speakers Bureau, and literary workshops" (http://www.realchangenews.org/index.php/site/about/org/). The residents of Nickelsville released a Homeless Manifesto at this press conference.

In the absence of long-term solutions that get to the root of the problem of urban poverty, short-term solutions are put into place, such as the "Ten-Minute Plan to End Homelessness" initiated by the Citizens Commission for Ending Homelessness in Portland, Oregon, to provide shelter in the winter months for everyone living on the streets. Such short-term plans are well-intentioned, yet they nevertheless fall short in terms of creating sustainable housing solutions for the homeless in the longer run, and ultimately do not get to the bottom of deeply-rooted structural problems in financial and urban planning.[17] At Tent City 4 on the East Side of Lake Washington in King County, the sister community of Tent City 3, for example, residents are issued conditional use permits by the local government to stay on each host site for a short period of ninety days. Despite the efforts of the organizations sponsoring Tent City 4 since its establishment in May 2004—the Seattle Housing and Resources Effort (SHARE) and Women's Housing Equality and Enhancement League (WHEEL)—the tent city has met with considerable resistance by local residents who have expressed concerns over issues of safety and health, a move that expresses a proprietary claim on the control of public space in the name of public security.

17 Juxtaposed to the "Ten-Minute Plan to End Homelessness" is the "Ten-*Year* Plan to End Homelessness in Portland and Multnomah County" published by the Citizens Commission on Homelessness in December 2004 which calls for the more effective usage of resources in working toward the provision of long-term affordable housing. The plan states, "To move from the institutionalization of homelessness, the institutions that serve homelessness must change. Rather than shuffling homeless people from service to service and back to the street, the aim of all government agencies, nonprofits, and institutions in the homeless system must be to first get homeless people into permanent housing" (3).

Tent City 3 in Seattle with the Space Needle in the background. Photo courtesy of Marc Weinberg.

Tent City 3 in the snow, a U.S. Flag and a "Welcome Home" sign. Photo courtesy of Marc Weinberg.

The prevailing of such public attitudes to tent cities and their residents can be attributed, in no small part, to the grim nationwide statistics in this current period of economic crisis. According to the *U.S. Foreclosure Market Report* published by *RealtyTrac*, a major online marketplace for foreclosure properties, California has one of the highest rates of bank repossession, Notice of Default (NOD) and Notice of Trustee Sale (NTS) nationwide. Similarly, *RT*—the Russian 24/7 English-language news channel—reports an unemployment rate of 9.5% in the United States, and cites the U.S. Census Bureau's 2010 statistic that over 40 million Americans—or one in seven—are living in poverty.[18] Homeless shelters are packed every night, with demand exceeding supply, and government policies are not alleviating the problem. On February 13, 2009, for example, U.S. Congress passed the American Recovery and Reinvestment Act which included $1.5 billion for homelessness prevention and re-housing.[19] The spending package for 2010 included $4.2 billion in funds targeted for affordable housing and homelessness. According to the fiscal report for 2010 released by the U.S. Department of Housing and Urban Development,[20] the latter had requested $1.794 billion for Homeless Assistance Grants, an increase of $117 million over the fiscal year 2009 appropriated level. Despite these measures, however, homelessness and urban poverty continue to be a major problem in cities across the United States.

Conclusion

As modern-day amalgamations of Foucault's "heterotopias of crisis" and "heterotopias of deviation," tent cities across North America are, on the one hand, counter-sites that challenge the hegemonic norms by which dominant social spaces operate, yet, on the other, they are simultaneously testament to, and a result of, acts of economic and social exclusion that separate them from the public domain by their very nature of being "other" spaces. The latter ultimately undermines tent cities' challenges to, and re-negotiation of, the prevailing logics and functions inscribed onto public spaces, or renders these contestations temporary at best.

In his somewhat bleak yet acute study, *Planet of Slums*, urban theorist Mike Davis addresses the widespread global problem of urban poverty and homelessness. He blames the "neoliberal restructuring of Third World urban economies that has occurred since the late 1970s" (147) for

18 The report, published 17 September 2010, can be found here: http://rt.com/news/americans-poor-tent-city/.

19 http://www.recovery.gov/About/Pages/The_Act.aspx.

20 The report can be downloaded here: http://portal.hud.gov/portal/page/portal/HUD/program_offices/cfo/reports/cforept.

the current proliferation of *gecekondus*, *favelas*, and *chawls* around the world. In seeking to provide a deeper examination of tent cities and their reflection of urban poverty in North America as caused by economic exclusion, this essay has focused on tent cities in a North American context wherein the social dimensions of homelessness have a particular historical resonance, given the deep-seatedness of ideas of property and (land) ownership in an American, but also Canadian, context.[21] This is conveyed, for example, in the fifth Amendment to the U.S. Constitution which stipulates that "no person shall be [...] deprived of life, liberty, or property, without due process of law", and John Adams' statement that "[p]roperty is surely a right of mankind, as really as liberty" ("A Dissertation on the Canon and Feudal Law", 1765).

In a North American context, therefore, homelessness refers not simply to a lack of a psychological sense of home and belonging, but concretely to a lack of property ownership or tenable rights over property. Residents of tent cities have little or no claims on the urban public spaces they occupy, spaces that are inscribed with and operated according to a logic of maximum efficiency in a late capitalist framework. Recent depictions of tent cities in the media, literature and art have played a crucial role in reversing the act of social disappearance, restoring a certain amount of visibility to a section of society—the urban poor—who have to stay out of sight and keep on the move. This coverage therefore potentially challenges prevalent perceptions of homelessness in the social imagination, and renegotiates the "official" functions of public space. The danger, however, as elaborated in this essay, is that such attempts could also unintentionally disseminate and reinforce stereotypical notions of the urban poor, and therefore dangerously lead to the institutionalization of homelessness[22] in North America. With the globalizing processes of late capitalism coming full circle to impact on local spaces of American culture, the need to de-criminalize homelessness and support long-term af-

21 It is a commonly-held view, for example, that, among other reasons, it was a series of property disputes that led to both the American Revolution and the Constitutional Convention itself (see, for example, Rick Lynch's article, "Property Rights, Freedom, and the Constitution").

22 Erving Goffman's critique of the institutionalization of people with mental health problems in asylums is also relevant here in so far as "[t]he self . . . is not a property of the person to whom it is attributed, but dwells rather in the pattern of social control that is exerted in the person by himself and those around him" (168).

fordable housing in the United States and Canada are pressing needs that need to be addressed, now more than ever.

Works Cited

Arias, Santa and Barney Warf, eds. *The Spatial Turn: Interdisciplinary Perspectives*. London and New York: Routledge, 2008.

"America's Poor and Impoverished Turn to the Forest." 17 Sept. 2010. *RT*. 01 Dec. 2010. <http://rt.com/news/americans-poor-tent-city/>.

Armstrong, Tom. *Sacramento Homeless Blog*. 09 Dec. 2010. <http://sacramentohomeless.blogspot.com>.

Christensen, Karen and David Levinson. "Homelessness". *Encyclopedia of Community: From the Village to the Virtual World. Vol. 1*. Thousand Oaks: Sage Publications, 2003. 596-600.

Davis, Mike. *Planet of Slums*. New York: Verso, 2006.

"Declaration of a State of Emergency in 2010 by and for Homeless People in Seattle & King County." *Www*. 11 Nov. 2010. <http://www.nickelsvilleseattle.org/>.

Dignity Village official website. <http://www.dignityvillage.org/>.

Döring, Jörg and Tristan Thielmann, eds. *Spatial Turn. Das Raumparadigma in den Kultur- und Sozialwissenschaften*. Bielefeld: Transcript Verlag, 2008.

Dünne, Jörg, Stephan Günzel, et al., eds. *Raumtheorie: Grundlagentexte aus Philosophie und Kulturwissenschaften.* Frankfurt am Main: Suhrkamp Verlag, 2006.

Foucault, Michel. "Of Other Spaces." *Diacritics* 16 (1986): 22-27.

Ginsberg, Allen. "Howl". *Collected Poems 1947-1985*. New York: Penguin Books, 1987; 1995. 126-133.

Goffman, Erving. *Asylums*. New York: Anchor, 1961.

Green, John. "The Road to Tent City". *Save Feral Human Habitat*. 6 May 2009. 09 Dec. 2010. <http://bullsheet.wordpress.com/2009/05/06/the-road-to-tent-city/>.

"Foreclosure Activity Hits Record High in Third Quarter". *Foreclosure Real Estate Listings RealtyTrac*. 15 Oct. 2009. 15 Nov. 2010. <http://www.realtytrac.com/foreclosure/foreclosure-rates.html>.

Home Again: A Ten-Year Plan to End Homelessness in Portland and Multnomah County. Rep. Portland/Multnomah County Coordinating Committee to End Homelessness (CCEH), March 2010. 9 Dec. 2010.

Hopper, Kim and Jim Baumohl. "Held in Abeyance: Rethinking Homelessness and Advocacy". *American Behavioral Scientist* 37.4 (February 1994): 522-52.

Kawash, Samira. "The Homeless Body". *Public Culture* 10 (1998): 319-39.

Lazarus, Emma. "The New Colossus". *Selected Poems*. Ed. John Hollander. New York: Library of America, 2005. 58.

Lefebvre, Henri, *The Production of Space*. Trans. Donald Nicholson-Smith. Oxford and Malden, MA: Blackwell, 1991.

Ling, Lisa. *Tent Cities in America: A Lisa Ling Special Report*. Rep. 25 Feb. 2009. 30 Oct. 2010. <http://www.oprah.com/showinfo/Tent-Cities-in-America-A-Lisa-Ling-Special-Report>.

Lynch, Rick. "Property Rights, Freedom, and the Constitution". *Freedom Daily*. Nov. 2008. <http://www.fff.org/freedom/fd0811e.asp>.

Marin, Peter. "Helping and Hating the Homeless". *Harper's*. Jan. 1987. 39-49. <https://www.msu.edu/~jdowell/135/PMarin.html>.

Martin, Drew. "Homeless Art: Can You Spare Some Change?" *The Museum of Peripheral Art*. 13 Mar. 2010. 09 Dec. 2010. <http://museumofperipheralart.blogspot.com/2010/03/homelessart.html>.

Nickelsville. Official website. < http://www.nickelsvilleseattle.org/>.

Orta, Lucy. "Lecture: November 25, 2002". *Unboxed: Engagements in Social Space*. Eds. Jen Budney and Adrian Blackwell. Ottawa: Gallerie 101, 2005. 52-65.

---. Official website. <http://www.studio-orta.com>.

Pratt, Mary Louise. "Arts of the Contact Zone". *Profession* 91 (1991): 33-40.

Sacramento Homeless Blog. <http://sacramentohomeless.blogspot.com>.

Shortell, Sheila. "Friday Night in Dignity Village". *Dignity Village*. 10 Apr. 2001. 9 Dec. 2010. <http://www.dignityvillage.org/poems/sheila.html>.

Soja, Edward. *Postmodern Geographies: the Reassertion of Space in Critical Social Theory*. New York: Verso, 1989.

---. *Thirdspace: Journeys to Los Angeles and Other Real-and-imagined Places*. Oxford and Malden, MA: Blackwell, 1996.

---. *Seeking Spatial Justice*. Minneapolis: University of Minnesota Press, 2010.

Stern, Mark J. "The Emergence of the Homeless as a Public Problem". *The Social Service Review*. 58.2 (June 1984): 291-301.

Sullivan, Justin. *From Boom Time to Tent City*. MSNBC: Picture Stories, Mar. 2009. <http://www.msnbc.msn.com/id/29528182/displaymode/1107/s/2/>.

---. "Just Trying to Survive". Web log post. *At Home and on the Road: Stories and Observations from a Working Photojournalist*. 6 Mar. 2009. 09 Dec. 2010. <http://sullyfoto.blogspot.com/2009/03/just-trying-to-survive.html>.

Tent Cities in America: A Pacific Coast Report. Rep. Washington DC: National Coalition for the Homeless, 2010. 30 Oct. 2010. <http://nationalhomeless.org/publications/tent_cities_pr.html>.

The Golden Door. 11 Nov. 2009. 09 Dec. 2010. <http://www.tentcitiestoolkit.org/index.html>.

"The Recovery Act". *Recovery.gov - Track the Money*. 09 Dec. 2010. <http://www.recovery.gov/About/Pages/The_Act.aspx>.

Tone, Lilian. "Placeless Place". *Los Carpinteros*. 09 Dec. 2010. <http://www.loscarpinteros.net/index/placeless-place/>.

Vater, Regina. "Artist Statement". *Women Artists of Color: A Bio-Critical Sourcebook to 20th Century Artists in the Americas*. Ed. Phoebe Farris. Westport, CT: Greenwood Press, 1999. 229.

Networlds: Localizing Silicon Valley

Eugen Banauch, Astrid M. Fellner, and Susanne Hamscha

Contact within the mediated internet space is the main theme of Eugen Banauch, Astrid M. Fellner, and Susanne Hamscha's contribution. Drawing on Mizuko Ito's concept of "network localities," their essay reads the imaginary relations on Social Network Sites (SNSs) such as Facebook as evidence of a new concept of locality which is not bound to a specific location but to the affiliations among the network users. By geographically locating the phenomenon of SNSs in California's Silicon Valley, they highlight the American-ness of SNSs on the one hand but insist that this American-ness takes on a new form through the global reach of these SNSs.

Introduction: Network Localities

"We lived on farms, then we lived in cities, and now we're going to live on the internet!" This is how internet technology businessman and entrepreneur Sean Parker (Justin Timberlake) painted the future to Facebook founder Mark Zuckerberg in *The Social Network* (2010). And indeed, not even a decade after Parker and Zuckerberg started to collaborate, global networks form an important part of our work and social life, and we are challenged to understand the scope and implications of the powerful transformations that global connectivity entails. Since the founding of Social Network Sites (SNSs) such as Facebook and YouTube, we have witnessed the tremendous rise and overwhelming global popularity of social interaction on the internet.[1] SNSs are "web-based services" that allow registered users "to (1) construct a public or semi-public profile within a bounded system, (2) articulate a list of other users with whom they share a connection, and (3) view and traverse their

---

1 Google purchased the internet video sharing platform YouTube on October 11, 2006 when it was still an unprofitable start-up enterprise. This is sometimes seen as a watershed moment towards the general realization that web 2.0 is 'here to stay.' 26 September 2010 <http://www.msnbc.msn.com/id/15196982/>

list of connections and those made by others within the system" (Boyd and Ellison). Hundreds of millions of users worldwide have embedded those services into the daily routines of their practices of social interaction.

Social network sites have also attracted the attention of academic researchers who have explored the impact of communication media and the Internet on connectivity between people. Scholars from various fields have examined SNSs and the fascination and engagement of users with social network sites in order to understand the practices and meanings of the services they provide (Haythornthwaite 2005, Boyd and Ellison 2007, and Vie 2007). In this paper, we want to take a look at the kinds of spaces global networking creates, analyzing the ways in which these networks allow users to form connections and linkages. As technology becomes a social space, it is interesting to explore how human interactions in networlds and on networks bear an imaginary quality and foster the formation of imagined communities. In order to understand localized affiliations that are made possible by new media networks such as SNSs, the Japanese cultural anthropologist Mizuko Ito has suggested the term "network localities," which she uses "as a way of describing local places and identifications constructed upon media infrastructures" ("Network Localities" 2).[2] These localities constitute affiliations and affective encounters that are grounded in concrete geographical places, practices, and material relations.

In this essay we want to investigate in which ways network localities are structured by imaginary relations that are connected to notions of "American-ness." In attempting to localize the multiple affiliations that are enabled by new media networks, we want to envision SNSs as localities that constitute imaginary relations that, in turn, challenge a bounded notion of locality. Our argument is twofold: First, we claim that although SNSs constitute affiliations that are not geographically localized, they engage the signifier "America." The way we see it, SNSs construct a new sense of "America," an "America" that is not necessarily tied to the geographic place but rather to one that forms itself at the intersection of reinscription and displacement. Secondly, we will use the example of Facebook as our case study for a network localization that promotes forms of affiliations that span geography, producing "new forms of trans-

2 The authors have asked Mizuko Ito to grant permission to use the quotes used in the article. (Mail to Eugen Banauch from December 8, 2010)

geographic localization" (ibid.). We make our argument by theorizing one specific network locality—Silicon Valley—a place and non-place, which constitutes a technologically mediated social place that fosters imaginary communities.

2) Locating Silicon Valley

Culture and social relations are disseminated across space and are structured by translocal forces that create what Arjun Appadurai has called "global cultural flows" (33). Due to the development of communication technologies of the last 150 years, human encounter is no longer place-dependent. In fact, as Linda M. Harasim states, it is common practice now to use the term face-to-face (2-3) in order to distinguish real-place meetings from those held on telephones or global networks (5). As we rethink dynamics of identity and place, the question arises under which theoretical paradigm we can analyze the connections and affiliations formed in these networked relationships. Should SNSs be envisioned as locales of hybridity and transculturation, intersections of (cultural) flows, as a boundary-less system of sharing, a ludic give and take? Do they provide the perfect tool for proffering enhanced agency for the individual—as suggested by *Time* magazine three years ago, when the editors decided to declare "YOU" *Time*'s person of the year 2006?[3] Or should they rather be envisioned as a tool of acculturation, a one-sided cultural ex/change, an instance in which globalization works in a reductive manner? Do they lead to what Linda Stone famously named a "continuous partial attention"[4] for those who participate in this expanding online social community and locale, without being ever fully there, functioning "[a]s a node on a network, […] continually projecting our own status, scanning the surface and alighting briefly for short intervals of time" (5). Do they, and we in them, function as sites that permanently broadcast our continuously processual identity projects—and formations? In talking about these theoretical challenges posed by networked places

3 That way, *Time* celebrated the unprecedented rise of pro-active media and internet technology generally labeled as web 2.0 in the year 2006.

4 Stone uses this term to describe a mode of paying superficial attention to numerous things at the same time, characteristic for much of today's cyber culture and differentiates this mode from the notion of multitasking. For an ongoing discussion of the concept, see her blog: <http://lindastone.net/> 16 October 2010.

and localities, we suggest that we heed Ito's advice and also "ground the seemingly unrestrained currents and minglings of media flows" ("Network Localities" 3). In particular, we want to focus on one network locality, Silicon Valley, which is not a geographical place but rather a nickname given to the San Francisco peninsula around Stanford University. The rise of networking technologies, one could say, is primarily rooted in this particular place, or non-place. The term Silicon Valley was coined in 1971 by Ralph Vaerst, a Central California entrepreneur, in order to refer to the "congeries of electronics firms mushrooming in Santa Clara county" (Gromov). As the leading hub for high-tech innovation and development, Silicon Valley is also the home of Facebook. As such, Silicon Valley serves as a metaphor for the space that Facebook creates.

Although, strictly speaking, Silicon Valley does not refer to a particular geographic locale, it can also not really be referred to as a non-place as Marc Augé understands it. Rather, it can be seen as a network locality that provides a geographic referent to an imagined place of localized affiliation enabled by networks. According to Augé, "places" are encrusted with history and social life, while he sees "non-places" as spaces of transition (not location) that have no history or social life. Highways, airports, airplanes, shopping malls constitute such non-places. They are in-between places that embody the paradox of neither "here" nor "there." As he states: "If a place can be defined as relational, historical and concerned with identity, then a space which cannot be defined as relational, or historical, or concerned with identity will be a nonplace" (63). If we follow Augé's definitions, then Silicon Valley is an intermediate between a place and a non-place. It is not a space of specific location but rather a space one can take along wherever one goes: one can access one's social networking profile from virtually any computer in the world, turning SNSs into spaces that are always "here" and never "there." SNSs constitute something like a "portable social life" and, as such, they are by definition relational and concerned with identity and fulfill Augé's criteria for a "place." Locations like Silicon Valley, we believe, necessitate a reconfiguration of Augé's binary model, which includes virtual space as an ungraspable space of transition that, nevertheless, creates individual and collective identities.

Cultural and local identities are formed in different realms where art, politics, and mass culture intertwine. In current reflections on the ways in which relations between people, places, and cultures are expanding, the buzzwords of transnationalism and translocal cultures often evoke the term "globalization," which, in turn, has often been used interchangeably with the term "Americanization" (Ritzer and Stillman). Ito identifies the emergence of SNSs (such as Friendster, Myspace, and Facebook) as a "second wave of youth adoption of networked media [...] centered on the *US social media space* rather than mobile communications" ("Media Literacy" 6, our italics). Mass culture is the site where Americanization becomes explicitly visible. Siliconization as a specific form of Americanization—the global impact of high tech business and network technologies—can be recognized as a dynamic cultural process, negating cultural binaries of high/low and producer/receiver, and leading both to cultural homogenization among different national states, as well as foregrounding different ways of cultural appropriation. As a site of complex cultural exchanges, Siliconization suggests itself as a particularly productive concept in which the increasing importance of "affect," associated with mass culture in general and new media in particular, can be seen in relation to national and transnational identity formations.

As Ito argues, the Internet is an imagined globality that works as an imagined community in similar fashion as Benedict Anderson has described the concept of nation as an imagined community. Ito states:

> Like standardized print technologies enabling identification at the scale of the nation-state, discourses of globality are a product of two separate processes: the compression of distance through technological implementation, and the production of an imagination that posits a difference in the scale of identification. Technologies like the Internet enable one to imagine global interconnection without realizing it in practice. ("Network Localities" 6)

Silicon Valley commonly signifies the proliferation of technology and capitalism, while its association with Bill Gates, Steve Jobs, and more recently, Mark Zuckerberg evokes stories of the American Dream turned reality. In this sense, Silicon Valley is a very "American" locale that epitomizes mythical imaginings of America as the land of opportunity and that reaffirms the notion that modernity finds its most direct expression in the context of American (mass) culture.[5] Siliconization then describes the

5 The conflation of "America" with "modernity" found its culmination in Horkheimer and Adorno's *Dialectic of Enlightenment*, in which modernity is understood to signify increasing rationalization, commodification, technologization, mass production, and self-alienation. According to Horkheimer and Adorno, who both fled Nazi Germany and spent the war years in the U.S., America anticipated the cultural and social

process of the displacement and subsequent reinscription of "America" into different localities. As a stand-in for America, Silicon Valley thus needs to be approached as a transnational and transcultural concept, which is grounded in imaginary affective relations and constructed through appropriations and performances of Americanness.

Theorizing Affective Imaginary Relations

As global platforms that reconceptualize human encounters and that create new forms of interaction which are not dependent on the occupation of the same physical space, SNSs raise two questions concerning a re-theorization of locality. First, how can we theorize the realm in which social interaction takes place? And second, how can we negotiate the formation of (collective) identities that emerge out of those social interactions? In other words, where can we locate both the site of interaction and the communities that are formed?

In all SNSs, the site of interaction is a virtual space that actually none of the participants physically occupies but that everyone can symbolically inhabit and partake of. This virtual space is a space of imaginary linkages and networks, for which there does not exist any geographical or material correspondent. Users can communicate and form relations without ever meeting "in person," which constructs a reality in which human encounters are completely dissolved from bodily presence and materiality. "Real" and "imaginary" are not mutually exclusive; indeed, in social network interactions, reality constitutes itself to a great extent in the realm of the imaginary.

Our usage of the term "imaginary" is grounded in the work of Wolfgang Iser and Cornelius Castoriadis rather than on the Lacanian notion of the imaginary.[6] Iser's seminal study *Das Fiktive und das Imaginäre* [The

developments of post-WWII Europe. As Richard Leppert points out, Adorno's "experience in the American 'paradise' suggested what was to come [in Europe] after the defeat of fascism, a world dominated by technologically accomplished forms of mass culture whose purpose was to sell" (514).

6 The Lacanian Imaginary is a pre-verbal register whose moment of formation has been named "mirror stage" and describes the moment between six and eighteen months in which an infant first recognizes his/her image in the mirror. In other words, it designates the moment in which the child is first able to make a connection between its own motricity and the images moving in the mirror. For Lacan, the mirror stage

Fictive and the Imaginary] (1991) seeks to chart literature anthropologically and establishes a triadic model of the real, the fictive, and the imaginary, which are inextricably intertwined and cannot exist in isolation. Iser argues that the opposition between "real" and "fictive" does not hold because these two concepts merge in literary texts. Iser thus introduces the imaginary as the link that connects and feeds both the "real" and the "fictive." A text, Iser argues, can be neither confined to its fictional features, nor to its elements taken from the reality it refers to, because such an approach would presuppose that fictional features are a closed entity characterized by an absence of the "real." A more differentiated approach to literature shows that texts reproduce items of reality, which again bring forward purposes that are not part of the reality reproduced and are thus products of a fictionalizing act. This fictionalizing act, in turn, cannot be deduced from reality. This is where, according to Iser, the imaginary, as a quality that does not belong to the reproduced reality but that also cannot be separated from it, comes into play (Iser 18-19).

If we replace Iser's "fictive" with the term "virtual," we can establish a triadic model similar to his, a model which explains the workings of cultural exchange in SNSs. Human encounters and interaction that take place in SNSs bear an imaginary quality as the reality produced in social networks is somewhat removed from one's day-to-day reality (at home, at the workplace, etc.), yet "virtual reality" cannot be completely divorced from "real reality." Items of reality are reproduced in virtual space (in the form of status updates, for instance, in sharing links, or in the uploading of videos, photos, etc.), but in their consumption by other users, these items may be appropriated, shared, commented on, or linked to other contents and thus gain new meaning and produce new realities.

As both Iser and Castoriadis, to whom Iser's notion of the imaginary is indebted, emphasize, the imaginary manifests itself in a diffuse manner and in fleeting, spontaneous impressions. Castoriadis notes that

---

describes a fundamental and unbridgeable gap between the subject and its own self (*Écrits* 2-3). The Lacanian Imaginary describes the formation of an individual's subjectivity as a process that takes place in isolation, while Iser's notion of the imaginary takes into account the individual's situatedness within culture and understands the formation of subjectivity as a process that takes place in an individual's relations to others, be those relations real or imagined. Thus, Iser's notion of the imaginary allows us to theorize the affective dimension of the formation of an individual's subjectivity and of collective identities.

> representations (and affects, and intentions or desires) emerge in an "absolutely spontaneous" way, and even more: we have intentions (desires, drives) which are creations of this a-causal *vis formandi* in their sheer being, their mode of being and their being-thus (*Sosein*). And, for all we know, this stream of representations *cum* affects *cum* desires is absolutely singular for each singular human being. (Castoriadis 143-44)

Cultural productions and interactions provide the means to bring the imaginary into form, attributing the imaginary with a determinacy it actually does not possess (Iser 22). Affects, images, and desires can thus be articulated and, as Winfried Fluck explains, lead to an empowerment of the individual: "Das Imaginäre erhält eine intentionale Struktur und wird Teil eines fortlaufenden Prozesses kultureller Selbstverständigung, durch den eine Aufwertung (*empowerment*) des Individuums erfolgt, weil dessen 'insgeheime' Vorstellungs- und Gefühlswelt Gestalt gewinnt und damit ausdrucksfähig wird" (20). The empowerment of the individual is undoubtedly a crucial issue when we talk about SNSs. Sites like Facebook, Twitter, YouTube, or Myspace provide a platform and outlet for self-expression as users put themselves onto display and, in customizing their online profiles, virtually "type themselves into being" (Sundén 3). And—it is of course not only typing. There is an arsenal of possibilities for sharing or mashing content which is always already bearing the imprint of individual choice and affective relationship. In view of life writing and processual formation of identities it becomes a semi-private process of selection, an active and visible process of self formation, most condensed and best expressed in the tag line of YouTube: "BROADCAST YOURSELF." Its double meaning might not even be intentional, but it taps both into the realm of empowerment brought about by the technological means of web 2.0 (as well as digital cameras and other high tech paraphernalia that have simultaneously become readily available for so many) and as *live* life writing, with an immediacy and intensity as never witnessed before in history.

The self-expression and empowerment of the individual depends, however, on the apprehension of the individual by others. As Fluck contends, the individual imaginary needs to undergo a process of "socialization" to become readable to others, that is, the imaginary needs to be articulated within the boundaries of cultural rules and conventions (20). On a broader cultural level, the imaginary then describes "those vast networks of interlinking discursive themes, images, motifs, and narrative forms that are publicly available within a culture at any one time, and articulate its psychic and social dimensions" (Dawson 48). Social networks foster the formation of global, trans-geographic cultures that rely upon shared sets of symbols and codes of behavior, specific narrative forms, and their own practices and conventions. Affective imaginary relations define the reality of social networking and they are, in fact, essential to the construction of global cultures, as they transcend concepts such as citizenship, race, ethnicity, or religion, which traditionally mark and delineate a culture. The formation of communities and collective identities facilitated by human encounters on SNSs is increasingly marked by affect, that is, by sentiments and emotions that connect individuals in a given moment as partakers of the same cultural system of communication.

In order to grasp and theorize the space of the imaginary in which these collective identities emerge, we might conceive of Silicon Valley as a metaphor that allows us to localize and control the diffuseness of the imaginary that structures understandings of "America." In the imaginary realm of social networking, the world becomes Silicon Valley and Silicon Valley becomes the world in the meeting and merging of the individual, local, and global. We will illustrate the process of Siliconization by drawing on Facebook, currently the most popular Social Network Site, in the next section.

Facebook: One Case of Network Localization

The following case study reads today's most popular SNS Facebook[7] as a realm deliberately designed for the purpose that collective identities can be formed via social interaction. Different to blogs, vlogs, or amateur online tutorials, with which users share original content (knowledge, practices, or know-how), the sharing and communication that occurs via social platforms such as Facebook are less content- or theme-driven than they are person- and community-driven. They are expressive of an egalitarian principle in which the producer-audience separation evaporates—a separation which is still strongly visible in blogs, even if comments are

7 Founder Mark Zuckerberg announced in July 2010 that 500 million people have a Facebook account worldwide. About 70% of all Facebook users (about 350 million people) reside outside the United States. <http://blog.facebook.com/blog.php?post=409753352130> 26 September 2010.

enabled. It is the communal aspect that actually writes them into existence which is also the incentive behind the continuous re/formulation of the countless and everchanging collective "Facebook narratives."

What makes SNSs unique is that "they enable users to articulate and make visible their [already existing] social networks," while at the same time enabling the formation of "connections between individuals that would not otherwise be made" (Boyd and Ellison). A subscription to a specific YouTube channel is usually done out of interest in the channel's content. A Facebook user, however, befriends other users out of interest in the person: primarily, communication takes place between people who are already part of each other's extended offline social network and serves to maintain pre-existing social relations. Although SNSs also facilitate connections between strangers, based on shared interests, political views, or activities, they are mainly used by registered members to articulate and display their social networks, which suggests that the interest in other users overwrites the interest in the content that gets posted. Finally, users of SNSs are able to partake of imaginary relationships and communities, that is, to form new and maintain already existing social relations, or become part of specific interest groups and collectives, without necessarily engaging with others on a face-to-face basis.

Although SNSs allow users to send each other private messages and engage in one-on-one interactions, communication among users primarily takes place in the form of posting items on one's profile and sharing these items with others. It is generic to sites such as YouTube and Facebook to encourage comments to posted items. This interactive set-up suggests that recognition is a vital motivation in posting material in general. The act of posting or broadcasting user-generated content will usually look for, and incite, some sort of response from the imagined audience. Whereas more content-driven sites such as YouTube or open blogs will allow this response from any other registered user, Facebook users can customize their privacy settings and choose whether they want to make their profiles publicly available or restrict access to their profiles to the friends they have invited in their network locality, making it thus a mediated public/private sphere. In an egalitarian vein, the system does not distinguish between different degrees of relationships; all people added to one's profile are termed "friends," which is a misleading term as online connections do not necessarily mean "friendship" in its common sense and the reasons for linking people to one's profile can be varied. On SNSs which do not require a bi-directional confirmation of friendship, relationship ties are sometimes labeled "Followers" or "Fans" as to signal the one-sidedness of the investment in these relationships. The public display of one's connections is an essential part of SNSs, as it is implied that the number of "friends" or "followers" one has added is indicative of one's popularity and sociability.[8]

Facebook's facilitation of the creation and posting of user-generated content is unprecedented. Compared to Myspace and YouTube profiles, the set-up or layout of Facebook profiles is relatively strict and predetermined. Facebook provides a universal form or genre which enables the individual user to fill in individual content and create an individualized realm very easily. Users are asked to fill out forms that ask for an individual's age, gender, current location, profession, interests, and activities in the "about me" section. Facebook also encourages its members to upload a profile picture and allows them to enhance and personalize their profiles by adding applications that are supposed to simplify the sharing of information. Every time a user logs on to Facebook, s/he is invited to share with friends the answer to the question "What's on your mind?" Until March 2009, the question used to be "What are you doing right now?" The switch in this generic request from action to emotion arguably inscribes affect and immediacy even more into the core of the social exchange the site is designed for. Via the newsfeed function,[9] users are shown the activities of friends—another design to facilitate communication and or suggest comments on activities of friends, such as a status update, the uploading of a video or wall photo, or the "liking" of a com-

8 According to Facebook statistics, the average user has 130 friends and is connected to 80 community pages, groups, and events. Currently, the late Michael Jackson is the person with the most friends (roughly 19 million), Lady Gaga has the most friends of all living Facebook members (over 16 million), followed by Barack Obama, who can call almost 13 million people his friends. As of 21 August 2010, Lady Gaga is also the most popular Twitter user with 5.7 million followers. The previous frontrunner, Britney Spears, comes in a very close second with 5.6 million followers. See <http://www.facebook.com/press/info.php?statistics and http://twittercounter.com/> 10 October 2010.

9 The introduction of the newsfeed function in September, 2006 was for a short time heavily contested among users (Vie 36). Meanwhile it arguably has become the main day-to-day incentive to open one's Facebook page for most users. According to Facebook statistics, about 50% of all active users log on to Facebook in any given day. <http://www.facebook.com/press/info.php?statistics> 10 October 2010.

munity page.[10] An affective space is deliberately created and recognition of the other's action or content is enabled, even suggested by the invitation to post comments or to express one's sympathy and agreement via the "like"-button, symbolized with a "thumbs-up" icon. Significantly, there is no "don't like" or "thumbs-down" button, which underlines Facebook's positive, even "happy-go-lucky" approach to social exchange and communication, as thoughts and contents shared by friends can only be affirmed and agreed with. Similarly, users can display their interests by "liking" community pages (which replaced the "become a fan" function in April 2010), but they cannot display their dislikes—despite massive demands for such a function from countless members within the Facebook community, a "thumbs-down" button has not been implemented.

The (more or less) public display of one's taste in music and movies, hobbies, religious views, and political convictions significantly shapes one's online identity and allows users to (deliberately or subconsciously) create an "online-persona," as it were, which may to varying degrees be removed from their offline selves. Furthermore, community pages and interest groups link otherwise unrelated users and thus establish imagined communities of individuals who (in most cases) will never communicate with each other but create new senses of identification and belonging by becoming part of an interest-based network. In this way, Facebook can also serve as an enabling tool, as people who are constantly connected via networked social media can be easily mobilized for social intervention. In Austria, the success of "Es ist Zeit für eine Lichterkette,"[11] an appeal by two hitherto unknown students without any political affiliation that brought more than 3,500 people on the streets of Vienna to peacefully protest against right-wing statements by the third presiding officer of Austrian parliament was solely made possible by the enabling technologies of Facebook (ORF). On a more satirical note, the community page "Kann dieser seelenlose Ziegelstein mehr Freunde haben als H.C. Strache?" received considerable media attention when it was "liked" by over 100,000 people within a week after its founding and currently holds at

10 Community pages combine the old concept of fan pages with users' interests/activities and bring together "people who like this," which is Facebook's new term for "fans." There are community pages for celebrities and brand-products, but people also "like" avocados, sleeping in, and "Women's Curling: because the kitchen has already been wept."

11 See <http://www.facebook.com/group.php?gid=81733713338&ref=search&sid=1367558838.89546699> 30 October 2010.

over 174,000 "people who like this."[12] Although this group was founded to entertain, as is stated in the group's profile, it has a clear political agenda and mobilizes users to be politically active and set a sign against right-wing ideologies.[13] Facebook lends itself as a tool for protest events and social mobilization because of its easy handling (anyone can found a community page or a group within a few minutes) and because community pages can quickly accumulate many members. The strength of Facebook is its ability to motivate users to "like" a group, share this activity with their friends and thus forward information about new groups and events within a very short period of time. Its power lies both in its speed and potential reach, but also in the low threshold participation. However, as the membership in Facebook groups and community pages is non-committal, people tend to politically position themselves more readily than in "real life." While the group "Es ist Zeit für eine Lichterkette" counted at times over 11,000 Facebook members, for instance, only a third attended the actual protest event.

As the above examples demonstrate, SNSs such as Facebook continuously challenge the notions of private and public, personal and political, as well as "real" and "virtual" all around the globe. Facebook is the paradigmatic example of a markedly American product (the generic Facebook site was initially created as a tool for communication between Harvard students, then opened to college students in general, and finally to everyone),[14] which has been globally appropriated for self-expression and glocally used for localized affiliations. The blocking of access to Facebook in Iran just before the 2009 presidential elections, for instance, demonstrates the political power attributed to new technologies and the importance of new media as a source for information (CNN). The Iranian case is of particular interest for our understanding of the "Americanness" of Facebook because it implies that Facebook is perceived as an instance of Westernization/Americanization which is rejected by the Iranian polit-

---

12 See<http://www.facebook.com/pages/Kann-dieser-seelenlose-Ziegelstein-mehr-Freunde-haben-als-HC-Strache/290967602506> 26 October 2010.

13 The group's status updates right before the election of the Austrian Federal President read, for instance: "Ich bin als Ziegelstein leider nicht wahlberechtigt... Ich bestehe aber vehement darauf, dass jede und jeder Einzelne von euch den Urnengang beschreitet!!!" (status update on 25 April 2010), or "Möchte alle—'egal wie sie sich entscheiden—'eindringlich zum Urnengang aufrufen! Für eine tiefgehende Demokratisierung unserer Gesellschaft!" (status update on 22 April 2010).

14 See <http://www.facebook.com/press/info.php?timeline> 8 September 2010.

ical establishment. The "Facebook scandal" put the global (or Western) spotlight on the elections in Iran and showed how Facebook is seen and also feared by some countries as a democratizing tool.

Arguably, there are also specific features in the layout of Facebook that can be linked to notions of Americanness: the egalitarian approach towards the system of friends or the explicit suggestion to share your immediate feelings via the status update function on the generic level, the use of the "thumbs-up" sign on a symbolic level. Other long-standing ingredients of perceived Americanness to be found in the Facebook imaginary include means of self-expression, individualism, and freedom of speech. Also, the effective, quick and efficient form of communication enabled by Facebook might be related to a particular time-is-money attitude prevalent in a global (Americanized) economy. But it is also the empowerment of the individual made possible by a SNS such as Facebook that should not be overlooked. It might be a long stretch to compare the creator of a site such as "Kann dieser seelenlose Ziegelstein mehr Freunde haben als H.C. Strache" to US (movie) icons of lonely outsiders fighting the establishment such as, e.g., Erin Brockovich, but a site such as Facebook is certainly a tool enabling stories of such individual success and empowerment. Clearly, Facebook invites affective encounters and is a constant encouragement for interaction and participation. It serves as a network locality that helps constitute and foster imaginary relations, an imaginary space to be recognized and to belong to.

Conclusion

In this paper, we have envisioned SNSs as localities that constitute imaginary relations that are connected to notions of "Americanness." SNSs like Facebook are produced by and are productive of localized social relations and they enable their users to imagine global interconnection. The term global, as Ito reminds us, refers to a "set of linked particularities that span geographic distance, and yet often connotes a singularizing context" (Ito, "Network Localities" 6). As she explains: "The Internet is actually global only in the sense that it enables information circulation and accessibility between different places *around* the globe, and not in the sense that it creates a context that is shared or homogeneous *across* the globe. The distinction, dare I say, makes all the difference in the world" (ibid.). As we have shown with the example of

Facebook, SNSs create interconnection and accessibility between peoples and different geographic locales and can actually offer an opportunity for "the production of difference and new forms of trans-geographic localization" (ibid. 2). In our age marked by immense technological advances and increasing globalization, phenomena such as SNSs demonstrate the necessity for a radical reconceptualization of identity formation and cultural interaction. As we have shown, social networking is defined by affective imaginary relations that transcend traditional markers of cultural specificity; SNSs thus advance the formation of global cultures and transnational collective identities, which largely rely on shared sentiments, emotions, and interests that connect individual users from all around the world as partakers of one and the same cultural system of communication. In a web 2.0 world, traditional notions of "space" and "place" consequently do not suffice anymore when we theorize human interaction and cultural processes of identity formation. To be able to account for the role SNSs play in cultural practice, physical space needs to be supplemented with virtual space and the binary oppositions of "place" versus "non-place" and "here" versus "there" need to be expanded to include the in-between, because as we have shown, networlds are not either "here" or "there," but they are really here, there, and everywhere.

Works Cited

Adorno, Theodor W. *Essays on Music*. Trans. Susan H. Gillespie. Ed. Richard Leppert. Berkeley: U of California P, 2007.

Appadurai, Arjun. *Modernity at Large: Cultural Dimensions of Globalization*. Minneapolis: U of Minnesota P, 1996.

Augé, Marc. *Non-places: Introduction to an Anthropology of Supermodernity*. Trans. John Howe. London: Verso, 2008.

Boyd, Danah M., and Nicole B. Ellison. "Social Network Sites: Definition, History, and Scholarship." *Journal of Computer-Mediated Communication* 13.1 (2007). Web. 8 September 2010.

Castoriadis, Cornelius. "Radical Imagination and the Social Instituting Imaginary." *Rethinking Imagination: Culture and Creativity*. Eds. Gillian Robinson and John Rundell. London: Routledge, 1994. 136-54.

CNN. "Report: Iran blocks Facebook ahead of presidential election". CNN.com/world, May 23, 2009. http://edition.cnn.com/2009/WORLD

/meast/05/23/iran.elections.facebook/index.html. 2009 (accessed on 8 September 2010).

Dawson, Graham. *Soldier Heroes: British Adventure, Empire, and the Imaginings of Masculinities*. London: Routledge, 1994.

Fluck, Winfried. *Das kulturelle Imaginäre: Zur Funktionsgeschichte des amerikanischen Romans 1790-1900*. Frankfurt/Main: Suhrkamp, 1997.

Gromov, Gregory. "Don Hoefler." *NetValley*. Web. 16 October 2010. <http://www.netvalley.com/silicon_valley/Don_Hoefler_coined_the_phrase_Silicon_Valley.html>.

Haythornthwaite, Caroline. "Social networks and Internet connectivity effects." *Information, Communication, & Society,* 8.2 (2005): 125-47.

Harasim, Linda M. "Global Networks: An Introduction." *Global Networlds: Computers and International Communication*. Ed. Linda M. Harasim. Cambridge: The MIT P, 1993. 15-34.

Horkheimer, Max, and Theodor W. Adorno. *Dialectic of Enlightenment*. Trans. Edmund Jephcott. Palo Alto: Stanford UP, 2002.

Iser, Wolfgang. *Das Fiktive und das Imaginäre: Perspektiven literarischer Anthropologie*. Frankfurt/Main: Suhrkamp, 1991.

Ito, Mizuko. "Network Localities: Identity, Place, and Digital Media." 6 August 2010. <http://www.itofisher.com/PEOPLE/mito/locality.pdf>.

-----. "Media Literacy and Social Action in a Post-Pokemon World". 6 August 2010 <http://www.itofisher.com/mito/publications/media_literacy.html>.

Lacan, Jacques. *Écrits: A Selection*. 1966. Trans. Alan Sheridan. London: Routledge, 2001.

Leppert, Richard. "Commentary." Theodor W. Adorno. *Essays on Music*. Trans. Susan H. Gillespie. Ed. Richard Leppert. Berkeley: U of California P, 2007. 513-63.

ORF. " 3.500 Menschen bei Lichterkette". ORF.at/Wien. June 19, 2009. <http://wien.orf.at/stories/369218/>. (accessed on 26 Oct, 2010).

Ritzer, George, and Todd Stillman. "McDonaldisierung, Amerikanisierung und Globalisierung: Eine vergleichende Analyse." *Globales Amerika? Die kulturellen Folgen der Globalisierung.* Trans. Henning Thies. Eds. Ulrich Beck et al. Bielefeld: Transcript, 2003. 44-68.

Sundén, Jenny. *Material Virtualities*. New York: Peter Lang, 2003.

Vie, Stephanie. "Engaging Others in Online Social Networking Sites: Rhetorical Practices in Myspace and Facebook". Dissertation, U of Arizona, 2007.

Playing Indian in Austria: Waterloo and the Transnational Performance of America

Leo Lippert

Leo Lippert starts his theoretical probing into transnational contact on the example of "Waterloo," an Austrian singer-songwriter who often appears in "Native American" costume. Lippert analyzes two instances, a TV appearance and a musical performance in Vienna, Austria. Lippert argues that such an act cannot be adequately grasped through national ("American Studies") nor even transnational models ("globalization"), but have to be understood as performance, in which "America" is an ever-elusive effigy (here, the performing of "American-ness" through "Native American-ness" which is, however channeled both through global stereotypes and national Austrian narremes). Lippert thereby critically challenges Pratt's concept of the "contact space" as too localized, too binding and argues in favor of a consideration of these performances as more fleeting and more deterritorialized than traditional disciplinary approaches allow for.[1]

In recent years, the increasing interdependency—cultural, political, and economic—of the United States and other countries has precipitated the emergence of what Shelley Fisher Fishkin names in her 2004 presidential address to the ASA, "the transnational turn in American Studies" (17). Despite the neat summarization of a vast array of theoretical approaches under one umbrella "turn," Fishkin appropriately identifies the current impulse in American Studies scholarship to adopt frames of analysis that go beyond the boundaries of the nation-state. Acknowledging that "[n]ation-states, as units in a complex interactive system, are not very likely to be the long-term arbiters of the relationship between globality and modernity" (Appadurai 19), American Studies scholars have found it particularly necessary to adjust their traditional lines of inquiry. The es-

1 Work on this article has been made possible by the "Forschungsstipendium 2011" of the University of Vienna. I want to thank Chris Tedjasukmana, Julia Schilly, and Judith Kohlenberger for their valuable suggestions on this piece in various stages of its development.

tablished search for "exceptional" national characteristics has gradually given way to the analysis of how these seemingly exceptional cultural constructions have been circulated, mediated, and reworked in the transnational domain. For Fishkin, the challenge presented to American Studies scholarship is to "see the inside and outside, domestic and foreign, national and international, as interpenetrating" (21).[2]

Fishkin's call for the interpenetration of disciplinary dichotomies, however, entails a significant problem of legitimacy for American Studies as a field. The rise of new transnational perspectives, obviously, has put into perspective "America" as a (highly contested and culturally constructed) national framework related to the United States.[3] If our research is to be located at the hybrid interpenetration points of cultures, at the liminal contact spaces of transnational cultural rearticulation, why should we still call our (inter-)discipline *American* studies? What specificity is there left to the institutionalized American culture studies which, as George Lipsitz claims, "are tied to connections between culture and place that no longer may be operative" (27)? Why should we not speak of "global culture studies" instead? These problems have preoccupied scholars at least since the New Americanists urged for a post-national conception of the field in the early 1990s.[4] Tellingly, in her 1998 presidential address to the ASA, Janice Radway asks, "What's in a Name?," and goes on to deliberate possible names for both American Studies and the ASA at a time when "the notion of a bounded national territory and a concomitant national identity deriving isomorphically from it are called into ques-

---

2 Among the most influential theoretical approaches to transnational American Studies, I would place Günter Lenz' call for a "dialogics of international American culture studies" (475) or Jane Desmond and Virginia Domínguez' "critical internationalism [...] that resituates the United States in a global context on a number of terrains simultaneously" (475). Both Mary Louise Pratt's "contact zones," the much-quoted "social spaces where cultures meet, clash, and grapple with each other" (34) and Gloria Anzaldúa's "borderlands," the liminal space where "the lifeblood of two worlds merg[es] to form a third country—a border culture" (25) have also been hugely influential concepts.

3 Whenever I use "America" (or "Americanness," for that matter) in this essay, I refer to it as exactly this inherently contested national framework. Although quotation marks are usually employed to indicate the cultural contingency of the term, I will refrain from this practice here, as it unnecessarily complicates the reading process.

4 These calls can be found in two widely-read edited collections, namely Donald Pease's *National Identities and Post-Americanist Narratives* and later, John Carlos Rowe's *Post-Nationalist American Studies.*

tion" (16-17). In order to accommodate diverse perspectival outlooks, she proposes, for instance, "United States Studies" (18), the hemispheric "Inter-American Studies" (20), or the deterritorialized "Intercultural Studies" (22). In the end, however, Radway dismisses all three approaches and instead opts for a clichéd pledge of allegiance to traditional American Studies terminology. "I do not think this field or this association need to fear change," she states. "Together they have fostered it in the past and embraced its effects; they can do so again" (23). Although it is difficult to speculate about the exact nature of her motivations, Radway's refusal is significant, as it points to the complex tension between the national and various notions of the transnational as conceptual frameworks for American Studies scholarship. Despite the recent fad for the production of transnational knowledges, the nation, as a distinctly modern phenomenon, still holds considerable critical currency and has precluded a more thorough exploration of the challenges posed by globalization and postmodernity. What the transnational turn has revealed, then, are still unre-unresolved issues concerning the social production of locality, or more generally, the links between culture and place.

In the following deliberations, I will enter the debate by situating the current preoccupation with transnational American Studies vis-à-vis the ongoing epistemic shift from *discipline* to *performance* as primary modality for the production of contemporary knowledge. In my subsequent reading of the significance of the Austrian singer/entertainer Waterloo, a former Eurovision Song Contest participant who has made his career performing "Indianness" [5] on various stages, therefore, I will suggest that we approach Americanness in the transnational realm along the epistemological lines of performance. Such an advance is not necessarily at odds with comparative or dialogic conceptualizations of the transnational; however, my focus in this essay will be on the epistemological challenge posed by transnational processes to both America as a national framework and American Studies as an institutionalized (inter-)discipline.

5 Whenever I use "Indian" or "Indianness" in this essay, I employ the term as a marker for the cultural representation of allegedly Native American traits. The ascription "Indian" (as well as, of course, the similarly problematic designation "Native American") must always be understood as a legacy of violent and unjust colonial power dynamics. As with "America" above, I will refrain from putting the word into quotation marks so as to render my writing more reader-friendly.

Waterloo's Audience with the *Kaiser*

The April 2, 2009, episode of the Austrian national broadcasting company ORF's successful late night comedy show *Wir Sind Kaiser* (literally: We Are Emperor) featured a memorable encounter. The *Kaiser* Robert Heinrich I, a regally adorned mock impersonation of the somewhat legendary Austrian emperor Francis Joseph I, has invited Hans Kreuzmayr, better known to the Austrian public as Waterloo, to a royal audience. The audience with the *Kaiser* constitutes the centerpiece of each episode and involves the humorously orchestrated visits of Austrian celebrities to Robert Heinrich, played by the Viennese actor and comedian Robert Palfrader. *Wir Sind Kaiser*, a format that represents a comedic engagement with post-imperial Austria's national inferiority complexes, seems to be the ORF's satirical tapping into the profitable nostalgia industry surrounding the Austrian monarchy. The show's title is of course a pun on the famous "Wir Sind Papst!" (We Are Pope!) headline, which the German newspaper *Bild* ran on April 20, 2005, the day after the German cardinal Joseph Ratzinger was elected Pope of the Roman Catholic Church. *Wir Sind Kaiser* was broadcast for four seasons from 2007 to 2010, when Palfrader switched to the other side of the social spectrum of imperial Vienna and performed the title role in Franz Molnár's *Liliom* at the Viennese Volkstheater.[6]

As the press information accompanying the April 2 broadcast informs us, the *Kaiser* wanted "to immerse in other cultures and enter a spiritual exchange on the meaning of life" ("Seine Majestät").[7] The cross-cultural aspect of the quotation, probably cryptic at first, must be regarded as an allusion to Kreuzmayr's public persona: Waterloo is Austria's number one impersonator of Indian characters of all kinds and is consequently expected to *play Indian* with Robert Heinrich. It is at this point that the relationship of the royal audience with the transnational American Studies project becomes explicit: As an Indian character on Austrian national television, Waterloo participates in a transcultural conversation about Americanness on a mock imperial stage. The skit, accordingly, employs the symbolic vernacular of what I will refer to as Indianness, that is, the

6 A version of the April 2 episode that contains Waterloo's royal audience is available on YouTube. See specialagent, or: http://www.youtube.com/watch?v=PX7RBrBRrJg.

7 In order to facilitate the reading process, I have silently translated to English all quotations from German sources that appear in this essay.

socially mediated construction of Native American cultures. For the audience, the *Kaiser*'s baroque auditorium has been adroitly refurnished in order to suit the visitor's alleged taste: a teepee has been erected at the center of the room, and a green cactus lingers in the background; the *Kaiser*'s attractive yet silent female personal assistant wears buckskin leather clothes and Robert Heinrich himself, finally, dons a feathery headdress.

Kreuzmayr himself has a relatively profane interest in appearing on the show: His visit is part of the promotion tour for his new book, a semi-autobiographical Indian self-help guide titled *Das Geheime Wissen der Lakota: Die 7 Wege zu einem Besseren Leben (The Secret Knowledge of the Lakota: The 7 Ways to a Better Life).* The book contains, as Waterloo explains to Robert Heinrich in a somewhat enigmatic construction, "pieces of wisdom about life between Austria and the Indians of North America." In fact, *The Secret Knowledge of the Lakota* opens with Waterloo's chapter-long allegation "I am an Indian," and continues to outline seven virtues allegedly treasured by the Lakota. These virtues—generosity, steadfastness, courage, sagacity, love, respectfulness, and modesty—are illustrated by exemplary Indian stories, while a final "Waterloo Recommends"-section suggests their applicability to everyday life. Generosity, for instance, is to be shown through tips, small gifts, caring for the elderly, or a friendly smile. The book is rounded up by a test section, entitled "How Much of an Indian am I?," which allows readers to find out whether they are competent enough to apply the secret Lakota knowledge adequately.

In order to advertise his book, Kreuzmayr is required to engage in a ten-minute conversation with the *Kaiser*, an exchange that is clearly intended for laughs, yet emerges as a compelling vortex through which a variety of transnational cultural discourses of empire, masculinity, race, and civilization are channeled.[8] As it turns out, Robert Heinrich is deeply suspicious of Waterloo's Indian masculinity, and examines him accordingly. However, due to the dramaturgical conventions of the audience, which always position the *Kaiser* as the more powerful, indeed sovereign subject, Kreuzmayr is doomed to fail. Already Waterloo's early years as owner of a small boutique for ladies' fashion cast him in an unmanly (read: homosexual) light, an impression that is only intensified by the live

8 For a sustained understanding of the links between the cultural construction of masculinity, civilization, and nation in an American context, see Gail Bederman's *Manliness and Civilization.*

falsetto performance of the "Erzherzog Johann Jodler," a well-known Styrian yodel. Although Waterloo has even discarded his usual Indian-style clothing and has opted for a traditional green Styrian jacket instead, the *Kaiser* cringes, interrupts the yodel, and retorts, "No wonder the Indians lost the war." Waterloo's failures proliferate: when examined by the *Kaiser* on the contents of *The Secret Knowledge of the Lakota*, he is only able to come up with two of the seven Lakota virtues, which puts his knowledge of Indian wisdom into serious doubt. The skit climaxes when the *Kaiser* and Waterloo decide to become blood brothers and initiate a phallic exchange that would eventually lead to the transnational merging of royal and Indian blood. The first knife that Waterloo is given, however, turns out to be too small for the purpose: it is, as the *Kaiser* puts it, "a woman's knife." The second one, more a dagger than a knife, seems to be masculine enough for the ritualized slitting of wrists. With a bold movement, Waterloo pretends to cut his arm and offers it to the emperor when Robert Heinrich mockingly interrupts and exclaims, "Well, that was the wrong edge of the blade." Waterloo "cuts" his wrist for a second time, but is again refused by the emperor, who sarcastically comments, "One can't even see a little bit of blood". Apologetically, Waterloo mumbles that the "white man's knives aren't sharp enough," but Robert Heinrich is disappointed, abandons the plan, and officially dismisses Waterloo.

When we attempt to interpret Waterloo's audience with the *Kaiser* as an intercultural dialogue about Americanness in the transnational realm, it would certainly be awkward to read the scene as a conversation between two nationally-identified social actors. But then, what kind of exchange is it that takes place here? What is the *domestic*, what the *foreign* in this global performance arena? Where do we locate America in a skit that was never even broadcast in the United States? And in what ways can American Studies account for this creative yet strangely deterritorialized cultural production? How should we speak of transnational Americanness in the encounter of an Austrian singer (usually dressed up as Native American but this time dressed up as Styrian *Erzherzog*) with an Austrian actor (dressed up as Austrian emperor) on Austrian national television? Or shouldn't we? It is the *Kaiser*'s relentless testing (and Waterloo's repeated failure), I would argue, that directs us to an essential characteristic of the event: it is a showcasing of *performance*. What is at stake here is neither "authentic" Indianness nor a "real" exchange of bodily fluids, but the fundamental ability to *perform* in the globalized domain; what is at stake is not the viability of modern nation-frames such as

"America" or "Austria" and an all too easily assumed correspondence of culture and place, but the power to reenact, embody and concomitantly replace; what is at stake, finally, is not the study of cultural interaction across national boundaries, but the study of culture *beyond* the disciplinarity of the nation-state. For to study the Americanness of *playing Indian in Austria* more accurately, we need to study it for what it is: a performance.

Understanding America as Performance

In his 2001 book *Perform or Else: From Discipline to Performance*, Jon McKenzie ponders the ubiquity of *performance* in contemporary discourse and embarks on a daunting project: "*to rehearse a general theory of performance*" (4). A general theory, for McKenzie, would recognize *performance* not only as a descriptive term for a number of cultural performance events on a spectrum ranging from ritual to theater, but would encompass a much broader terrain. To cultural performance, McKenzie adds organizational and technological performance and concludes that the curious recurrence of the term in seemingly distinct disciplines points to a larger epistemic shift that has been under way since the end of World War II. Gradually developing his project, McKenzie provocatively asks,

> What if the diversification and proliferation of researchers, projects, and fields over the past fifty years signal not only a quantitative leap in research initiative, but also a qualitative mutation in what we call knowledge, the becoming-performative of knowledge itself? (13-14)

McKenzie's general theory of performance, then, proposes a modification of our thinking about knowledge. The ongoing transition from modernity to what Lyotard has called *the postmodern condition* and Appadurai *modernity at large*, he claims, has been accompanied by a transition in epistemology and power as well. The disciplinary regime that Foucault famously placed at the center of the modern Western knowledge project, the "disciplinary modality of power [which] has infiltrated the others" (*Discipline* 216), has steadily decreased in relevance. Instead, McKenzie suggests that "*performance will be to the twentieth and twenty-first centuries what discipline was to the eighteenth and nineteenth, that is, an onto-historical formation of power and knowledge*" (18). McKenzie's epistemic shift from discipline to performance, accordingly, necessitates a gradual desertion of disciplinary thought systems and technologies of power. While modern knowledge is produced in "hospitals, workshops, schools, prisons" (Foucault, *Discipline* 205) through techniques of normalization and subversion, the prototypical institution of postmodernity is the stage, offering a much simpler epistemological challenge: to *perform or else.*

It is important to realize that McKenzie's shift from discipline to performance does not constitute a radical break, but rather, a gradual transition. Although this essay will concentrate on the transnational *performance* of America, I do not want to imply that there are no longer any disciplinary, national American knowledges being produced. But what would it mean for American Studies, as a distinctly modern, national project, to go *transnational*? What would happen in a transnational realm to the discipline's securely institutionalized endeavors to produce national subjectivities and American bodies, endeavors that ultimately refuse to address the *becoming-performative* of power and knowledge? In these reflections, then, I am interested in what the study of the *performance* of America in the transnational realm would entail. How can we consider *performance,* in Diana Taylor's words, "a way of knowing, not simply an object of analysis" (xvi)? And finally, what importance would earlier disciplinary terms like America and Americanness still have, and how should we conceptualize them?

Marvin Carlson's *Performance: A Critical Introduction* provides first clues to the understanding of performance. Carlson opens his extensive overview that covers writings in linguistics, anthropology, and traditional theater studies with the now familiar claim that "the rise of an interest in performance reflects a major shift in many cultural fields from the what of culture to the how" (ix). The question, however, remains: what exactly is performance other than the obvious—embodied behavior—that would help us adjust our epistemologies? Carlson points to a crucial fact:

> performance is associated not just with doing but also with re-doing …—its embodiment of the tension between a given form or content from the past and the inevitable adjustments of an ever-changing present make it an operation of particular interest at a time of widespread interest in cultural negotiations—how human patterns of activity are reinforced or changed within a culture and how they are adjusted when various different cultures interact. (ix)

Without a doubt, Carlson's introductory remarks place his ruminations on performance at the heart of the American Studies project and its methodological difficulties. The *cultural negotiations* highlighted by Carlson are central to the transnational turn in the field, which has focused on the very adjustments undertaken by interacting, or *interpenetrating* cultures. Performance, it seems, points not merely to embodied behaviors but to the *tension* between different versions of embodiment. To study performance, then, involves the examination not only of "doing," but of why, when, where, and in what ways things are "re-done," and re-done differently.

Performance theorist Richard Schechner is even more explicit. When he recommends that we think of performance as "restored behavior" (35), he specifies that "[p]erformance means: never for the first time. It means: for the second to the *n*th time" (37). For Schechner, performance is a constant restoration of an irretrievable "first time," a lost original. It serves as a powerful echo of an authentic source, though a source never to be pinpointed exactly. Recognizing the still considerable fascination exerted by the "first time" over all performances, Schechner argues that "[t]he original 'truth' or 'source' of the behavior may be lost, ignored, or contradicted—even while this truth or source is apparently being honored and observed" (35). That the original is always an elusive entity has not only been theorized in Performance Studies, but is also one of the central arguments in Michel Foucault's reflections on history in his well-known essay, "Nietzsche, Genealogy, History," in which he claims that "[w]hat is found at the historical beginning of things is not the inviolable identity of their origin; it is the dissension of other things. It is disparity" ("Nietzsche" 142). In a related claim, theater historian Joseph Roach also concludes that an "original" is always out of reach, and argues for elusiveness as a crucial feature of performance. Roach claims that performance "stands in for an elusive entity that it is not but that it must vainly aspire both to embody and replace" (3). As *n*th-time embodiment, performance must be understood as the unlimited and exhausting reenactment of seemingly original "behaviors," that is, again in Foucaultian terms, the social actions contingent on the (disciplinary) workings of power and knowledge. Performances never literally repeat existing social structures or cultural arrangements; instead, they continuously actualize potentialities. To read America as performance, then, means to pay attention not to the disciplinary and institutionalized production of "national" knowledges, but to the constant and outrageously self-referential feedback loops created by performances from the *second to the* n*th time.*[9]

In order to possess a methodological tool to study performance, Joseph Roach has introduced the concept of the "effigy". The *effigy*, as performative device, "fills by means of surrogation a vacancy created by the absence of an original" (36). The effigy represents the mechanism through which the workings of performance, the processes of reiteration and replacement, manifest themselves. "Beyond ostensibly inanimate effigies fashioned from wood or cloth," Roach continues, "there are more elusive but more powerful effigies fashioned from flesh" (36). As with all epistemologies, their effects become visible first and foremost on the human body. Living effigies, that is, social actors of all kinds, function as surrogate entities that reveal the workings of performance on their bodies. As scholars of performance, accordingly, we must pay close attention to what S. Paige Baty calls "representative characters" (8), cultural figures that strike us as exemplary, for it is by means of these figures that we are able to determine the operations of the power/knowledge matrix through the performance episteme.

In the context of American Studies, this outline of the epistemology of performance raises the following questions: What is it of Americanness that is retained when we think of it as performance in the transnational realm? And, on a more analytical note, in what ways can we think of Waterloo's performances as American? Or can't we? My suggestion would be to consider Waterloo's Indian performances in Austrian venues of all kinds as "American-in-effigy," as futile yet creative attempts to tap into what Lauren Berlant has called the American "National Symbolic."[10] Wa-

---

9 Indeed, a central problem for scholars of performance is whether Performance Studies constitutes a discipline that itself reproduces disciplinary power/knowledge structures. Carlson quotes responses to this question from the then directors of the Performance Studies programs at NYU and Northwestern University, Joseph Roach and Dwight Conquergood. Roach considers Performance Studies, if there is such a formation, "of course an antidiscipline," while Dwight Conquergood calls "the trickster the 'guru' of this new antidiscipline." For Carlson himself, it is important to recognize that "[p]erformance by its nature resists conclusions, just as it resists the sort of definitions, boundaries, and limits so useful to traditional academic writing and academic structures" (206).

10 In her 1991 book *The Anatomy of National Fantasy*, Lauren Berlant develops the idea of a "National Symbolic" which she describes as "the order of discursive practices whose reign within a national space produces, and also refers to, the 'law' in which the accident of birth within a geographic/political boundary transforms individuals into

terloo's continuous cultural reenactments merely actualize a *potential* Americanness, they faintly echo America, but, as the *Kaiser* so aptly pointed out, they must always fail to embody exactly the exceptional American characteristics so important to a traditional American Studies project. Thinking about America as performance in the transnational realm, then, we have to realize how systemic power and knowledge are increasingly channeled through self-referential and always already processual *echoes* rather than through direct exchanges between national frameworks.The performances of America in unexpected global settings must accordingly be considered as "representation[s] without reproduction," as performance theorist Peggy Phelan has described the "ontology of performance" (146). Phelan's oft-quoted dictum that "[p]erformance's being ... becomes itself through disappearance" (146) implies a paradoxical methodological directive: As scholars of performance, we need to seek Americanness through its very disappearances. No longer considered a self-fulfilling promise of disciplinary inquiry, America must be traced as a continuous disappearance, a fleeting performance that is of a different ontological order. The disappearance of America through performance, however, always introduces a ghostly presence that strangely haunts the transnational cultural landscape. Like performance, ghosts are always experienced, says Avery Gordon in her study of *Ghostly Matters*, "not as cold knowledge, but as a transformative recognition" (8). Therefore, it might be appropriate to speak of the "ghost" of America, a faint echo of a lost original that is never to be reproduced exactly yet always represented, or rather, re-presented anew. Inherently fleeting and transitory, the ghost of America *becomes itself* only through performance, through the frustrated restorations of an always already elusive Americanness. As scholars of America in the transnational realm, our task is to decode these ghostly messages, and pay attention to those *representative characters* who take up the challenge to constantly reenact, rephrase, and rework; characters who take up, in short, the challenge of performance.

---

subjects of a collectively-held history. Its traditional icons, its metaphors, its heroes, its rituals, and its narratives provide an alphabet for a collective consciousness or national subjectivity [...] This pseudo-genetic condition not only affects profoundly the citizen's subjective experience of her/his political rights, but also of civil life, private life, the life of the body itself" (20).

Playing Indian, Performing Americanness

When Waterloo takes up the challenge to perform, a challenge that is always predicated on its necessary failure, he invokes an American ghost that has haunted Philip Deloria in the form of "a five-hundred-year-old headache," which signifies "disrespect, injustice, and oppression" (*Unexpected* 224). Deloria's headache is brought about by the recognition that "the imaginative superstructure that helped define modern American senses of self relied heavily on long histories of nationalism and primitivism figured around Indianness" (*Unexpected* 232). In other words, what has come to be regarded as Americanness has always been constituted vis-à-vis its projections of the Indian. "Native Americans were and are real," Robert Berkhofer insists, "but the *Indian* was a White invention and still remains largely a White image, if not stereotype" (3). Obviously, the fact that these projections served the hegemonic construction of certain (exceptional) American characteristics and national qualities only furthered the representational (and, of course, violently real) injustice towards the Native American peoples inhabiting the territory of the emerging United States. The various representations of Indianness by White settlers, then, were unapologetically utilized to further the colonial project of the United States.

Already in 1953, Roy Harvey Pearce argues that the foundational construction of Americanness relied on the (imagined) polarity of "savagism and civilization," a dichotomy that enabled White settlers to think of themselves as the "civilized" counterpart to a "savage" Native American population. Such thinking, unfortunately, produced devastating results. As Pearce illustrates, "[t]he way to begin to know savagism, and through it civilization, was, simply enough, to destroy savages" (58). Relentlessly perpetuated through centuries, the savagism/primitivism-dichotomy produced a vast and discrepant representational archive of Indianness, while at the same time it actively outlined the highly conflictual representations of Americanness itself. It is the ghostly presence of this representational archive, with its complex negotiation (and negation) processes, that is still haunting the contemporary global performance culture (and Waterloo's performances in particular) addressed in this essay.

Academic literature has identified the "noble savage" and the "ignoble savage" as the two most pervasive and iconic Indian stereotypes. Although both are based on the strategic allegation of Indian primitivism, they possess almost oppositional character traits. L. G. Moses points out that the noble savage was always associated with "good" nature, the harmonious and idyllic pastures of the prairies; the noble savage, for Moses, "appeared handsome in features, dignified in manner, and brave in battle" (3). Although still uncivilized, noble savages were curiously admired as they were provided the opportunity to shun the burdens and obligations of civilization. The ignoble savage, on the other hand, was considered treacherous, disgraceful, and "in life and demeanor more closely resembled the brute beasts with which he shared the howling wilderness" (Moses 3). Most significantly, images of both noble and ignoble savages abounded at the *frontier*, this mythical place of continuous American rejuvenation, where they sparked the representational zest of White U.S. citizens, who were constantly reaffirming their Americanness in the process.

Whether good or bad, noble or ignoble, animalistic warriors or hallowed possessors of mythic and spiritual wisdom, Indians have not only been imagined, but always performed. In his *Playing Indian*, the book to which the title of this essay (and this subsection's heading) refers, Philip Deloria presents a narrative of performed Indianness throughout American history. Stressing the *performative* nature of culture, the act of *playing Indian*, and by extension, the act of *playing American*, Deloria states:

> Play was powerful, for it not only made meanings, it made them *real*. The donning of Indian clothes moved ideas from brains to bodies, from the realm of abstraction to the physical world of concrete experience. There, identity was not so much imagined as it was performed, materialized through one's body and through the witness and recognition of others. (*Playing* 184)

Deloria's history outlines the various and contradictory performances of Indianness that have shaped American national identity from the revolutionary period to the 20th century. Although his study is tied to the territory of the United States in scope, it is a remarkable description of how Americanness is acted out through the concrete bodies of national performers at large. Deloria's *playing Indian* is an examination of a nationwide *re-doing*, a conflicted search for an authentic indigeneity that never succeeds, but produces highly charged meanings, both hegemonic and counter-hegemonic, along the way. In *Going Native*, Shari Huhndorf describes a related phenomenon that must also be understood as a performance practice. "[T]hroughout the twentieth century," Huhndorf claims, "white America has repeatedly enacted rites of conquest to confirm and extend its power over Native America, and these racial dynamics continue to shape contemporary American life" (15). The *going native* in various guises, an endeavor that is also to some extent undertaken by Hans Kreuzmayr appearing as Waterloo in a transnational cultural context, must be understood as "rite of conquest," a *performance* that represents a futile attempt to embody an authentic Indian original and thus to conquest Native American identity. These reenactments, all uncannily haunted by the ghost of America, illustrate the importance of performance for the understanding of Americanness as a highly contested, utterly discriminatory, and always transformative national category.

For German-speaking audiences, the novels of the 19th century German novelist Karl May, which themselves have been adapted for a variety of performance events, present a related and extremely popular narrative of conquest. As Susanne Zantop reports in her introduction to an edited collection on *Germans and Indians*, "May's works, since their inception, have generated a whole culture industry that almost obsessively reiterates and thereby reproduces the idea of a special affinity between Germans and Native Americans based on shared experiences" (4). The Indian culture industry, certainly present in Austria as well, has generated and profited from what Hartmut Lutz calls "Indianthusiasm" (167), a fervent passion for all things Indian that has found its manifestations in various open-air performances of Karl May's novels (especially of the *Winnetou*-trilogy), Indian hobby groups, or concerts which feature Indian lore and music. Waterloo's performative engagement with the ghost of America in transnational spaces, historical yet untimely, deterritorialized yet strangely local, adds a further "Indianthusiastic" link to the long chain of globalized performances of Indianness. From Deloria's revolutionary Indians to Karl May's Winnetou to Waterloo's royal audience: The global performance of America has already created a vast and inherently contradictory archive.

In Waterloo's audience with the *Kaiser*, it becomes impossible to determine an "original," categorical Americanness. America, in this skit, merely appears as an apparition, a constantly disappearing ghostly presence haunted by a century-old performance archive. Reading Waterloo's performance *as performance*, or more specific, as performance of America, necessitates a rethinking of our epistemologies. Rather than framing the audience within the disciplinary parameters of the nation-state, we need to understand how knowledge is produced transnationally through the constant reiterations, reproductions, and re-doings of performance.

Essentially an open-ended, inconclusive, and oddly transhistorical performance process rather than an exceptional national concept produced by the disciplinary technologies of modernity, America is constantly disappearing in the global domain. Untimely, ghostly, it hovers over Waterloo's royal audience, opening up a creative global cultural space in which powerful effigies engage in a complex renegotiation and resignification of national knowledge.

Resisting Conclusions: "Heya Heya" at *Meidlinger Markt*

On June 12, 2010, a couple of friends and I attended an early afternoon concert performance of Waterloo's at *Meidlinger Markt* in Vienna's 12th district. The location, which is close to where I live, houses a traditional food market situated at what can be considered the district center, close to the subway station Niederhofstraße, the local shopping street Meidlinger Hauptstraße, and the Amtshaus Meidling, the district administration. Meidling itself is often regarded as a "typical" Viennese working class district, and the "Meidlinger L," an allegedly salient linguistic feature, has secured a dubious popularity throughout Austria. Waterloo's performance was part of the local *Bezirksfest* and was heavily advertised in the surrounding neighborhoods. In fact, it was a flyer I found in my mailbox that directed me to the performance (Fig.1). The concert featured Waterloo as singer and two musicians, a guitarist and a drummer. As Waterloo's musical repertoire is diverse and certainly not limited to Indian music, the concert performance included a variety of songs such as the cheerful "*So ein Wunderschönes Leben*" ("Such a Wonderful Life"), the environmentally concerned "Blue Planet Blue," or the already mentioned "*Erzherzog Johann Jodler*." The concert was remarkably integrated into the everyday Meidling traffic, as there was no real stage and Waterloo literally performed among his audience (Fig.2). Such a setting, naturally, created an unusually intimate atmosphere with a high amount of audience interaction.

Figure 1. Promotional flyer for Waterloo's concert at Meidlinger Markt on 12 June 2010. Author's collection

It is only toward the end of the concert that Waterloo plays his signature Indian song "Heya Heya," a five-minute "war chant" built on a formulaic Indian tom-tom beat.[11] The song is arranged around the creative tension between a duplet beat ("He-ya He-ya") and a triplet beat ("Ha-ya-ya"), which are alternated throughout. Philip Deloria describes this simple pattern, complete with the "war drum," as "simplified and stereotypical Indian sound" (*Unexpected* 192) that has shaped dominant conceptions of Indianness. More generally, Deloria states:

11 I have filmed the performance of "Heya Heya" with my small snapshot camera and put the video on YouTube, where it is publicly accessible. See mrwasserklo, or http://www.youtube.com/watch?v=JMYdhWzu2fU.

> Music, which often exhibits an uneasy tension between sonic abstraction and the representation of ideas and things, has been a primary way of evoking, not simply sounds, or even images, but complete worlds of expectation concerning Indian people, rich with narratives and symbolic meanings. (*Unexpected* 184)

Figure 2. Waterloo performing at Meidlinger Markt on 12 June 2010. Author's photograph.

Waterloo's performance certainly capitalizes on these "worlds of expectation," as he re-enacts a powerful but obviously lost Indianness in the Viennese food market and, in the process, attempts to summon the ghost of America. In order to expose his tanned and hairy chest, Waterloo takes his shirt off and begins a sort of "war dance" that is becoming more and more ecstatic as the song progresses. Despite the high temperatures (I remember more than 30° Celsius in the early afternoon heat), and despite his advanced age of sixty-five, he puts enormous strain on his body: Waterloo's musical engagement with Indianness turns out to be a sweaty enterprise. In this transnational performance, however, America gradually disappears. The simple "Heya Heya," as an embodied practice, is used to restore discourses of masculinity, race, and modernity that are no longer American in a disciplinary, national sense. Rather, Waterloo's performance is always recognizable *as performance*, not as an attempt to embody exactly exceptionally Indian or American characteristics. The dance emerges as a *trans*national and highly inconclusive performance event, an recreation of an archaic manhood in the Meidling summer heat which can never be fully rationalized by the nation-oriented routines of traditional American Studies. Performed abroad, then, America only exists *in effigy*, strangely haunting the transnational realm through an ontologically elusive and never exactly determinable presence.

In this sense, it is hardly surprising that over the summer, "Heya Heya" took on a life of its own. Slowly but surely, it began to re-appear in conversations among my friends, as brief performative inflections with increasingly incongruous meanings. What started out as a memory marker that reminded us of the concert performance turned into, variously, a synonym for Waterloo himself, a mocking comment on (what for some seemed ill-conceived) Austrian *Indianthusiasm*, a disturbing remark on the misrepresentation of Native Americans, or—to my rising uneasiness—an alternative descriptive term for my research as such. "Heya Heya," however, was not only circulating among Waterloo's concert audience, but even appeared at the Viennese Burgtheater in early fall, when director Stephan Kimmig had the Spanish king enact an Indian dance in his staging of Franz Grillparzer's *The Jewess of Toledo*. As a performative tag of Indianness in the transnational arena, it seems, "Heya Heya" is still undergoing constant reinterpretation. Like all performance, it "resists conclusions, just as it resists the sort of definitions, boundaries, and limits so useful to traditional academic writing and academic structures" (Carlson 206). Like all performance, it participates in the re-presentation of behavior *from the second to the* n*th time*, repeatedly attempting to access an original, first-time America—an America, however, that can never be completely recreated. Instead, we find transnational performances haunted by the ghost of America, a ghost which merely echoes the faint howls of lost origins, of national characteristics, and disciplinary epistemologies. The challenge posed to us as scholars of this transnational culture conundrum is a continuous challenge to study the reenactments, recreations, and restorations of America, the haunting presences of American ghosts, and the Indian war cries that (dis)appear through unexpected bodies in unexpected locales. As we enter the transnational realm through the epistemology of performance, then, we must resist the disciplinary certainties provided by nation-based frameworks and simply continue to rewrite, rephrase, and rethink.

Works Cited

Anzaldúa, Gloria. *Borderlands/La Frontera: The New Mestiza.* 1987. 2nd ed. San Francisco: Aunt Lute Books, 1999.

Appadurai, Arjun. *Modernity at Large: Cultural Dimensions of Globalization.* Minneapolis: Uof Minnesota P, 1996.

Baty, S. Paige. *American Monroe: The Making of a Body Politic.* Berkeley: U of California P, 1995.

Bederman, Gail. *Manliness and Civilization: A Cultural History of Gender and Race in the United States, 1880-1917.* 1995. Pb. ed. Chicago: U of Chicago P, 1996.

Berkhofer, Robert F., Jr. *The White Man's Indian: Images of the American Indian from Columbus to the Present.* 1978. 1st Vintage Books ed. New York: Vintage Books, 1979.

Berlant, Lauren. *The Anatomy of National Fantasy: Hawthorne, Utopia, and Everyday Life.* Chicago: U of Chicago P, 1991.

Carlson, Marvin. *Performance: A Critical Introduction.* 1996. 2nd ed. New York: Routledge, 2004.

Deloria, Philip J. *Indians in Unexpected Places.* Lawrence: UP of Kansas, 2004.

---. *Playing Indian.* New Haven: Yale UP, 1998.

Desmond, Jane C. and Virginia R. Domínguez. "Resituating American Studies in a Critical Internationalism." *American Quarterly* 48.3 (1996): 475-90.

Fishkin, Shelley Fisher. "Crossroads of Cultures: The Transnational Turn in American Studies—Presidential Address to the American Studies Association, November 12, 2004." *American Quarterly* 57.1 (2005): 17-57.

Foucault, Michel. *Discipline and Punish: The Birth of the Prison.* 1975. trans. Alan Sheridan. 2nd Vintage Books ed. New York: Vintage Books, 1995.

---. "Nietzsche, Genealogy, History." 1971. trans. Donald F. Bouchard and Sherry Simon. *Language, Counter-Memory, Practice: Selected Essays and Interviews.* Ed. Donald F. Bouchard. Ithaca: Cornell UP, 1977. 139-64.

Gordon, Avery F. *Ghostly Matters: Haunting and the Sociological Imagination.* 1997. New U of MN P ed. Minneapolis: U of Minnesota P, 2008.

Huhndorf, Shari M. *Going Native: Indians in the American Cultural Imagination.* Ithaca: Cornell UP, 2001.

Lenz, Günter H. "Toward a Dialogics of International American Culture Studies: Transnationality, Border Discourses, and Public Culture(s)."

The Futures of American Studies. Eds. Donald E. Pease and Robyn Wiegman. Durham: Duke UP, 2002. 461-85.

Lipsitz, George. *American Studies in a Moment of Danger.* Minneapolis: U of Minnesota P, 2001.

Lutz, Hartmut. "German Indianthusiasm: A Socially Constructed German National(ist) Myth." *Germans and Indians: Fantasies, Encounters, Projections.* Eds. Colin G. Galloway, Gerd Gemünden and Susanne Zantop. Lincoln: U of Nebraska P, 2002. 167-84.

Lyotard, Jean François. *The Postmodern Condition: A Report on Knowledge.* 1979. trans. Geoff Bennington and Brian Massumi. Minneapolis: U of Minnesota P, 1984.

McKenzie, Jon. *Perform or Else: From Discipline to Performance.* London: Routledge, 2001.

Moses, L.G. *Wild West Shows and the Images of American Indians, 1883-1933.* Albuquerque: U of New Mexico P, 1996.

mrwasserklo. "Waterloo in Meidling." *YouTube.com.* YouTube, LLC, 12 June 2010. Web. 27 Sep 2010. URL: http://www.youtube.com/watch?v=JMYdhWzu2fU.

Pearce, Roy Harvey. *Savagism and Civilization: A Study of the Indian and the American Mind.* 1953. Pb. ed. Baltimore: The Johns Hopkins P, 1967.

Pease, Donald, ed. *National Identities and Post-Americanist Narratives.* Durham: Duke U P, 1994.

Phelan, Peggy. *Unmarked: The Politics of Performance*. London: Routledge, 1993.

Pratt, Mary Louise. "Arts of the Contact Zone." *Profession* 91 (1991): 33-40.

Radway, Janice. "What's in a Name? Presidential Address to the American Studies Association, 20 November, 1998." *American Quarterly* 51.1 (1999): 1-32.

Roach, Joseph. *Cities of the Dead: Circum-Atlantic Performance*. New York: Columbia U P, 1996.

Rowe, John Carlos, ed. *Post-Nationalist American Studies*. Berkeley: U of California P, 2000.

Schechner, Richard. *Between Theater and Anthropology*. Philadelphia: U of Pennsylvania P, 1985.

"Seine Majestät auf den Spuren fremder Kulturen in der 'Donnerstag Nacht'." *programm.orf.at.* ORF, n.d. Web. 27 Sep. 2010. URL: http://programm.orf.at/?story=3193.

specialagent. "waterloo bei wir sind kaiser." YouTube.com. YouTube, LLC, 3 Apr. 2009. Web. 27 Sep. 2010. URL: http://www.you tube.com/watch?v=PX7RBrBRrJg.

Taylor, Diana. *The Archive and the Repertoire: Performing Cultural Memory in the Americas*. Durham: Duke UP, 2003.
Waterloo and Thomas Jeier. *Das Geheime Wissen der Lakota: Die 7 Wege zu einem Besseren Leben*. Wien: Ueberreuter, 2009.
Zantop, Susanne. "Close Encounters: Deutsche and Indianer." *Germans and Indians: Fantasies, Encounters, Projections*. Eds. Colin G. Galloway, Gerd Gemünden and Susanne Zantop. Lincoln: U of Nebraska P, 2002. 3-14.

CONTRIBUTORS

Eugen Banauch studied at the Universities of Vienna, Brighton, UK, and Ottawa, ON. He works at the University of Vienna at the Department for English and American Studies and teaches literary and cultural studies, but currently acts as a Visiting Professor at Hebrew University, Jerusalem where he teaches courses at the European Forum and works at the Center for Austrian Studies. Recent publications include the monograph *Fluid Exile* (Universitätsverlag Winter, 2009), and the co-ed volumes *Almighty Dollar* (LIT Verlag, 2010) and *Apropos Canada* (Peter Lang, 2010). In May 2011, he organized the international conference "Refractions of Bob Dylan - Cultural Appropriations of an American Icon" (www.dylan-vienna.at) in Vienna.

Georg Drennig studied North American Studies at the University of Vienna, Austria, and Georgetown University, U.S., and is now a PhD candidate in the Advanced Research in Urban Studies program at the University of Duisburg-Essen. There, he works on the Utopian Imaginaries of Vancouver and the cultural production of space. His main interests are spatially-turned Cultural Studies and "stone-kicking-realist" Ecocriticism.

Petra Eckhard is Assistant Professor at the Institute of Art History and Cultural Studies at the University of Technology in Graz. She also teaches courses in American Cultural Studies at the Department of English and American Studies at the Alpen-Adria Universität Klagenfurt. Her fields of research include 20th century American literature and culture, postmodern theory, urban studies, architectural history, the city in literature (especially New York), and gothic fiction. She is the author of *Chronotopes of the Uncanny: Time and Space in Postmodern New York Novels* (Transcript, 2011).

Eric C. Erbacher is a doctoral candidate in American Studies at the Technical University of Dresden, Germany. He is currently working as a research associate and lecturer in American Studies and TEFL at the University of Paderborn and the Westfälische Wilhelms-Universität Münster, Germany. His research interests are urban studies, media studies, and cultural studies, with a particular focus on the intersection of these fields with issues of visual culture, economic restructuring, popular culture, and class.

Astrid M. Fellner is Professor and Chair of North American Studies at Saarland University in Saarbruecken, Germany. From 2008-09 she was "Distinguished Visiting Austrian Chair" at Stanford University and before that she taught at the University of Vienna, Austria. Her publications include *Articulating Selves: Contemporary Chicana Self-Representation* (Braumüller, 2002) and several articles in the fields of U.S. Latino/a literature, Colonial American Literatures, Canadian literature, Gender Studies, and Cultural Studies. She has also finished a study entitled *Bodily Sensations: The Female Body in Late-Eighteenth-Century American Culture*. She is the co-editor of *(Anti-) Americanisms* (LIT Verlag, 2005) and *Making National Bodies: Cultural Identity and the Politics of the Body in (Post) Revolutionary America* (WVT, 2010), and the editor of *Body Signs: The Body in Latino/a Cultural Production* (LIT Verlag, 2011).

Laura R. Fisher is a Ph.D. candidate in American Literature at New York University, where she is also a Graduate Fellow of the Humanities Initiative. Her dissertation, entitled Pedagogies of Uplift: Reform Institutions and U.S. Literary Production, examines the mutual relationship between institutions of education and social reform and American literature in the late-nineteenth and early-twentieth centuries. Her research looks across different kinds of media to explore the social work of literature within emergent U.S. reading publics.

Alexandra Ganser studied English and American Studies, History, and Art History at the University of Vienna, the University of Trieste and the University of Oklahoma at Norman (Fulbright). She holds a doctoral degree in American Studies from the University of Erlangen-Nuremberg, where she also works as an assistant professor for American literary and cultural studies. Her dissertation was published as *Roads of Her Own: Gendered Space and Mobility in American Women's Road Narratives, 1970-2000* (Rodopi, 2009). She has published mainly in the fields of gender studies, film and visual culture, transatlantic and transnational studies, and Native American studies. Her current book project examines textual representations of piracy in transatlantic literatures from the late 17th century to the Civil War.

Susanne Hamscha is a Ph.D. candidate at the Graduate School of North American Studies (FU Berlin). She studied English and American Studies at the University of Vienna and at the University of Massachusetts at Amherst, where she was a fellow in the "Graduate Certificate in Advanced Feminist Studies." In 2008, she received a three-year scholarship from the German Research Foundation for the completion of her doctoral degree. In her dissertation she analyzes how the "Americanness" of American culture is performatively constituted in nineteenth-century American literature and contemporary pop culture. Her research interests include the American Renaissance, American Modernism, feminist literature, popular culture, film studies, and gender theory.

Louis J. Kern is Chair of the History Department and Director of the American Studies Program at Hofstra University. He is a cultural and intellectual historian who has strong interests in literature, film, and popular culture He is the author of *An Ordered Love* (The University of North Carolina Press, 1981), a study of sex and sexuality in three nineteenth-century utopian communities. His recent work has focused on issues related to sexuality and the body. He is currently working on a history of the early eugenics movement in relation to free love advocacy, feminism, and the defense of free speech.

Leopold Lippert is a PhD candidate in American Studies at the University of Vienna and is currently working as a research assistant at the Department of American Studies of the University of Graz. His PhD project, tentatively entitled "Performing America Abroad," deals with the "Americanness" of Austrian cultural and academic practice. He has published on American drama and queer film and situates his research at the intersection of Queer Theory, Performance Studies, and Transnational American Studies.

Lisa Lowe is Professor of Comparative Literature at University of California - San Diego. She is the author of several books on orientalism, immigration, and globalization, including *Immigrant Acts: On Asian American Cultural Politics* (Duke, 1997). Her current project, *The Intimacies of Four Continents*, examines the convergence of African slavery and Asian indentured labor in the Americas as the conditions for modern liberal freedom.

Ana Mª Manzanas Calvo teaches American Literature and Culture at the Universidad de Salamanca, Spain. Her research centers on Ethnic American Literatures, a field she approaches from a comparative, intercultural perspective. Her publications include *Cities, Borders, and Spaces in Intercultural American Literature and* Film (Routledge, 2011), with J. Benito, *Uncertain Mirrors: Magical Realism in US Ethnic Literatures* (Rodopi, 2009), with J. Benito and B. Simal, and *Intercultural Mediations: Mimesis and Hybridity in American Literatures* (LIT Verlag 2003), with J. Benito. She has edited collections of essays, such as *Literature and Ethnicity in the Cultural Borderlands* (Rodopi, 2002), *The Dynamics of the Threshold: Essays on Liminal Negotiations* (Gateway Press, 2006), and *Border Transits: Literature and Culture across the Line* (Rodopi, 2007). With J. Benito she is general editor of the Rodopi Series "Critical Approaches to Ethnic American Literature."

Sina A. Nitzsche is Research Associate at the Institute of English and American Studies at Dortmund University of Technology, Germany. In the academic year 2011-12, she is a Visiting Scholar at Oglethorpe University, Atlanta, GA. She organized the international and interdisciplinary conference *HipHop im Revier* in the framework of the European Capital of Culture *Ruhr.2010* and is currently editing a volume on Hip-Hop in Europe. Using the Bronx as a prime example, her dissertation examines the contested interrelationship between space and the media in the late 1970s and early 1980s. Her research interests include popular cultures, postmodernism, and New York City as well as international educational and cultural exchange.

Klaus Rieser is Associate Professor of American Studies at the University of Graz, Austria, where he teaches in cultural studies and in film studies and – since 2007 – acts as department chair. His major areas of research comprise US film, representations of gender and ethnicity, and cultural studies. He is the author of *Filmische Passagen in die Neue Welt: Entwürfe ethno-amerikanischer Kulturen im Migrationsfilm* (WVT, 1996) and *Borderlines and Passages: Liminal Masculinities in Film* (Die Blaue Eule, 2006) and the co-author of *Daughter Rite (1978) und Daughters of Chaos (1980): Filmanalysen* (WVT, 1996, with Susanne Rieser). Beyond that, he published a number of articles on film and co-edited volumes on cultural and literary studies. He is a long-standing board member of the Austrian Association of American Studies (over which he also presided), and co-edits the book series "American Studies in Austria."

Silvia Schultermandl is an assistant professor of American Studies at the University of Graz. Her research and teaching interests are in transnational American Studies, early American literature, gender studies, narrative fiction and life writing, and 9/11. She is the author of *Transnational Matrilineage: Mother-Daughter Relationships in Asian American Literature* (LIT Verlag, 2009) and the co-editor of *A Fluid Sense of Self: The Politics of Transnational Identity* (LIT Verlag, 2010), and *Growing Up Transnational: Identity and Kinship in a Global Era* (University of Toronto Press, 2011). Together with Erin Kenny (Drury University), she is the series editor of LIT Verlag's book series *Contributions to Transnational Feminism.*

Kathy-Ann Tan is an assistant professor in the American Studies department at the University of Tübingen, Germany, where she teaches courses on contemporary American and Canadian literature, Language poetry, and diasporic writing, especially Caribbean Canadian fiction and poetry. Her first book is titled *The Nonconformist's Poem: Radical "Poetics of Autobiography" in the Works of Lyn Hejinian, Susan Howe and Leslie Scalapino* (WVT, 2008). She is currently working on her second book project (Habilitation) on globalization and citizenship in contemporary North American fiction.

Susanne Wegener completed her MA in American Studies at Ludwig Maximilians Universität in Munich in 2008. She has been a research assistant and a Ph.D. student at the Department of English and American Studies at Paris Lodron Universität in Salzburg since October 2008. Her doctoral thesis is concerned with concepts of 'risk' and 'speculation' in contemporary speculative fictions of the North-American Pacific Rim. Susanne Wegener has published on the work of Truman Capote, Siri Hustvedt, Larissa Lai and Karen Tei Yamashita. Her research interests are theories of fictionality, narratology, economic criticism, law and literature, and transnationalism.